The Green Stubborn Bud:
Women's Culture at Century's Close

edited by
Kathryn F. Clarenbach
and
Edward L. Kamarck

Introduction by Betty Friedan

The Scarecrow Press, Inc.
Metuchen, N.J., & London
1987

The title "The Green Stubborn Bud" is drawn from the
poem "Peony" in <u>Depth Perception: New Poems and a
Masque</u>, by Robin Morgan, Doubleday/Anchor Books,
© 1984 by Robin Morgan and reprinted here with the
author's permission.

Library of Congress Cataloging-in-Publication Data

The Green stubborn bud.

   Proceedings of the Second National Conference
on Women and Arts, held June 3-6, 1985, Madison,
Wis., and sponsored by University of Wisconsin
Extension.
   Includes index.
   1. Feminism and the arts--United States--
Congresses. 2. Feminism and the arts--Congresses.
I. Clarenbach, Kathryn F. II. Kamarck, Edward L.
III. National Conference on Women and Arts
(2nd : 1985 : Madison, Wis.) IV. University of
Wisconsin--Extension.
NX180.F4G7 1987 700'.1'03 86-31649
ISBN 0-8108-1981-3

"The Conference's Accomplishments" by Florence Howe,
Copyright © 1987 by Florence Howe

....who dare, tenacious,
to nibble toward such blossoming
of this green stubborn bud
some call a world.

from "Peony,"
a poem by Robin Morgan

Acknowledgments

Special thanks to Robin Morgan for giving us
permission to use the singularly appropriate metaphor from
her poem, "Peony," as the title of this book. "Peony" was
published in Ms. Morgan's Depth Perception: New Poems
and a Masque, Garden City, N.Y., Anchor
Press/Doubleday, 1982. The entire poem also appears in
Ms. Morgan's article in this book.

We are particularly honored to present Betty
Friedan's insightful analysis of the inevitable intertwining
of the Feminist movement and the flowering of women in
the arts. As the Introduction to this volume, Ms. Friedan's
provocative essay provides a message of hope and a spur to
redoubled commitment to a more egalitarian, humane
world. We are deeply indebted to her.

We are grateful to the following for grants given in
support of the planning and implementation of the Second
National Conference on Women and the Arts: The Ford
Foundation, New York City; the Johnson Foundation,
Racine, Wisconsin; the Miller Brewing Company,
Milwaukee, Wisconsin; the Wisconsin Arts Board, with
funds from the State of Wisconsin and the National
Endowment for the Arts; and the University of
Wisconsin-Extension.

We are also grateful to all the Conference participants
as well as the network of women in the arts in all parts of
the country whose knowledge and insights were crucial
assets in the planning for the Conference.

Mention should be made of three individuals who had
key roles in the development of the Conference: Genevieve
Lewis as administrative coordinator, Elizabeth Durbin as
researcher, and Lori Untulis O'Neill as administrative
assistant. Our warm thanks to them and also to three
others who backed up their efforts: Sue Hermanson, Kathy
Krueger, and Elaine Penpek.

v

CONTENTS

THE GREEN STUBBORN BUD:
Women's Culture at Century's Close

INTRODUCTION

One of the first clues to me of what I later called "the feminine mystique," was the discovery that in the years after World War II there was a great increase in the number of Americans that wrote "artist" on the census forms. But this increase was all male. There were, if anything, slightly fewer American women than ever who wrote "artist" on the census blank. That was puzzling. It used to be, of course, that art was considered not a manly, masculine thing to do, and people wanted their sons to be businessmen or lawyers or titans of one sort or another. If a man discovered his son was an artist, he considered him a sissy. So it was a sign of the maturity of the society that men would now write "artist" on the census blank.

But why not women? And I thought to myself, "Oh well, how could women do it, with motherhood?" Still, art is something you can practice at home. When you think of all the women taking art classes, a great many were interested in art. Of course, you have to take yourself seriously when you're an artist. You really have to risk, you have to trust your own inner voice, your own talent. You can't be creative unless you trust yourself enough to say "no" to an existing tradition, and be willing to risk a new direction. It was the presence of what I named the "feminine mystique," that kept women from taking themselves seriously enough as people to become artists. So it's a great satisfaction to me now to discover this wonderful flowering of women in the arts.

This flowering is a direct result of the women's movement, and of the battle for equality that we have made. We have opened doors of opportunity, and more than that, given women self-respect, self-determination and autonomy. Oh, the talent was always there. I'm sure artistic talent is distributed with equal diversity among men and women. But most women, up until very recently, couldn't get the training, and it was not always even a question of overt sex discrimination. It was that the society didn't encourage women to take themselves seriously enough to be artists. This is why there have not been that many great women artists in the past, in any field. Women in the society as a whole were defined completely by their biological role, and in fact, had their lives curtailed by that role and were not allowed to move as full people beyond the home.

How many artists do we know from the past, who only managed to sell their work by putting their brother's name to it? Or writers that had to take a man's name to get their books reviewed? And how many women artists paid a terrible price, were literally driven mad when they tried to use their talent seriously? So, it was the women's movement for equality—for the personhood of women—that is responsible for the flowering of women artists in the last fifteen years. Yes, it is her own genius, yes, it is her own talent, of course. But how many would have had the guts to use that talent to find out what the limits of their genius were, thirty, forty, fifty, sixty years ago?

At the same time women as artists have given vision to the women's movement. The books that I and others wrote helped propel the women's movement forward, gave a name to the problems. All serious women artists are also serving the cause of women. The more the women's movement makes it possible for women to be free, the more likely that women artists will create new visions for society as a whole, based on their authentic experience of life as women.

I've always had a bit of a problem with terms like "feminist art," and "feminist writers." In the era when we had broken through the feminine mystique and for a time were locked in a reaction against it, there was almost a denigrating of certain experiences common to women, such as motherhood, and art that celebrated the domestic parts of life wasn't considered important enough to be labelled "feminist art." Nonsense. All experiences of women,

xii

provided they are treated honestly and authentically, provide grist for art. Feminism has made it possible for women to write their own name and to paint their own name—as people—free to take themselves seriously in their complex totality, encompassing and transcending tradition, as they now create new tradition out of their different voices as women. And that process is beginning to reach critical mass.

I also have a little trouble with the distinction that's made between woman's culture and male culture. We live in a human culture, the American culture of the 1980s. It is true that women have come into that culture in a different place, that women's experience is not always the same as men's, and that we have a different history. Also there are whole dimensions of every artistic field that have been somehow buried, ignored, and made invisible, because until recently, culture was defined only by men and in terms of male experience. Now we have women beginning to define their own dimensions, and we have women's experience being brought out from obscurity, from invisibility, or from its false pedestals, and becoming a part of the mainstream of art. If it is necessary in order for women to get on the stage at all, to have a special, separate, alternate theatre, all right, that is or was a temporary necessity. But I will not be satisfied until women's experience and women's talents are used fully in the mainstream and are redefining that mainstream. As far as I'm concerned, this is the direction that we must go.

While I look to a flowering of women artists in every field, I think we have to be careful of talk about a woman's culture. We know that we can't have equality based only on a male model. But let us beware of new mystiques, let's beware of idealizing or even wanting to perpetuate certain aspects of women's experience that come from our oppression. For instance, I think that it is wrong to deify the anonymity that was the only way that women (e.g., quilt makers) were able to express their art in an earlier era. With our new self-confidence, we are now moving beyond that anonymity.

There is a certain kind of novel of manners, a novel that dealt with the minutiae of daily life, of emotional life, that has been called a woman's novel. That was the sphere, the ultimate to which women were confined. Some of that was great writing; Jane Austen, for instance, and it defined a very basic part of life. Now I wait to see what will happen when women begin to do the great social novels and the great political novels, not just novels that deal with manners and emotions and domestic life. But the problems in our society are so complex now, and so intimidating that you find that even few male writers are dealing with them. In fact, males are now limiting themselves to the novel of manners and even a narcissistic self-absorption and angst. They are unable to take on the larger questions. Maybe the next step is that women, freed from a narrow sphere, will emerge from what has been called woman's culture to take on the questions of life and death that are threatening our whole society. I am for women's experience being used authentically as part of the whole culture, dealing with and defining that culture.

It was a shock to learn that at the 1986 International PEN Conference that out of 117 readings of novels, poems, essays, and panel discussions, only sixteen were by women. Not that there was a conspiracy, it was just a blindness on the part of the men who ran that conference. But when it was called to their attention, their excuse was that because women didn't have the intellectual stature of the men (of Norman Mailer! of Gay Talese!) they would have had to lower their intellectual standards to put women on the panels. The women were rightly outraged and protested; I trust it will not happen again. And now the new president of PEN is a woman. She didn't need any feminist push, she's a great writer. But if in 1986 there could have been blindness to women's intellect among America's socially conscious writers, then women are still not being taken as seriously as they should.

We must know our history. A woman artist today who is not interested in how women fit into the history of art, who is not interested in questions of why we weren't allowed to be serious enough about art for there to have been many great women artists, suffers a kind of blindness. In whatever your field, unbury the history of those women who had to sell paintings under their brother's name; the women who were in no way permitted to be serious in their art's pursuit; the women, married, who had to keep the children quiet so their husbands would have the freedom to paint or to practice their art. We must know their history to realize that today we are in a unique situation. In great numbers women now have the freedom and the opportunity to take ourselves seriously as people, and to get the training. Now artists who are women must also work out new patterns of life so they can enjoy their right to love and choose to have children, and also to keep their commitment to their art. That requires not only new patterns of domestic life but new structures for society. No matter how well we have individually solved these problems ourselves, as exceptions, or what degree of fame we have reached, as exceptions, it is our obligation to reach back and keep the door open for the generation that comes after us, and to encourage them to take on the problems that we weren't able to solve.

At the moment we face a backlash against women's hard-won basic right to legal choice in abortion, when or whether to have children, and the right to sexual preference. It is surely the obligation of women artists to join with other women in defense of these fundamental rights. But for most women to have real choices, we must go beyond this defense. If you do a survey, I don't care what field it is, and you look at the men who achieved recognition as senior artists, senior scientists, whatever, you will find that the great majority of them are living comfortable home lives with first or second or third wives, and have children. You will find relatively few prominent women artists and scientists who are living with spouses and have children. This is still a price that women have to pay. Or they pay the price the other way, they have to go easy on their ambition, they have to down peddle their art. In my generation, many suppressed their art altogether in the interest of domestic bliss. Now it's more accepted that a woman can take herself seriously to be an artist, but the possibility to make that work in real life and still have real choices about love and children, is still not there for many.

We cannot deal adequately with the problems of today with the rhetoric of yesterday. To some extent too much dwelling on woman's culture is a retreat from the complex problems of the mainstream of our society today. Women want, and have a right to want, continued progress in the mainstream. But more than that, the mainstream itself, in any art, will be moved from sterility by the dimensions that come from female experience. We have to continue fighting for that. I see in every field now women who have come up to the glass ceiling. They know the field, they know the craft, and at a certain point they aren't allowed to get any further. So they can't really use their experience fully to define the field. It's important that women break through that glass ceiling. Because I think there is a different dimension that does come from woman's experience, and that difference has never been allowed to express itself openly in the mainstream. So in a sense we still have a male defined universe of television, we have a male defined museum. I don't want an alternate woman's museum, I don't want an alternate woman's television network. I want a television network and a museum equally defined by man's and woman's vision, the dimensions of male and female experience. And that can't happen if women are always kept below the glass ceiling.

Of course, young women grow up taking things for granted now. "I can be a great artist, I can go to study in Rome or Paris, I'll spend years working at my art." They wouldn't have been able to do that twenty years ago. It should be a part of women's new freedom as artists to feel some continuity with the movement that freed them, and the women that will come after them. Because women's liberation is still an unfinished thing it should be a part of their sensitivity as artists that they contribute in some way through their vision, through their activism, through identification simply with the larger goals of the woman's movement, to the continuing freedom and the personhood of women.

In still other circles, there are very negative attitudes toward feminists, especially among young women. This refusal to identify with the movement that opened the doors to them is not an accident. We are in a period of political repression and backlash. The Reagan administration has made it subtly or not so subtly clear that the only really permissible direction for young people to take today if they want to get somewhere in their career, and if they want to enjoy the material accoutrements of the economy, is to keep their eye on the goals of power and affluence within the status quo. And the larger considerations of human evolution, the noble movements that extend life, the marvelous movements of preserving the environment, of responsibility to the future, of ecology, of feminism, of humanism, of liberalism, of social welfare, of social progress, all the movements for equality, for civil rights: all of these have been made dirty words.

Those young women who say "I'm not a feminist but I intend to use these opportunities that feminists won to advance my career, as a television producer, as a literary critic, or whatever," may not realize that they have bought the message that's coming to them from Washington, from the Reagan administration, from the fundamentalist right wing church hierarchies and from the media. That message is that it's not good for your career to think beyond your own very narrow limits.

We have blind spots about our own progress and the progress of women as artists. We haven't recognized that what stands in our way is not just sex discrimination, but lack of structures in the whole society that enable women who are the people that give birth to children to have choices in that regard and still be able to take themselves seriously as artists. Because the crucial years in the development of an artist coincide with child bearing, child rearing years, they need structures for child care and parental leave. Women artists and men artists who have children with the new women must face these problems.

Parenting has to be taken into account in a new way, not the way it was in the past, with the male artist doing some of his greatest work in his thirties or his late twenties, while his wife had to keep the children out of his hair.

There is also that question of the freedom to develop throughout an eighty year life span. In many fields of art the woman more than the man is somehow denigrated when she's past youth. Women are sometimes free to really devote themselves fully and seriously to their art only after the child rearing years, and this is the point where they face the double bind of sex and age discrimination. Can a woman who never had a chance to fully develop her art, begin at the age of 45? Recognizing the difficulty in this, there have to be structures in the society so that more women can continue to practice and develop in their art during the years when they are having children, unless we are going to make women pay a price that men are never expected to pay.

There are also new questions here about the relationship of art to life. There has been the cliche of the male artist in his solitary studio or ivory tower, protected from the distractions of life by the wife or the monastery. It might be that all of art will flourish in a new way when none of it is protected from the distractions of life. When for women and men alike, the artist has to deal with life in the daily way, the art that comes from pen or brush or chisel will reflect that. In the future, we are talking about new roles for women, new roles for men, and new dimensions for art. If we are to be really free to practice our art, we are also talking about some very real mundane questions, the new political questions that have to be faced during the second stage of feminism.

Betty Friedan

THE CENTURY FOR WOMEN: Preface

We are nearing 2001, the advent of both another century and a brand new millennium. It is a prospect that has been long anticipated: this opportunity to experience an epic sense of history, when what is yet to be can be viewed in sharp contradistinction to what has been. Surely, the occasion will provide a heyday for philosophers, poets, politicians, and publicists. Already America's imagination is being challenged by varied and competing visions of the future, of what can and should be for one societal group or another.

Because of the broad base and maturity of their movement, women are uniquely positioned to make large claims on the 21st century. Those claims have been advanced and validated not only in the United States, but on every continent of the globe during the United Nations Decade for Women (1975-85). Forums of non-govermental organizations (NGO's), convened concurrently with U.N. conferences in Mexico City (1975), Copenhagen (1980) and Nairobi (1985), assembled international delegations of women numbering in the thousands. Diverse in their language, customs and economic condition, they nevertheless recognized as universal both the imperative of institutional change and the essential role of women in bringing about that change. The bolder dreamers have already insisted that the 21st will be the century for women, when many of their deepest aspirations for the achievement of a humane society will finally be realized.

Thus a prime objective of the Second National Conference on Women and the Arts was to formulate an agenda for leadership into the next century. Sponsored by the University of Wisconsin Extension, with the help of a major grant from the Ford Foundation, the four day meeting—June 3-6, 1985—brought together over a hundred influential women in the arts, as well as some men. Designed to identify and examine the critical issues of the future for women in the arts, the Conference's papers and proceedings provide the content of this book.

It should be noted that the Conference was a direct descendent of the First National Conference on Women and the Arts held in 1973 at Wingspread, the Johnson Foundation facility in Racine, Wisconsin. Also sponsored by the University of Wisconsin Extension, the earlier meeting is widely viewed as a watershed event, for it not only played an historic role in encouraging and giving recognition to women as artists, but it also had a signal influence in highlighting the pressing need for women to build their own institutional support systems.

As Elizabeth Durbin demonstrates in the Conference's working paper, "A Survey of Recent Progress," the growth of those women's alternative art groups has been spectacular. For example, there are now over 90 feminist theatre groups in the country, 116 women's presses and publishers, 45 feminist bookstores, and over 460 women's art periodicals. The Coalition of Women's Arts Organizations, a recently formed umbrella group, already lists more than 75 institutional affiliates.

There has been a concomitant growth—explosion!—in the number of women artists in all areas of the arts, and in the number of women ascending to professional recognition and achieving gratifying breakthroughs, with recent Pulitzer prizes being awarded to women for playwrighting, music composition, and novel writing. Particularly heartening has been the emergence of a number of extremely talented minority women writers, such as Alice Walker, Toni Morrison, Paule Marshall, and Maxine Hong Kingston.

There has also been a proliferation of women's imagery in the content of all the arts. This in turn has begun to have an impact on the subject matter of the mass media, notably commercial television and film fare. Women are now writing, producing, directing, and starring in dramatic vehicles that especially illuminate women's experience and aspiration. While the number of such women-centered productions is far from satisfying, still those that are presented are seen by audiences that number in the tens of millions.

The picture, of course, is not all rosy. Women's progress has been uneven across the arts. As Ruth Dean's Conference paper indicates, women in theatre and music have experienced only isolated breakthroughs and most still face many of the traditional problems of discrimination. There are still scant opportunities for women critics. Relatively few women have ascended to positions of power and influence in our major arts institutions or in the media. The reluctance of museums and galleries to recognize and display women's visual art continues!

As one would perhaps expect after a period of such persistent confrontation of the establishment, we are now also seeing a number of retroactive developments: a backlash against women activists, particularly in the visual arts—the price exacted of those who would militantly pursue change; major cutback in support to women's groups by the two National Endowments and by other funding agencies; a complacent acceptance by younger women in the arts of the gains that have been won, that complacency all too often characterized by outright anti-feminism; a growing tendency of some of the women's alternative institutions to become comfortable but insular ghettos rather than places of liberation.

There is also the continuing pattern of women being co-opted by the governance systems of the traditional arts institutions, with the net result that a few more women come to share with men in the management of otherwise unchanged institutions—i.e., with no modification of unjust practices with respect to other women.

Nevertheless, there is evidence that the tidal wave that we have experienced during the last fifteen years may not have run its course. One can still perceive impressive swells of energy. The promise remains.

You will note that the papers and discussions of the Conference offer a dizzying array of new ideas for stimulating a second surge of growth. It is their overriding sense that "the green stubborn bud" of women's culture in America will one day flower.

Given the sorry state of the public art of the United States, and our inability as a nation to establish sound cultural objectives—unquestionably this represents one of our major failures as a democracy—it is not surprising that a predominant thematic note of this book is the importance of moving women's culture closer to the center of American life.

How? By making linkages. Linkages which root, linkages which unify, linkages which enrich, and linkages which augment. For example, linkages with the larger women's movement, and its panoply of aspirations, motivations, resources, and institutions.

In the Conference opening address Elizabeth Janeway stresses the urgency of women artists developing a language "which will announce our truths so powerfully and unmistakably that men will be able to hear them." She clearly has in mind a need for closer ties with the women's movement, for she also says: "We can't plan a new world, we can only create one. The tools we need for that include a language in which we can speak truly and truthfully and we don't have such a thing. But inventing a language is also a stage in inventing a world...."

Robin Morgan also sees women's culture and the building of the new society as being "inextricably interrelated." In addition she urges stronger recognition of the global dimensions of women's culture: "Our ignorance is profound in the West."

Gloria Orenstein through her own researches on the Goddess image aptly illustrates the rich possibilities for collaboration between Women's Studies Programs and women artists. She urges that this connection be highlighted: "I sincerely feel that the relationship between feminist creation and feminist research must be articulated so that we can appreciate the vast impact that the Women's Movement has made on the creative processes of contemporary women writers and artists and visa versa."

Yet another connection of concern to the Conference was the relationship of established arts institutions with the newer alternative groups. As Florence Howe points out in her summary paper, the question of autonomy versus integration came to a head—Florence Howe calls it "the most promising clash of the several worlds of the participants"—during discussion of the National Museum for Women in the Arts.

Dr. Anne-Imelda Radice, Director of the Museum, responds to fears that the NMWA might exclude from its policy and decision-making those who have been struggling to advance the women's art movement. Radice's assurances and openness give hope that the Museum might indeed aid in synthesizing the often conflicting approaches of mainstreaming and separation.

The imperative need for establishing linkages with one's creative heritage constitutes the theme of Paule Marshall's paper: "...there is this tremendous importance of the literary foremothers for the woman writer. All of those women—those few women, rather—of an earlier period, who wrote in the face of the most unimaginable odds, who forged the way, who set an example, who served as models, so that each book, novel, play, story, is informed by the efforts of those who have gone before."

Knowing one's own roots and acknowledging that one's heritage uniquely shapes her work are essential to the fullest unleashing of the artist's creativity. This message was a continuing thread throughout the Conference, highlighted especially by a panel of four women of color: Tisa Chang, Director of New York's Pan Asian Repertory Theatre; Sophie Rivera, Latino photographer; Jean La Marr, Native-American printmaker; and Nellie McKay, writer and Professor of Afro-American Studies and

Women's Studies. Their personal stories confirm once more the profound enrichment of our culture that diversity provides; in valuing that diversity we are all its beneficiaries.

Maryo Ewell views the countless communities of our country as a vital arena for women's arts leadership: "As the arts-via-technology become commonplace and accessible to all, the unique arts will be the live arts, produced at the community level, by and for neighbors." In effect, she is urging a deeper and more pervasive rooting in daily American life of the spirit and style of women's culture—a very important kind of linkage.

Implied in the above and discernible as well in the sub-text of all the discussion, is the assertion that women's culture has the responsibility, and, indeed, someday will have the capacity, to humanize society.

A quixotic quest?

Certainly the evidence is strong that women artists both in this country and abroad are growing in boldness, skill, and imaginative understanding, and that increasingly they are using their special sensitivity to delineate not only their own condition, but the condition of humankind everywhere. Further, because women are now among the most militant seekers of the freedom dream, should we not expect their art to contain the cutting edge and energy of social change?

Robin Morgan says it best: "Any concept, vision, let alone reality, of a new society is linked not only to women's culture, but feminist culture and I mean feminist in the broadest sense of the term. I believe that feminism, quite simply, is the politics of the 21st Century for the entire human species, the main hope of saving sentient life on our planet, just that simply."

This Conference in focusing on the responsibility of the artist to society and of the society to the artist reminds us that we must all —whether woman or man; whether artist, art leader, critic, scholar or teacher—critically examine the culture in which we live and act, and do battle against the culturally destructive forces—of which sexism and racism are among the more noxious—in order to help build a responsible and creative society.

Kathryn F. Clarenbach
Edward L. Kamarck

Madison, Wisconsin

A Language for Women
and What That Doesn't Mean

by Elizabeth Janeway

A negative title? Not really. I'd rather label it
"tentative." Inventing a language of verbal expression is a
difficult job which involves testing ways of saying. It's
harder than inventing a style of visual art or a musical
school. Of all the arts, the one that uses words is most
open to influence and invasion by the rest of life. We all
talk all the time about grocery lists and work schedules and
politics and money and squabbles with friends. We read
books and newspapers, all of them with points of view,
mostly masculine. Television swamps us with chatter
designed to keep the commercials far enough apart for us to
distinguish between the products they're pushing. So
creating a new language might be seen metaphorically as
building a sculpture out of garbage and trash. Painting,
considering its long history—back to the caves—has been
invaded only recently by messages of commerce while
music, even when coopted by martial commands, translates
them into its own tongue. Women need a language of their
own, one based deep in our experience. Women poets have
been working toward that end in this past generation, but
as one of the best, Marge Piercy, says:

> We sit around the table gambling against the house:
> the power hidden under the green felt,
> the television camera that reads your hand,
> the magnetic dice, the transistorized
> computer controlled deck that riffles
> with the sound of ice
> blowing on the wind against the glass.

("The Twelve-Spoked Wheel Flashing," <u>Circles on the
Water</u>, p. 185)

Playing against the house with cards stacked against

us is a marvelous metaphor; negative perhaps, since it lays out no coherent reasons for this strange pursuit. But Piercy is absolutely right in her negativistic report on experience. We can't plan a new world, we can only create one. The tools we need for that include a language in which we can speak to each other truly and truthfully and we don't yet have such a thing. But inventing a language is also a stage in creating a world.

Indeed, since I'm a cock-eyed optimist, I believe that the language women will create-invent-discover that will allow us to talk among ourselves will in time announce our truths so powerfully and unmistakably that men will be able to hear them. After all, they too are playing against the house with stacked decks, under the impression that they have stacked them themselves and have thus guaranteed that they will win. Look around, fellows, I want to say. Is that "winning" that's going on out there? I'm not trying to sell you on feminism as humanism, we'll have to give birth to both a language and a couple of male prophets before you'll be able to take that in. But take a look, boys, at the world you have made. Couldn't it stand a little improvement?

I fear that agreement will take a long time. Meanwhile women have various jobs to do, jobs that also need time. The negativeness in my title is there in part to discourage the idea that we will find it easy to develop a kind of speech that will be both universal and colloquial, refreshed by poets and valuable to scientists, rooted in experience and open to new usages. I believe that one of the problems we had with the last attempt to get ERA passed was precisely our language. It was readily subject to distortion and could easily be ignored. I don't mean that as an exercise in blaming the victim. We didn't have in our hands the right tools for making our case or the right weapons for defending it. We ran into potent, familiar falsehood and it prevailed. It won't do so always but to prevent its happening again we need a strong, flexible, creative tongue that will take account of where we have been as women and also let us think together toward where we are going; and we're going to have to work at this task very seriously. So the negativism in my title says, "Don't hurry." It says, "Be sure. Get it right. Sing it with other women and listen to what you hear." Our language should be so solid that it can be learned with ease and remembered in hard times. It will bring comfort in pain and in trouble. It will laugh us into courage.

That's not going to happen tomorrow. Some of you may be thinking, it won't happen at all, and that's true. But if it doesn't, nothing is going to matter because the world will end, in fire and ice. If that's frightening and worse than negative, I can only say that another ending depends on old survivors like ourselves. All we have to do is to use our strength and we have more strength today than ever before. It has been used in the past, but then it was harnessed for purposes not our own. To use it well—to unstack the deck—we need the common language that another poet, Adrienne Rich, dreams of, a language of strength that will not bend or weaken in the face of reality; it will be the first <u>human</u> language ever.

What a language for women that can become a language for humankind isn't, then, is one that exists already. We have fragments to build on but they are only fragments. We need to join them, find new ones, and interpret them in the light of our experience. So a beginning implies thinking back into experience. I wonder whether we might not try to do that here. What has our common experience been? Do you think we might devote some effort during our days together to letting our minds run back in time and unearthing some memories, or some hearsay from mothers and aunts and grandmothers, that are sharp, clear and detailed? We want more than general statements like "Our experience has been one of oppression," which is hardly a vivid presentation and certainly narrows our lives, for women have fought back and survived. How does, how did, gender roles work to limit our lives, what deceptions and self-deceptions did we undertake to fit ourselves into them, in this or that time and place? What were the mechanics and techniques used to hobble bodies and minds? Why did we agree, what implied threats, what real menaces were used? What sort of rationale did we dream up ourselves to justify the fact that we went on living in situations that ran from slavery to coddled femininity? How did we come to take for granted the dogma that we didn't have the option of doing differently? Why did we adjust to changes in the world that changed our lives without trying to change the world ourselves? Or did we in fact do so, only to have our memories of courage wiped out? What sacrifices did we make? What black and bitter humor sustained us in corners of whispering secrecy? Who, once in a while, got out? What happened to her?

Why am I asking for horror stories? Because we are at last strong enough to look at them objectively and practically. If in the past we told over our sorrows masochistically, we don't have to go on doing that. We can take such disasters as data for examining the ways patriarchy has used to maintain its grip on power. Observations like that can alert us to methods of countering such efforts. We have a real resource to turn to now, as compared to the first Conference on Women and the Arts held under these auspices. Women's history is being mined productively, forgotten literature has been brought to life, dance and painting and cinema and music have taken new directions even as they searched out their roots. But we need to go further with these explorations, we need to coordinate past and present in order to build a strong future that doesn't deny the past even while it witnesses the reversal of past conditions.

Let me then speak for the base of power to be found in history as a means of understanding the variety of social structures and cultural frameworks and political systems that human beings can invent. Where we are now in our increasingly multinational, multicultural society, grew out of many traditions and many different roles. We can learn from these variations in controlling women's power, and also from successful resistance to them. It's important to look seriously at our past and not let ourselves be bemused by injunctions to slough it off because it is past and somehow, therefore, irrelevant to the present. We've all heard the voices that say "Now that you're liberated, or something, why don't you just shut up and do the jobs you've been given at pay that's better than any you've had before! Oh sure, it's lower than what men get, but what do you expect? You spend all that time looking after the kids and the house, don't you? What do you mean you do that for free? That's your natural instinct, isn't it? Why do you want to go back into all that old stuff and make yourselves miserable? God, isn't that just like women!"

And women's history is full of misery and pain. Who can deny it? It does arouse rage, and shame too, over what happened and how women put up with it. It also distances us from our foremothers, just because they put up with it. How can we forgive them for failing to rebel and for handing us over on the same old terms to a world where the same old lies live on?

Going back can mean going through that kind of emotional storm and it is debilitating. It leaves us angry and ashamed over what seems to be centuries of failure. But anger isn't all that a disciplined reading of history can bring us. We can learn also about techniques of survival, we can learn about the networks of communication and supportive action women devised, and we can learn—very helpfully to our self-esteem—about the many ways in which men, those dominant patriarchs, managed to screw themselves up into magnificent mistakes and failures and overestimates of what could be done—of the mythic ambition that landed them, quite often, in the mud. In short, it gives us a good feel for human capabilities including human self-deception. All that is a good base for evaluating the present and imagining a future in which male myths can be broadened and re-written in terms of women's experience.

Let me dwell on history for a few minutes. True, it isn't art, which is what we've met here to talk about, but it's a wonderful data-base for art, a rich source of material, much of which is fresh because it has not been looked at from women's situation. Let me give you a couple of examples, random ones from books and journals I've just been reading. Both my references are by women and one is largely about women. The other definitely is not, but once your eye is attuned to considering what's being said here about society, I think you'll want to ask, "What are the implications about women's situation in that time and place?" and also, "What analogies with our present time and situation spring off these pages?"

First is a collection of Carroll Smith-Rosenberg's essays that Knopf will publish this month. Its title is enormously appealing to one who happens to be writing a book called Improper Behavior. Carroll Smith-Rosenberg's title, you see, is Disorderly Conduct. Coincidences like that suggest a whole train of thought and feeling stirring within women's minds, and I find them most revealing. Well. The subtitle of Smith-Rosenberg's collection is Visions of Gender in Victorian America. Included is her memorable piece from the first issues of Signs, "The Female World of Love and Ritual," in which she examined the strong bonds that women formed with kin and schoolmates during the 19th Century and the support that letters and visits from friends brought to women increasingly isolated within households by the processes of industrialization and urbanization. There is much more material here too, on female responses to the Cult of True Womanhood which worked to reduce them to representatives of Happy-Wife-and-Motherdom who had to express—or were supposed to express--all their other interests and capabilities vicariously. They did not do so. A wave of fundamentalist religion had the unexpected effect of producing women preachers and activist moral reformers, who attacked the double standard along with slavery, seeing a pretty good analogy between the two. Read also her studies on the role of the medical profession in illegalizing abortion a century ago and wrestling with the strange female disorder of hysteria—which the restrictions of the Cult of True Womanhood undoubtedly helped to create. And more. Here are the reactions to economic and social shifts by both genders, that are far from irrelevant to our own times.

Now come take a look at a society very distant from us in culture and in time: that of the Aztecs of Mexico, just before the Spanish Conquest. The subject here is the dominant male role; but while the shaping cultural force is certainly weird, it is not as strange as we might wish it were.

When we think of those years of conquest, we generally see them as a period of brutal European invasion and the destruction of native peoples. True. But these native peoples differed widely among themselves, and the cultures they produced were not all fruits and flowers. An Australian historian, Inga Clendinnen, has published a remarkable study called "The Cost of Courage in Aztec Society" in the current issues of an historical Journal, <u>Past and Present</u>.

All right, Aztec society. It bred warriors, not just as a separate caste apart from ordinary society. War, and the rituals that celebrated it, was the very core of its ceremonies and its art. "Here no one fears to die in war," ran one of its songs, "that is our glory." Clendinnen is looking at a people who had elevated disciplined violence into an esthetic compulsion that shaped the lives of men and clearly that of women too. Birth, for example, was defined as a form of battle. The spirits of women who died in childbirth went to a kind of Valhalla. Male children were at once dedicated to war. They were not placed in the arms of their mothers, but held by the midwife who greeted their arrival with war cries and a formal exhortation to the new-born consecrating him to war as his life-task, in the hope that his reward would be ritual sacrifice "by the obsidian knife" that cut out the heart so that a priest could hold it up to the god of the sun. That was their highest and most significant rite. It also appears that the closest, most meaningful relationship among them was neither that between men and women nor even that between the young men who had been reared together as warriors from boyhood on. No, it lay in a mythic area between the captor of an enemy warrior and his victim, who was sacrificed at a great public slaughter, which both honored the winner and foretold his own doom. In this mythology, by the way, Mother Earth had been dismembered and torn apart as an act of creation. I've seldom read such an insightful inquiry into male worship of violence and its institutionalization at the core of life.

I cite these examples of past behaviors, one from our own not-too-distant history and the other from a very alien society, for what they have to tell us about the ways that gender roles create paradigms of belief and behavior, and are also able to shift as time and circumstances influence beliefs and behavior. Art, we can see, can weight these prescriptive structures of propriety and desirable conduct with great meaning. There are lessons here for women who are committed to the pursuit of art as an affirmation of hope and purposeful aspiration. Art, whatever else it may be, is probably the most potent instrument of persuasion—yes, and that means also of propaganda—that exists in this world.

That brings me back to what a language for women should not be. As we work toward creating-discovering our language, we must disavow its use as conscious propaganda for a particular ideology, or we shall end with something uncomfortably like the works of socialist realism dear to the heart of Josef Stalin. Art is not only a way of stating but a way of inquiring too. What it asks about grows out of a deep conviction that such questions are important, it is linked with belief that does not limit the search for new concepts but inspires it. "Here I stand," said Martin Luther to the Diet of Worms, "I can do no other." Whether or not one agrees with Luther's tenets, one must respect the sincerity with which he held them, the pain through which he moved to discover them, and the remarkable historical consequences of these beliefs. I suppose any enduring religion is in part a work of art; at any rate, powerful art grows out of this kind of conviction, one that has been tested and grown stronger, incorporated new visions and translated old ones in order to find a way of saying something absolutely necessary to the artist and to the audience.

So in looking for, inventing, discovering our language, we have to proceed with a kind of intense concentration, focussed on what we have not yet found, in the certain belief that we will know it when we do find it. And even though artists work alone, the "we" used in that sentence must be present in the ambience of the spirit; I suppose that's why I took such pleasure in the coincidence of my title and that of Carroll Smith-Rosenberg; it was as if we were chorusing along in different places, but in the same musical vein.

Neither of us, I repeat, is creating a piece of art, we are analyzing history in terms of social psychology and feminist philosophy, plus a bit of politics. But the purpose here is to report on overlooked events and ways of dealing with them, and to suggest how we can explore them for significant meaning—which may be used in many ways, and can form a base for expression in art. Looking back is informative politically, as well; our new language and the interpretations based on it, which suggest new activity, will inescapably be subjected to every imaginative attack at cultural and political levels. Women's autonomous images of the world have always faced such attack from the protean power of patriarchy. In confronting that power, we are not trying to do anything simple or easy. We had better not kid ourselves about that. We have got ourselves involved in making the most revolutionary revolution in human history. We need to know all that we can about defensive strategy and female techniques for survival, about the ways in which our foremothers managed to live as something much more than passive slaves and submissive housewives.

All right, our language will have to come out of women's experience, and that means experience broader than personal, broader than that which is contemporary today. We know the past was extremely diverse, why imagine that the future will be any less complex? Our own complex defenses should be at hand if we need them. And we do have defenses and advantages. One of them is what I named, in by book-before-last, the first power of the weak (of whom women form the oldest, largest, and most central group). That power is distrust—negative, you see, but oh, how valuable. Don't believe everything they tell you, it warns. Don't believe that you've come a long way, baby. If you have, why the hell are they calling you "baby"? Don't believe that the way to a world of equality leads through a region of learning, believing and practicing male tricks that will win you trophies that represent male-defined success. Isn't the correlation of "equality" with "winning success" in itself an example of patriarchal double-think, double-think that pollutes communication and distorts our lives? A language for women, which may in time become a human language, will have to reject the central intent of today's public, masculine language that we have all learned as our patriarchal tongue.

To find our mother tongue, then, we need to look at private language, both past and present. Perhaps we could also try to do some such research while we're here. Why, for instance, is our chosen name for menstruation "the curse"? That's sheer mother-tongue. The label certainly isn't used because we are aware of guilt-for-being female but because, in our secret hearts, it's exactly what we expect to receive from Himself up there in his hierarchical heaven: stuffy old creature hiding behind His whiskers, tee-ed off at Eve because of her disorderly conduct, improper behavior. "Curse her! She broke the rules! She tried something new!" And new, it appears, is bad, bad, bad—unless Himself does it Himself. Thus speaks patriarchy. Female black humor adopts its words as mockery.

Humor, like distrust, however, is only a first line of defense. Male language is effective, male patterns of thinking and conceptual relationships do get into our heads as we move out into man's world, and we ought to be very wary about accepting the standards of operation that go along with these ways of seeing and saying. Women's studies, as a discipline, has finally got itself a place on a number of campuses, though not a very high place. Well, being there is not enough. Courteous apologies for the presence of this unheard of discipline will get us nowhere, indeed are likely to diminish the bare tolerance with which it was received. Now, of course, newcomers to a field don't want to be discourteous. And academia is a prideful, even arrogant, enterprise which has however always felt itself menaced by philistinism and consequently reacts to ideas from outside with fear and loathing. In dealing with these paranoid creatures, newcomers will want to be politic—but that does not mean demure, recessive, and apologetic. Let us rather be apologists. Politics demands that we deal with the situations we confront, and a stance of apology isn't a form of dealing. What we need is more propaganda from full, convinced minds and hearts. We want to be bold about our feminine concerns—such matters as money and places on a tenure track, and the demands of raising children laid on those who do most of the raising, and such public needs as better control of violence at home and abroad—all those little matters that women worry about in their feminine way.

In our dealing, too, I believe that we will help ourselves to see more clearly where we stand if we resist putting feminist philosophy into masculinist forms of thought. The true Sons of Patriarchy believe in strict analysis, which separates layers of meaning, deconstructs form into its details of content, and destroys the patterns that are present only when interaction is taking place. I hate to see the language that goes with this Thomist-Talmudic interpretation spread too widely in the way women academics discuss their findings. No doubt being able to use male language is an advantage—bi-lingualism in general is an advantage. But I hope we are not seduced into finding it sufficient for our purposes.

I'm not suggesting that we should elect to be illogical, or sibylline, or mysterious—unless we have to be; unless there is no other way to speak truly. And when we have to talk in these ways, we—to come back to our reason for being here—we will be communicating through the various forms of art that incorporate the knowledge we want to make manifest to others. Academia doesn't trust art until it's been wrestled to the classroom floor and, preferably the artist or poet is dead—preferably, again, by suicide. And no wonder. They are at cross purposes. Art is that marvelous means of communication which is illogical in academic terms because it has its own logic. It connects, it brings together, it resists deconstruction, it knows that the sum is greater than its parts because the sum includes and celebrates form.

Distrust, black humor, resistance to the forms of thinking that carry seeds of separation and distancing, these are the defensive guards we should bear in mind as we work toward inventing-discovering our own language. Let me go a step further and ask whether they are so totally negative as they seem on the surface. Why do we distrust this description of reality? What is the knowledge we hide behind bitter humor? Why do we resist certain ways of analyzing the world, what positive sense makes us feel that they are false or destructive? When we begin to

look at our responses to patriarchal descriptions and
prescriptions we are on the road to understanding them and
the needs and purposes that created them and exploits
them. It might be worth using academic deconstructive
criticism briefly to ask the authors of myth, "What is it
that you are really up to? I find your public agenda
decidedly unpersuasive. That leads me to believe that you
have a private, hidden agenda.
Perhaps I'll have a shot at using your weapons in the right
place to analyze your arguments and the prescriptions for
proper behavior that got me into this position, which I have
decided to leave."

In doing that kind of deconstructive work, I come back
to the need to rely on our experience, past and present, as a
source of validation. If we are going to take apart
patriarchal myth, we need something else to compare it to,
and I guess that has to be our own hard-learned
understanding of reality. Women's experience is rooted in
everyday life; and one of the interesting things that has
been happening in the years since the first Conference on
Women and the Arts is a growing respect for creative
activity that is part of ordinary life. In my opinion, one of
the sad consequences of recent history has been the
separation between high art and ordinary, everyday
creativity so that crafts are pointedly separated off from
high-price, high status "works of art." Even the male
establishment has grown aware of the detrimental effects of
canonizing one kind of creativity and stigmatizing another;
but my feeling is that it has not gone about bringing them
together in a really fruitful way. It has, I think, been
looking merely for "something new," rather than something
true.

Women artists, on the other hand, have been looking
at the traditional world in order to reinterpret it. What is
new isn't a surface newness, but a different way of seeing
into reality so that a transformation is revealed; something
that has been there all along becomes an opening into a
more profound reality. The structure shifts. I've spoken of
history and its value as a data base for art; but in looking
back, we are not simply observing what happened. We are
also trying to understand the how and the why of this

happening. Where right-wing traditionalists want to
reinstate the past, we want to study the creation of
traditions and the way in which they prescribe
behavior—particularly the behavior supported by gender
roles—in order to create different traditions that are
broader and more fully human.

Question: Can we human beings actually "create"
traditions? Answer: Yes, if we know what we're doing.
After all, where did those we have been living with come
from?

If, for example, we believe that the gender roles of the
past have been severely limiting and distorting, if we wish
to change them and build flexibility and new processes that
give rise to choice into tradition, we can't simply declare
that this is a good idea. A conviction of the value of
flexibility and choice in human life must be felt and
communicated, and ways of living this conviction imagined.
I think that's possible. Can people be habituated to change?
Yes, I'm sure of it. It's exactly what has been happening
in our recent history. But at present, change has become
frightening instead of exciting and promising. The old
structure is resisting. I say again, the creativity of art can
work toward such ends better than any other kind of
persuasion.

But for us the message of this persuasion, this
propaganda, is not that "New is better," or that times have
changed and you'd better be trendy in order to keep up with
them. Certainly times have changed; but we can't just be
satisfied with keeping up. Change can run amuck if human
beings don't struggle to control and direct it. Change is
part of a process. It comes out of a past, it will make its
own future. If we hope for a better future, we have to try
to take a hand in what is going on. Political intervention is
certainly important, but vision comes first. Art is in some
form a way of prophesying; but prophecy that ignores the
past, where the processes of change began, falls away from
truth into fantasy.

In our lives today political fantasies are trying to
disconnect acts from the processes of which they are a
part. Communication has turned into public relations.
Everything comes up "instant" and therefore, everything

loses its meaning and life becomes incoherent; it has been deconstructed. Our patriarchal establishment has forgotten the facts of the past, except as they have been embalmed in mythic tradition, which is actually false to the past in many ways. The Establishment is consequently unable to think forward responsibly. It simply presents itself, and asks for public response in immediate approval or disapproval. Another presentation will be offered tomorrow if today's response is cold.

Now, the disciplines of art know better than that. Even if they deal in "instantness," they are asking about its significance. If they present violence and disruption, they are exploring the meaning of the widespread presence of these characteristics of our age. If the arts, from time to time, are declared to have no "meaning," what is being denied is the logical structure of a current system of concepts, not the significance of life and acts and processes and correspondences and responses. Like Martin Luther, I don't see how artists can do other—understanding the world and communicating understanding, in whatever "mysterious" or "sibylline" way is what art does and exists to do. It "can do no other."

Inventing a language for women, then, is a task of the first order of magnitude and one that must turn to art for its central direction. What's there? we ask of our experience. What does it mean? How do your processes interact? we say to reality. How has truth been adulterated? we ask history. What can we learn from the techniques that made falsity so convincing? Can we adapt them to support new ways of seeing that are less false?

There's no way to answer such questions by appealing to codified traditions. Responses must come from creative interaction between the world out there and the person struggling to reply. The very fact of new answers will incorporate wider vision into the language we are making, will keep it flexible even as it develops into a common way of speaking.

I began with a quotation from Marge Piercy. Let me end with one from Adrienne Rich:

No one ever told us we had to study our lives,

make of our lives a study, as if learning natural
history
or music, that we should begin
with the simple exercises first
and slowly go on trying
the hard ones, practicing till strength
and accuracy become one with the daring
to leap into transcendence, take the chance
of breaking down in wild arpeggio
or faulting the full sentence of the fugue.

I have to add that being a good poet and a speaker of
truth, she goes on:

And in fact we can't live like that: we take on
everything at once before we've even begun
to read or mark time, we're forced to begin
in the midst of the hardest movement,
the one already sounding as we were born.

("Transcendental Etude", The Dream of a Common
Language, p. 74.)

Well, back to Martin Luther. We can do no other.
The language demands to be made, as a child demands to
be born.

DISCUSSIONS—A RETROSPECTIVE LOOK

The Conference's working paper, Elizabeth Durbin's <u>Women and the Arts: A Survey of Recent Progress</u>, traces the phenomenal growth of women's culture since the early 1970's. The first set of discussion sessions were constituted to take the measure of the issues, problems, and opportunities presented by that growth from the standpoints of five different cultural perspectives:

- The Aesthetic Perspective
- The Political Perspective
- The Economic Perspective
- The Institutional Perspective
- The Educational Perspective

The Aesthetic Perspective

Leader: Gayle Kimball

Rapporteur: Estella Lauter

<u>Excerpts from the discussion</u>

<u>Gayle Kimball</u>: I explored themes in women's culture in
the first chapter of my book, <u>Women's Culture</u>. Let me
briefly describe the themes:

- one of the central messages is dealing with power in a
  new way, of talking about empowerment (you hear a
  lot in the women's movement now about "power with"
  not "over," and arriving at decisions through
  consensus).
- looking at love, sexuality, and family in terms of
  multiple options—not having one form that's proper,
  but many many choices.
- women's experience as the source of a new vision; half
  of human experience has been neglected, and we need
  to look at that with honor and respect. Jessie
  Bernard, the sociologist, talks about the female ethos,
  and Robin Morgan talks about female values saving
  the planet.
- regaining control of women's bodies and the planetary
  body. Both have been raped, both have been abused
  and treated with disrespect. There's a thrust toward
  regaining control of our bodies, our sensuality, and of
  protecting mother earth.
- integrated thought process, a movement towards what
  Mary Daley calls "spiral thinking" rather than "linear
  thinking," including intuition, the spiritual, the occult.

<u>Margie Adam</u>: One of the things that has happened in
women's music over the past ten years is the development
of a whole system of production and distribution for music.
There has been a deep commitment in this effort to reach
out to women of different economic, social and cultural

backgrounds—a desire to create a circle of community. I think that is one of the central values which is different about women working in culture: this desire to make the circle bigger, to include more people, to have more discussion rather than make an exclusive club which will then set up the rules to exclude more and more people from a definition of art which is "truly important."

Karen Winzenz: Another woman-identified value that informs not just the making of art but also culture in general is the notion that the *process* of making art is as significant as the result. The male value system seems to pay attention only to the end product. For example, in the educational setting it is clear that the male strategy for determining policy usually has to do with the legitimacy of the end product. It does not matter how you get there. If it means destroying people, if it means being totally callous to the individuals involved, it does not matter, so long as we proceed toward these wonderful goals that are supposedly "humanistic," but frequently are simply not.

Elizabeth Janeway: I'm so glad you raised the question of male values, because I don't think we can talk in a vacuum about female values without talking about where we are. I'd like to suggest to you that I've been coming to think more and more that something that is very oppressive to men and that distorts their view of the world is the fact that they have to be oppressors.

If you're going to divide the world in two by gender and have one be top dog, then the people who are named to be top dog have to distance themselves from the people who aren't. They, then, have to institute a dichotomy and see some people as others. This puts quite a burden on the way they can think about themselves. Women can look to be empowered and see it as something valuable and admirable. But if you are told you have to be the people in power, that can be very frightening, and that produces a tendency to institute oppression and to see the way to solve problems as confrontational—and you know, you argue and somebody wins.

Another thing, I think, is a tendency to create

hierarchies. This is a direct enemy of the sense of community. Well, I don't think you can ever accomplish everything by a consensus opinion—you have to have some kind of structure that can listen and can say, "this is what most people feel. Let's try it this way." But to set up a hierarchial system, in which there are slots and people fit in them, and if you don't fit in them you fall through the cracks, is the result, I think, of this laying upon the male sex of the need to be powerful and therefore of the need to oppress. I don't believe we can talk about aesthetics without getting into politics, because we're not just working away from politics; I think we have to be working against it.

Unidentified: I agree that it is more hurtful to be an oppressor than it is to be the oppressed. If we could get that in perspective, things would change very fast. We are, in fact, more hurt humanly than the people we are oppressing. Men are more hurt on a human level than females.

Betsy Damon: I actually think there are no new aesthetics. I think there's new content all the time, because we live in a communicating, dialoguing world, and we are all stretching to do the best we can to make things better. So as women we are creating new content according to our visions of how we want to make things better and better.

Estella Lauter: If you consider the arts as part of culture, then women have had a tremendous impact, and I think what we've done primarily is to broaden people's definitions of art. I'm not saying that this is an exclusively female or feminist enterprise. At the turn of the century, modernism also broadened our definitions. But unfortunately, in the formalist period afterward, ideas of art narrowed tremendously again. Women have now forced people to recognize the crafts as arts instead of simply as crafts. We've taken a critical look at phenomena in the art world that were hierarchically arranged during the period from the first World War until into the sixties, and we've attacked that hierarchy. Now we haven't destroyed it completely, but we've made serious inroads into hierarchical thinking about visual art, maybe to some extent about music, and certainly about literature.

So I don't agree that the only thing that we've done is to change content. The values we've asserted are very important. We're on our way to working out a very different definition of art than the formalist one which has dominated twentieth century thinking. And we're on our way toward a different sense of how to appraise art. We evaluate much more in terms of audience response. We go all the way back to the Greeks to create a renewed awareness of the power the arts have to move an audience. I don't see this as exclusively female or exclusively feminist, but I do see women as having played a terribly important role in broadening the role of the arts within culture.

Summary

The group agreed that there have been feminist messages in art. They have to do with the empowerment of women, with the development or preservation of a female ethos, with the nature of women's experience, particularly of the female body and its relationship to the life of the planet; and with the importance of integrative thought processes or "spiral thinking." To be sure, we will not know the full extent of what we have to say as women artists until the system of distributing our work develops to make our ideas more accessible. But we do share some values: a concern for community, a tendency to be inclusive, and an orientation toward the process of making.

We have altered the stereotypes of women to admit a new sense of women's power and sensuality; the image of women now emphasizes "doing," rather than "serving," in part because of our work. We have at least begun to influence the culture to think less androcentrically in a variety of ways. In the arts we have an effort to broaden the definition of art (i.e., to include the crafts), so that it is less hierarchical. We have begun to change the valuation system that governs the acceptance of works, making it more responsive to the audience. We have used our cooperative alternative institutions to share information about issues that concern all women, to initiate an exchange of power. Our art seeks to be more responsive to the rituals, the life experiences, and the political concerns of a broad range of human beings. We're developing a strong sense of social responsibility in the presentation of our art, if not always in its content or form. It's hard to identify "new" or exclusively "feminist" techniques of art-making, but perhaps "newness" is not the most important issue. Our work certainly is "significant."

But, like it or not, we are engaged in a battle for control of information—not only control of the system of distribution, but also of who is going to understand (interpret) how art is made, or defined, or evaluated. And in that battle, we need to develop a medium of exchange. Money would help. Alternative ideas are welcome.

One danger of our situation is that as we become more oriented toward collectivity we may stop listening to our own individual voices. We must not stop daring to be alone, different and excellent.

The Political Perspective

Leader: Susan Friedman

Rapporteur: Susan Searing

<u>Excerpts from the discussion</u>

<u>Susan Friedman</u>: Conventional definitions have talked about politics as being about the structures of power, particularly power in the public sphere. In this view, you don't have politics in the private sphere—what goes on there is apolitical—and politics is about governments and organizations and groups whose objectives are directed toward the use and retention of power or attacking other institutions of power.

Conventional or mainstream aesthetics relates that kind of definition to the arts, and concludes that the arts and politics are mutually exclusive. They don't have anything to do with each other. So when during the twenties a graphic artist like Kathe Kollwitz did lithographs about starving children in Germany and passed out hundreds of them, her work was dismissed as not being artistic but rather "political."

Feminism has redefined our traditional concepts of the political. One of the major theoretical statements was made by Kate Millet in her 1970 book, <u>Sexual Politics</u>. Primarily, she brought politics into the private sphere, asserting that politics is not just something that happens between governmental or institutional organizations out there in the public sphere, but that it happens right in the home. It happens during sexual intimacies. In every dimension of human experience, there is something political going on.

Kate Millet talks about politics as being concerned about the uses of power as it's been organized along a gender hierarchy in both the public and private spheres. Her book was enormously important in feminist criticism because it highlighted a relationship between power and the issue of creativity. She would, in fact, argue that not only is Kathe Kollwitz's art political but so is Picasso's, so is that of every artist. We had the rallying cry in the feminist movement of "the personal is political." In this view, there is no domain of human experience which is outside of politics, because in fact human beings exist in culture, and culture is organized in many different ways.

One of the ways in which all cultures organize is along gender lines. In fact, there is no society in which men and women have had equal power and equal access, particularly in the public sphere. The implication for the arts is that no creative act can stand outside of culture, can stand outside of the political organization of that culture; it must be weighed within a cultural context that reflects a gender system. There is a political implication in all creative expression, whether done by men or women. Nothing is neutral, nothing stands outside of culture.

Last night Elizabeth Janeway described two kinds of political art. She said that art as propaganda can be the most potent instrument of persuasion—a use that she associated with socialist realism and Stalin. She said that art can also be a protest, a form of inquiring, asking, not making a statement.

Lourna Bourg: I'm reminded of the effort we made in Louisiana to collect stories of plantation women. At first, when they were only viewed as individual stories people found them absolutely fascinating. Then they were brought together as a group and put on display in the little library in the local community and they took on a new meaning: Black women telling their own stories about struggle and success and survival under the oppressive planation system. Suddenly there was a community explosion. There were Black women trailing in from the countryside eager to see the display because the library had never done anything like this before. You had some white people sort of applauding—this was a minority of them—saying it's about time. You had others turning very red as they read the materials. You had newspapers dealing with some of the topics. It was a time when the community in a sense confronted itself.

<u>Kristine Cottam</u>: In the visual arts we've been
experiencing several kinds of political activity. One has to
do with the art itself, with respect to its having so-called
political content. At another level there have been the
organizational efforts that have occurred, and the kind of
revolutionary activities that artists have been involved in.
I'm talking about as far back as the sixties when women
artists first banded together and said, "it's no longer a
crime to be female and an artist. We acknowledge this fact
and we acknowledge it publicly, even though it is risky to
our careers." And it was very very risky to say," yes, I'm
a woman artist and I identify as a woman artist, and I'm
willing to stand up and say, My name is not K. L. Cottam,
my name is Kristine. And that's female. And, yes I am a
female. And, yes, that is a positive part of my identity."
When women started doing that, we had the beginnings of
very dramatic political activity in the visual arts. At the
next stage women started to acknowledge to one another,
"Our opportunities in the art world are not what they
should be. Let us create our own opportunities." And they
started banding together and founded women-run,
women-owned galleries like AIR in New York and WARM
in Minnesota. Then various groups of minority women
banded together as artists to put on independent shows. I
think that is the level of political involvement that's been
most effective.

<u>Ruth Dean</u>: I have to say that I can't see the connection
between politics and creativity. I think creativity is such an
inherent part of the artist, it's such a subjective thing, it's a
gut feeling artists have to express themselves.

<u>BUTO</u>: Personally I view any intimate statement as
political, in the sense that it makes a comment on one's
position in the world. I feel, in fact, it's important for
individuals to make such statements.

<u>Margot Kernan</u>: I've been teaching recently and I had an
interesting experience. I assigned the writing of a screen
play to my class—it was a very small class of five women
students—and I said it should reflect a personal problem

and a political problem, because I was interested in trying to get at some of these schisms that we're talking about. They all wrote about personal problems. None of them could summon up a political problem to deal with. The closest they got was drunken driving as a political problem—you know, legislation against drunken driving. I said what about nuclear war, abortion, civil rights, minority rights, pornography, foreign policy, the draft, and so forth and so on? And these were as remote to them as if these were problems of Soviet or Japanese youth.

Lorna Bourg's work with the women farm workers of Louisiana is very political even though it isn't agitational per se. It is very political because it is dealing with the valorization of experience, which then leads to the sense of need to change that experience.

I find from my own observation as a teacher and video maker that the key problem in the arts is really the depoliticization of American life. This is a time when American history and American structures are being buried and lost. And not just women's history but political history in general.

I think we really need not be afraid of politics in art because I don't think we have that problem. I think our problem is the other, that we venerate the mystification of experience rather than the analysis of it.

* * * * * * * * * * * * * *

Kristine Cottam: Many women artists have been absolutely stripped out of history because it was socially unacceptable for women to be artists—socially unacceptable for them to have a place in the power structure. So you have to be very careful of this concept of universality, because it is not necessarily true that all important work survives over time. If it has survived time, it has survived political structure, societal pressure, and the emotional needs of the people with the power to buy and keep that work in production. If art has not survived time we have to consider whether it may have been unacceptable because of who produced it, how it was produced, what the subject matter was, and what the form of the art work was. We also have to look at who did not want those things said, and why not.

Margot Kernan: If you want an example of universal art, or something that is universally appealing right now, look at network television. This is something that blankets our culture, and it is universally appealing to a large bank of Americans. It's a very political art form, because nothing in our society better expresses and perpetuates the forms and needs and structures of late twentieth century capitalism better than network television.

Ted Shannon: And leads to the alienation you spoke of...and to the depoliticization of human beings.

Margot Kernan: Exactly! And to a loss of history, and a loss of connectedness.

Summary

The discussion moved between two ways of seeing the relation between art and politics: the content of the art itself; and the role of the artist (as individual or in organizations) as a political agent in the traditional sense. There was general agreement on the latter; all felt the artists should be more active in the legislative process.

Participants expressed a broader spectrum of opinion of the relation of politics to the content and form of art—from the minority stance that art is intimate, subjective, and unrelated to politics, to various perspectives that incorporated a feminist definition of politics (i.e., that the private is as political as the public, and that all art, indeed all human experience, exists within a cultural system that is also a gender system and a power hierarchy).

Much of the discussion centered on definitions of "universal" as a criterion for good art. Some saw universality as a "trap," a cover-up for white male middle-class taste and values. Experience (as rendered in art) must always be defined in terms of race, culture, generation, etc. The notion of the universal is also tied to our sense of history and tradition, e.g., ancient Greek art and literature feels universal to us because our own present day culture derives from it; we do not have the same sense about other cultural histories. Moreover, what we praise as universal excludes the experiences of ancient Greek women and slaves.

A definition of the universal as that which has "staying power through the ages" was critiqued. We know that women's art has been suppressed historically, not for reasons of quality but for its social or political unacceptability. The content, form, or the very fact that a woman created it can guarantee that art fails to stand the test of time.

"Politics" has become a dirty word to artists; it carries connotations of "vulgar marxism and socialist realism." There is a wider problem, too, in the depoliticization of American life. Art must valorize political issues, and must venerate the analysis of experience, rather than the mystification of experience.

Has feminist art history and practice become prescriptive? Must artists conform to certain standards of content or form (e.g., circular or vulval images) in order to genuinely paint "as a woman?" Most participants felt that such prescriptions are troubling but that they were more evident during the '70's than today.

For women composers, separatism remains an issue. Most would prefer to have their works performed by mixed orchestras for mixed audiences, but often women-only concerts are the only way to have their music heard. We need what Alice Ostriker has termed "both/and" thinking, a way for women artists from diverse perspectives to work together and still be part of the larger culture.

In sum, political questions are central to all of the following: 1) the definition of art; 2) the self-identity of the artist; 3) the content of artworks; 4) the form of the art (to what extent and how it encodes female experience); 5) the audience; 6) the art's impact; 7) organizational advocacy by and for the arts; 8) art institutions, both mainstream and alternative; 9) the canonization of "great" artists; and 10) the relation of art in the broadest sense to general society and human issues, including nuclear war.

The Economic Perspective

Leader: Karen Dobbs

Rapporteur: Cara Chell

Excerpts from the discussion

Karen Dobbs: I think the first order of business is to get the opinion of this group: are we in fact paid less than men?

Kathryn Clarenbach: Next question!

Karen Dobbs: O.K. Why are we paid less?

Jacqueline Bradley: Speaking as a representative of a performing arts union whose purpose and reason for existence is to negotiate wages and working conditions with our employer groups, theoretically women in the union should be earning the same amount of money as men because there are minimums below which nobody can go. What we have found is that even though those minimums are set, women's ability to negotiate upscale contracts—especially in the film area—is severely hampered by the fact that we are women. The attitude often is that women actors don't really need to work because they're all married and they have husbands supporting them, and acting is really sort of a hobby for most of them, so that they don't need to be paid as much—and there's always somebody else who can do the job and will work for scale.

Judith Lang Zaimont: As a composer I wish we had a union framework from which to negotiate. This is such an individual art form. I just wish we had scale and minimum and a salary schedule that was laid out, instead of having to scrimp from hand to mouth and negotiate conditions on a case by case basis.

Karen Dobbs: One of the primary questions we are to address is what have been the patterns of economic discrimination that women have experienced. Are conditions getting better? Women are making more than they were X number of years ago. Does the future bode well? Should we be encouraged by the number of women Pulitzer winners suddenly in various fields? Should we be encouraged by the fact that the New York Philharmonic has recently hired a couple of women as principals and has never done so before in history, etc? Should we be encouraged that so many of our students in the arts are women? Where does it all go? Are we moving? What is your perception? Is it going to get better?

Unidentified: I think that the male society is giving us a few things to pacify us, but I don't see things getting really better over a large picture.

Unidentified: Can I just challenge that? Is it the males who are doing that?

Unidentified: It's the whole society. It's men and females, because the females have a lot to do with other females getting work.

Judith Lang Zaimont: Part of the difficulty may be that many of the art forms we're talking about are centuries old—making music in groups, writing for traditional combinations. Now, in electronic music, which is a post World War II sub-speciality, women do not have a problem—nowhere near like the way composers of symphonic or regular acoustical instrumental music do. Many women have been founders and directors of electronic music studios. There are at least eleven women heading up electronic music studios in this country and they are now role models for other women composers coming to study with them. So, in the recently developed arts of the 20th century there is not the problem of a bias which has been inherited from centuries of cultural thinking. You're not dealing with a climate of mind that is perpetuated because the art form is dragging its history around with it.

Summary

We had a variety of perspectives on economic matters:
- creator vs. presenter
- those with institutional perspective vs. individual artist
- performing artist vs. visual/word (solitary) artist
- unionized vs. non unionized worker

Answer to the question "are we paid less than man"? was, of course, yes. Strategy (short-term) for improving this seemed to be learning better negotiating skills.

To the question of the necessity for blind reviewing and auditioning, most agreed that it was even more important to educate the individuals on the selection panels.

In a discussion of both politics and grants, it was pointed out that often the best strategy for finding support for individual women artists is to take the "back door" approach—namely, to form an all women's group (like At The Foot Of The Mountain, WARM) which then seeks funding.

The most fascinating point was that women in recently established art forms, like electronic media, graphic arts and photography, have a better chance at leadership, higher pay, and "star" positions, because these arts have not yet developed the patterns of male bias.

The Institutional Perspective

Leader: Ellouise Schoettler

Rapporteur: Alice Randlett

Excerpts from the Discussion

Ariel Dougherty: I have a strong feeling that the development of the arts in this country during the last twenty five, thirty years has been made on the backs of women. As the field now becomes more professional and there is more money in it, it seems likely that we will sink down into the lower echelons of power within the arts—exactly parallel to what happened to the educational movement in this country. I see that as a big problem.

Ellouise Schoettler: June Wayne has been the prophetess of the arts for ten years and she was dead right when she said that women began to make inroads for change when they presented the appearance of a strong, coherent force of people. The difficulty is that we don't stick with such efforts. We don't stay with them. You have to have that unity if you are going to deal with the government. You have to be able to make a statement that they can hear and understand.

Kirsten Beck: That's a very good point. But as I look at the difference between the Biddle administration and the Hodsell administration, the Biddle administration was prepared to respond to the concerted efforts of women and other identifiable groups. My sense of the Endowment now is that they are insulated against that kind of pressure.

I don't know what kind of a strategy you adopt when the Endowment or other institutions that are so important to us turn a deaf ear to our needs. Successful public relations campaigns make a big difference in this country, and successful use of the mass media makes a big difference. I don't know whether the time may have passed for concerted political pressure.

Summary

- Phenomenal growth in number of women artists in last fifteen years or so.
- National Endowment for the Arts recent turn to the right has hurt women artists. Their funding for women's art organizations declined 35% from 1982 to 1983 despite $13,000,000 more dollars.
- Do artists need to divorce themselves from dependence on institutional funding? Does such funding infantalize artists?
- What is the connection of the media to the arts? Should women who work in the media, for instance as producers, be considered artists?
- Recent advancements in the arts have been made on the backs of women. Now that this great leap forward has occurred, will women be left to languish as they were in, say, education?
- Bi-coastalism and (versus) regionalism: we need to build on regional strengths as well as investigate our differences. What would the study of our various regional cultures gain us?
- Relationships with males in various art areas appear to be better in those areas where females dominate the field as in dance.
- Because of young women's lack of a sense of history and commitment, our relationships with them are not flourishing.
- Women are still doing the menial work, (e.g. mailings) in art organizations that have both male and female members. This may be in return for the continued interest and support from the males, who when involved in an organization, bring a great deal of clout.

The Educational Perspective

Leader: Margaret Lynn

Rapporteur: Karen Merritt

Excerpts from the discussion

Gloria Link: I noted that all the way up the line as a
student that if one were bright it made no difference
whether you were male or a female. When I was working
on my Ph.D. I was thrilled to the reaction I received to
whatever I was doing, whether artistically or academically.
There was no question but that my credentials were fine.
During the graduate seminars I was always invited to read
my papers aloud, and my opinion was always asked for.
However, when it came time for me to move into the
professional world suddenly I became aware of a radical
change. I'd be walking down the corridor with one of the
male students and we'd run into the chairman. Direct
quote! He would say to the young man: "There's a job
opening at Princeton. I want you to pick up the form at the
office." Or: "We've got something nice at Cornell. I want
you to apply for it. I've set you up for an interview." I
was made to feel like a little girl again! I would say to the
Chairman, "Er...is there anything for me?" And this is the
answer I would get: "Oh, check with the secretary. She's
got a whole group of things!" He was referring to what we
called "the cattle desk"—the collection of jobs that were one
and two year turnovers, which meant that they were the
dogs.

And so I did not end up at Cornell. I did not end up at
Princeton. I should have! My academic credentials were
good enough in every way to have done so.

Margaret Lynn: Looking back over your academic career
and knowing what you know now, could you have made it
different? Could you have had a different kind of career?

Gloria Link: I don't think so, because even women who have come to my institution in recent years have also been swallowed up by the old boy network. It's brutal. There is nothing deadlier than the old boy network within the university!

Cherie Doyle: I'd like to give an update on Gloria's story. Starting out in my professional career I didn't feel second to anyone either, although in the last few years I couldn't help but notice other people were getting ahead, and I wasn't. Why does sexism exist in the academic community? I think it's because the power structure is so entrenched. Women can be a part of academic departments and administration as long as they are not a threat to the existing power structure.

Gill Miller: I guess I'm tired of having to play the political game in a man's world. I'm tired of having to have the best credentials, and I should have been at Princeton or Cornell. My point is this: my credentials are fine—as scholarly as my male colleagues. I should expect to get hired as often as they do. Why do I have to be "Superwoman?"

In dance departments, men often get hired because they are men. Departments are trying to find a gender balance. And yet, even when those men have the same credentials as their female colleagues, they never faced the same competition to get them. Men are nurtured and encouraged in dance, even when they're mediocre—because there are so few of them.

Unidentified: There's going to be quite a group of old boys retiring in the next few years. We have to prepare women to demand that women replace these men, so that we can have a much better balance in the departments.

Margaret Lynn: And I think it's terribly important that we don't seek all the little pedestrian positions, that we seek positions of authority that give us the power to hire people in the kind of jobs that help create a better balance. And I don't say we should proceed unfairly. Do it with integrity, do it with ethics, do it with a sense of fairness.

<u>Unidentified</u>: I want to spend my energies teaching, yet at the same time I see that if changes are going to take place I need to think about moving into decision-making roles. But if I do that, it cuts into my teaching time. I think there are an awful lot of people like me who are real torn about how exactly you go about working in the system in a way that changes it and yet doesn't dilute some of the good things that you're already doing.

<u>Karen Merritt</u>: It is true that when you go into administration, you're giving up a certain pleasure—and that's the pleasure of working with students. On the other hand, the impact that you can have as a person with hiring authority is just giant. Obviously, you're then able to more easily create the kind of work place that you want. The potential is there for making serious and long-lasting changes.

<u>Gloria Link</u>: I very strongly urge those of you who are in your twenties and your thirties to give up the joy of being in that class room, because what has been said here is very important. You do have to be in a decision-making position in order to have that long range chance. Now I think we've made some strides in our time, but if you younger women really want to make a difference, as Elizabeth Janeway said last night, you'd better pick it up from here on. What strategy can we use that is other than political?

<u>Margaret Lynn</u>: I think the fact that you don't use the political is part of the strategy. The fact that women are essentially non-political is part of the strategy—and that we fight! Yes, that does require an enormous amount of energy, an enormous amount of commitment, and an enormous amount of drive. Our strategy is to be visionary, our strategy is that each day we're going to foster the better opportunity for people—all people—not just women. We're for fairness for all people. We may feel the injustices of the unfair system more so than others—because the network among women has not been like the old boys'

system where they're all holding hands. So we feel more singular, but the unfair systems that many of us are seeing affect very good talent in the male population as well. Very strong and good men are often denied jobs, because they, too, are a threat, and they're given pretty much the same kind of treatment that women are.

Summary

The university is very supportive of women as students in the arts, but not of women who want to move into the academic hierarchy. How much have we let ourselves be intimidated, especially in the years before we developed a language of assertiveness?

The qualities of women as administrators as contrasted with men as administrators were discussed. Women have to develop strategies when men have predecided an outcome (before the meeting in the smoke-filled room).

At universities, we need to develop a critical mass of faculty working toward the same end (as in the case of the junior faculty conference at Macalester College). There is a psychological benefit of being a teacher: students idolize you. Women are attached to the package things come in (women work hard, but don't get things in packages the way men do. We look for approval—our package—while men accept that they receive things by right—their package). We need to test the criteria by which we are evaluated (male criteria, by male peers).

There is a problem of women administrators leaving many campuses, jeopardizing the gains we have made in the 1970s. There are many exciting things to attract women administrators outside academia. But there will be many male retirements inside academia in the next ten years. Women should prepare themselves to step into those positions.

Let's not forget or undervalue our impact on students, men and women, who will be the artists and academics of the future.

Historically, when women have entered a field in large numbers, the financial rewards of the field have dropped.

If women come to dominate university teaching and men leave, both prestige and salaries could drop.

Women may have to pay a price for standing up for what is right.

We need to foster a society that is fair for all people. Capable men have been denied in this society as well as capable women.

From Occultation to Politicization: The Evolution of the Goddess Image in Contemporary Feminist Art

by Gloria Feman Orenstein

Dedicated to the memory of Ana Mendieta whose incandescent work has always inspired my writing on the Goddess and whose passionate life recently came to a tragic ending.

As we survey women's artistic creation over the past decade the theme of the reclamation of the image of the Goddess in contemporary art and literature emerges as a salient feature of the new feminist iconography.

In fact, it is entirely logical that this should be the case, for the Goddess symbolizes creation and, therefore, by extension, the Goddess also represents artistic creation. Originally, it seemed as if the Fertility Goddess only represented Procreation, but we are now coming to understand this image as it appears in the arts in a more metaphorical way: as a symbol for three separate kinds of creation; procreation, cosmic creation, and artistic creation.

In the Goddess image there is no distinction drawn between woman as creator of nature and woman as creator of culture. The symbol of a Woman Creator bringing forth both life and art, nature and culture, seems to represent in the most poignant, powerful and concise way possible the point at which most of the themes espoused by contemporary Feminism converge.

The Goddess image implies a new feminist consciousness at the same time that it reveals a new knowledge of our most ancient historical past. This knowledge, obtained from studies made by excavations at archeological sites dating from the Upper Paleolithic through the Neolithic to the Copper Age, and elucidated largely by Archeologist Marija Gimbutas of U.C.L.A., informs us that for more than 20,000 years of human history the creator of life was imaged as a female in societies that had no weapons, and in which women had powerful roles, often as Priestesses of the Goddess Religion.

Thus, the Goddess symbol also reminds us that our legitimate history has been buried, and that through its excavation we are learning how short the patriarchal period in human history has been in comparison with the 20,000 or more years of matristic, women-centered, goddess-centered cultures that once flourished in Central Europe.

The Goddess then becomes a valid artistic symbol for women as Creator, for the reclaiming of a history in which women's creative powers were revered, as well as for a recognition that during those years of human history in which the Goddess was the central image of the Creation of life and of the arts, people did not engage in war. The Goddess emerges today as a symbol for the manifold changes that feminists hope to bring about in both consciousness and in the world which will restore the image of Woman to her rightful place in both history and society.

Indeed, it is this image alone that has now come to symbolize our feminist awakening to the new knowledge now being uncovered by feminist scholars around the globe, as well as to the political conclusions that must be drawn from the knowledge.

The return of the Goddess in art and literature today is not to be taken literally. It does not signify a plea for a return to the pagan religious practices of the pre-patriarchal past. Nevertheless, it does signal a new awareness of a kind of spirituality which does not separate heaven and earth, spirit and matter, human and animal; a spirituality which images the Earth as sacred and the Goddess as The Great Mother of all life.

I would like to outline the process that my own thinking has undergone with respect to the meaning of the Goddess image and describe the ways in which feminist scholarship about women's art works. I will use myself as a case history and trace at least four separate stages in the evolution of my own ideas about the re-emergence of the Goddess in women's art over this decade. These periods in my evolution are:

1. The Occultation of the Goddess in Art by Surrealist
    Women
2. My Jungian period and my Heresies article
3. The impact on my work of Marija Gimbutas'
    archeological writings
4. The Political Dimension: My collaboration with Irene
    Diamond

I sincerely feel that the relationship between feminist
creation and feminist research must be articulated so that
we can appreciate the vast impact that the Women's
Movement has made on the creative processes of
contemporary women writers and artists and vice versa.

In her paper, "The Dangerous Sex, Art Language and
Male Power," art historian Joanna Frueh critiques the
metaphors of war and miracles that permeate all art
historical writing. These metaphors define the artist as a
male, as a conquering hero in a war against the generation
of the Fathers to which the male artist must do violence in
order to achieve freedom, and as a miracle worker. The
male artist is sanctified by the language of miracles used in
art historical and critical writing. As Joanna Frueh
expresses it, the male artist "is the priest and prophet, a
missionary gaining converts...a seer, a saint. The artist is
divine."[1] Frueh reminds us how we are taught to worship
artists because the subtext of art history implies that great
artists are like God.

This is where the image of the Goddess emerges. Art
history's creation myth uses the male artist as a stand-in
for God the Father. In this case, God the Father and the
male artist both give birth to nature and culture.

It now becomes apparent that in the woman artist's
reappropriation of the Goddess image, she is at once
correcting two false creation myths:

1. The myth of God the Father as cosmic creator. In
    light of all the recent archeological evidence that
    shows how the very first divinity was imaged as a
    female Creatress, we must return to a Creation story
    in which the Goddess is recognized as the Mother of all
    living things.
2. The myth of the male artist giving birth to the work of
    art. This myth is based upon an erroneous and

rhetorical device in which the biological powers of procreation are transferred from the female to the male. Now it at once becomes clear that if we are to use the metaphors of Procreation and Creation legitimately, we will be led directly to the discoveries that:

a. The earliest image of a Creator was that of a female and

b. An artist who is both fecund and pregnant with, or who gives birth to a work of art might legitimately be or have been both historically and presently, a female.

In order to develop the sequence of my ideas on the re-emergence of the Goddess, I am obliged to narrate a personal anecdote which tells of the eruption of the theme of the Goddess in my own life. This story dates back to the summer of 1971 when I was concluding my dissertation on Surrealism in Contemporary Theatre and writing a chapter about the Surrealist painter and writer, Leonora Carrington. She had responded to my correspondence about her work and to the chapter that I sent to her by saying that I understood <u>nothing</u> about her art. She said that she lived in many dimensions, and it was as if I were describing an elephant having only seen its tail. I was despondent, since there were no books or articles about her that I could consult. How could I learn what her work was about without going to Mexico to visit her? I couldn't! So I decided to buy a Mexican dress, and I hoped that its magical vibrations would infuse my blood stream and ultimately illuminate my brain. On July 6, 1971 I put on the Mexican dress I had just bought, looked in the mirror, and said: "If I can't go to Mexico let Mexico come to me!" At that exact moment the phone rang and a deep English accent spoke to me from the other end of the line saying: "This is Leonora Carrington. I have just arrived in New York, and I would like to meet you." I trembled as I told her about my Magical Mexican dress. I said that she would probably never believe what had just happened. She replied: "Of course I believe it, Gloria, I'm a witch!" That evening I met her at the Chelsea Hotel in New York, and she greeted me with her fingers in the sign of a half-moon.

When I asked her what that meant, she said: "These are the holy horns of Consecration of the Great Goddess." Everyone has famous last words! Mine will go down as: "of the WHO?" As soon as I heard the word "Goddess" I knew that I had to find out what that meant. Until that moment I had only known about God. This was a great mystery to me and a great moment in my life. For the next eleven years I put everything aside and followed Leonora Carrington on a quest for the goddess vision in order to understand the occult meaning of her creative work. During that period I made several trips to Mexico and visited her almost on a daily basis when she lived in New York.

The first stage of my learning about the Goddess has to do with its occultation. I want to begin with an analysis of Leonora Carrington's occult Surrealist Goddess icon, Grandmother Moorhead's Aromatic Kitchen (1975). This painting is a coded cryptogram which on one level can "pass" for a surrealist oneiric dream image. Actually the image of Mother Goose is an emblem signifying the Mother Goddess. Note the resemblance in English between Goose and Goddess. The beings both otherworldly and mythological are preparing a meal within a magic circle which is decorated with a series of black strokes that would probably not interest the casual viewer. However, these inscriptions in mirror-writing contain the occult meaning of the work. When deciphered they read: "The Goddess Dana became and is the Sidhe." "The Old Races Died—Where did they go?" The painting imparts a visionary and scriptural revelation of the underworld land of the Sidhe from Celtic mythology where the Goddess Dana's tribe fled when it took refuge from the conquest of the patriarchal gods. The message of the painting is occulted precisely because goddess knowledge is threatening to a patriarchal culture. Witness the burning of the witches who believed in the religion of the Mother Goddess?

In my studies of the works of the Women of Surrealism I began to wonder about the rate at which these women artists committed suicide and went "mad," and so in a series of articles such as "Reclaiming the Great Mother: A Feminist Journey to Madness and Back in Search of A

Goddess Heritage"[2] and "Towards a Bifocal Vision in
Surrealist Aesthetics,"[3] I studied these two themes in
Surrealist women's art and writings. The results of my
research are as follows:

In the works of the Women of Surrealism who have
either had encounters with "madness" or committed suicide,
the image of the Goddess is encoded and occulted. It is a
symbol of female creation that has been repressed to such a
degree that when it surfaces, it looms so large that it is
easily confused with a "delusion of grandeur." Such is the
image of a woman giving birth to the city of Berlin in
surrealist writer, Unica Zurn's autobiographical novel The
Jasmin Man, which recounts her experience with madness.
I will just give one example of what I call the "bifocal vision
of Surrealist women." I want to discuss Leonora
Carrington's painting Rarvarok (1963). Here we see
clearly the dichotomy between a patriarchal and a
gynocentric vision. The woman on the floor on the right of
the painting may be judged "mad" by the male Priests,
Rabbis, and Choir Boys of the Judeo-Christian pantheon on
the left. Yet, from the gynocentric perspective this woman
may indeed be possessed by a vision of the Goddess. In this
case we may interpret the woman on the floor as being
possessed by the vision of the White Horse goddess Epona
from Celtic mythology, here depicted with breasts. In
Carrington's personal case, she too, was judged "mad" for
her goddess visions, and interned in a mental asylum in
Spain where she was injected with Cardiazol which induced
epileptic seizures. If Leonora Carrington occults the
meaning of the Goddess vision in her work, it is because to
articulate more fully this knowledge involves running the
risk of literal torture in a patriarchal culture.

Kay Sage, the Surrealist artist wife of Yves Tanguy,
committed suicide. In her painting Mother of Time we see
a hooded female figure shrouded in shadow, sitting
collapsed astride the gates of her city while the civilization
she has birthed crumbles before her eyes. Her painting The
Answer is No (1958) shows that in a world which has
erased all images of the female cosmic creator "the mother
of time" recognition of the woman artist as legitimate
creator is also impossible. Kay Sage and Leonora

Carrington visibly link the gender of the creator of the universe to the gender of the creator of art and show us poignantly how a patriarchal version of the creation myth blocks female creativity, virtually causing "madness" and even suicide in the lives of women artists who have no divine image from which to derive the legitimation of their creative powers. This sole fact often dooms their work to rejection.

II. My Jungian Period and the Heresies Collective

At the time I was formulating these ideas in their embryonic stages, the Heresies collective in New York invited me to do a piece for their Great Goddess issue on contemporary "goddess" artists. I called my article "The Re-emergence of the Archetype of the Great Goddess in Art by Contemporary Women,"[4] and my use of the word "archetype" signals that I was under the influence of Jung. At that time I had come to believe that the fact that so many contemporary women artists were expressing the goddess image in their works meant that they were turning into an "archetype" of the collective unconscious, one that Jung had called "The Archetype of the Great Mother." Moreover, the fact that the surrealist women artists had envisioned the Goddess in states of altered consciousness or moments of "madness" and "illumination" led me to conclude that, in fact, the archetype of the Great Mother emerged in dreams and in art just as Jung had described it. According to Erich Neumann's book The Great Mother: An Analysis Of An Archetype,[5] based upon Jungian psychology, the Great Mother represents the "feminine" in the human psyche. He would argue that the archaic world of the archetypes appears in myths and dreams of all humans throughout all time and space. According to Jungians, the archetype is an inward image at work in the psyche everywhere.

What I want to stress here is that at the time I wrote the Heresies piece, I believed this to be the case. Also, because on the subject of the Goddess, only Jungian literature existed, most women artists I interviewed

corroborated my beliefs since they had read the same books
I had. Architect Mimi Lobell had designed a Goddess
Temple (1975) in collaboration with a Jungian therapist.
She explained to me that she considered the shape of the
temple to be the externalization of an archetypal structure
that exists within the psyche.

Artist Carolee Schneeman also felt that her earliest
body images related to the ancient Cretan and Minoan
Goddesses, because she had been intuitively in touch with a
vision of the archetype. Buffie Johnson told me that her
work since the late 1940's had been drawn from the
Jungian concept of the collective unconscious. Her
paintings evoked mythic memories and served as sacred
icons to stimulate and resurrect the layers of consciousness
in which our most primordial and archaic images, such as
The Great Goddess in the images of Ariadne or The
Pomegranate recalling Demeter and Persephone, appear in
connection with the life-giving powers of "the feminine."

Donna Henes was doing process environmental
sculptures about "Spider Woman" from the Navaho
Emergence Myth. Sheila Moon in her study of the Navaho
Emergence Myth said that "Spider Woman is the
unobtrusive but powerful archetype of fate, not in the sense
of determination, but in the sense of the magical law of
one's own gravity which leads always beyond itself towards
wholeness."[6]

At that time we all believed in the existence of the
Jungian archetypes. We affirmed that, as the Jungian,
June Singer, maintains in Androgyny: Towards A New
Theory of Sexuality,[7] "When a psychological need arises it
seems inevitably the deeper layers of the collective
unconscious are activated and sooner or later the memory
of a myth of an event or an earlier psychic state emerges
into consciousness." There was a clear need for the
re-emergence of what we then called "the feminine," and it
seemed to us that the figure of The Great Goddess was
emerging from the collective unconscious via the works of
women artists. As a scholar I was able to fit almost any
Goddess image in the works of contemporary women into
this neat theory. Hence, I could analyze the image of the
Goddess as the Shekinah from the Kabbalah in the art of

Gilah Hirsch by stating that in mystical states of illumination this Kabbalistic image had emerged into her consciousness.

Donna Byars had a dream of the oracle of the Goddess, and concretized it in her piece Oracle Stone Grove. In her dream "A stone woman who sat in a grove of trees spoke to me in vapors not words... All of a sudden she slid from her chair into a hole in the under-ground. I grabbed her before she went underground, and when she came up she was no longer able to speak."[8] For Byars, the artist is a seer and a shaman who, in a visionary state or a dream, calls forth imagery about the Goddess from the unconscious.

Jovette Marschessault's Telluric Women: Women Of Hope And Resurrection represented for me the mythic images that appear in the ecstatic trance states of the Amerindian shamans.

III. The Impact on My Work of Marija Gimbutas' Archeological Writings

My departure from the Jungian hypothesis first began to take shape in my mind when I interviewed Mary Beth Edelson about her pilgrimage to the Grapcèva caves in Yugoslavia. She was a friend of Merlin Stone, and they were working together on the Heresies Great Goddess collective. I had read Merlin Stone's book When God Was A Woman,[9] too, and I began to realize that to describe the Goddess as an archetype in the psyche was both invalidating to the kind of research that Merlin Stone had done, and distorting to the literal genesis of the artistic work of Mary Beth Edelson. In her lecture at The Great Goddess Re-emerging Conference held at U.C. Santa Cruz in 1978, Merlin Stone discussed the difference between reading about a "goddess cult" in a patriarchal historical text and actually visiting the archeological site referred to in the text. At an archeological site one might find literally hundreds of goddess figurines and artifacts. The actual scale of the site, its dimensions, its profoundly awe-inspiring setting, etc., often led one to realize, on the spot, that these were no small "goddess cults," but rather

that this was once an important world religion that had
existed over a period of many thousands of years. Mary
Beth Edelson's readings about the Goddess and her travels
to Yugoslavia convinced me that her artistic and creative
imagination was fecundated by feminist scholarship and by
personal pilgrimages. The Goddess that appeared in her
work did not emerge from a trance state or as an archetype
from the collective unconscious. In fact, it emerged from a
knowledge of history and a familiarity with geography.
Also, politically, it seemed to me that talking about
archetypes emerging in the psyches of women was again
relegating women artists to the problematic status of
"inspired" or "mad" visionaries from which they were so
desperately struggling to emerge. It would be only too
convenient to discard this new artistic work as the work of
women mystics and "nature freaks" or "neo-pagans" who
were either "mad" or "illuminated" by the archetypes of the
collective unconscious, when, in my experience, I knew
them personally to be conscious creators, and even scholars
in their own right.

Before Cynthia Mailman did her Self-Portrait As God
for the Sister-Chapel, she undertook extensive research,
and showed me a huge collection of notebooks and
sketchbooks about her readings on the Goddess in
Prehistory. Similarly, Diana Kurz had studied Buddhism
for may years before she painted herself at The Durga.
Judy Chicago's Dinner Party was also in process at that
time, and we were constantly informed of her research on
the "Fertile Goddess," "The Eye Goddess," and "The Snake
Goddess." Indeed, Judy Chicago even made use of the
services of a group of women researchers who actually
sought out Goddess images for the plates in the project.
Helene de Beauvoir's Goddess paintings are based upon her
extensive readings about Crete and her travels to Crete.
The images she draws upon come to her from history and
are then artistically transformed into symbols for
contemporary women emerging into an era in which their
own creative powers are affirmed and flourish. Hence, it
became more and more evident that contemporary women
artists' goddess images did not emerge directly from dream
visions, but were rather creations inspired by new feminist

knowledge of our true and erased historical past.

Finally, I discovered the vast and profound body of archeological research and interpretation done by Marija Gimbutas. In her book The Goddesses and Gods of Old Europe,[10] Marija Gimbutas demonstrates that the ancient civilizations which endured from the Upper Paleolithic and Neolithic through the Copper age (from 26,000 BC to 3,000 BC) particularly in S.E. and Central Europe were distinct in every way from their Indo-European successors. They were matrifocal, peace-loving, and earth and sea-bound, whereas the Indo-European civilizations which followed were patrifocal, mobile, war-like and sky-oriented. The peoples of this "Old European" culture worshipped the Great Goddess Creatress, Giver of All, specifically in two aspects:

1. As Cosmogonic Creator—The Giver and Source of all Life, Fertility and Creation
2. As The Goddess of Death and Regeneration, The Symbol of All Renewal and Becoming.

At once I began to see that the works of contemporary feminist goddess artists also fell into these two categories. Yet, this was not because of a psychic archetypal connection, but because in their conscious creation of new feminist images of strength and creativity, they drew upon the most ancient sources of inspiration that they had come upon in their readings, research, and travels.

Thus, in my article "A Gynocentric Vision in Contemporary Feminist Art and Literature"[11] I was able to show that a variety of visual and literary works created by feminist artists from California to Cuba, from Canada to Nigeria, recapitulate the most ancient motifs and symbols connected to the pre-Indo European mythos of the Goddess—motifs such as the Snake Goddess, the Bird Goddess, The Primordial Egg, the Butterfly, caves, labyrinths, seeds, rivers, webs, vessels, horns, the Cow, the Double Ax, Earth Mounds, and the uplifted arms of the Cretan and Minoan Goddesses.

Visual artists such as Betsy Damon, Ana Mendieta, Faith Wilding, Miriam Sharon, Susan Schwalb and Judy Chicago, and writers such as Flora Nwapa (Nigeria), Meridel Le Sueur, Jovette Marchessault (Quebec), Robin

Morgan, Jeanne Hyvrard (France), and Diane di Prima, all use the symbol of the Goddess to create a link with the vision of an ancient past in which the Earth was experienced as the living incarnation of the body of the Great Mother.

The literal reclamation of our ancient historic past was reenacted by Betsy Damon in her piece The 7,000 Year Old Woman, just as Mary Beth Edelson's Proposal for: Memorials to the 9,000,000 Women Burned as Witches in the Christian Era commemorated a tragic era in the history of women who revered the goddess. Monica Sjoo's numerous goddess images were all based upon the various forms that the Great Goddess has taken in myths and religions of different cultures from Egypt to Crete and Celtic Ireland. Judy Baca has studied the goddess Califia, for whom California was named. Nancy Spero is inspired by the ancient cave paintings of the Paleolithic. Jean Edelstein has studied the Cretan sites and the Cretan Goddess.

Today literary critics Estella Lauter and Carol Schreirer Rupprecht are revising Jungian archetypal theory to make it more malleable to feminist analysis. Their recent book Feminist Archetypal Theory[12] is written in response to Naomi Goldenberg's challenging critique of Jungian theory for Feminism in her book Changing of The Gods[13]. Lauter and Rupprecht's revision of the archetype concept marks a huge step forward in archetypal analysis, for they maintain that "the archetype assumes different forms according to the personal and social history of the person who manifests it." They feel that the archetype is a useful concept because it refers to something real in our experience, that it may uncover a tendency shared by a great number of women across time, space, and human culture. They also maintain that image and behavior are inextricably linked. Yet, their ultimate goal is to study what women imagine, dream, fantasize, feel and think by studying their art and their dreams.

Where my ideas now differ from theirs and from my own previous "archetypal" approach is in the understanding I now have of the ways in which these "goddess" images were actually inspired by the new knowledge of history,

archeology, and anthropology uncovered within the context
of Feminist scholarship. It seems to me that the recurrence
of Goddess imagery today shows us precisely to what
degree feminist scholarship has actively influenced the
creative processes of women artists by providing them with
new materials about which to dream, to muse, to imagine
and to create.

These artists all seem to be saying: "Remember: Our
true history has been erased! People once imaged the deity
as female. We are not making visible a mere fantasy of the
imagination; we are consciously creating an imaginative
rendition of what was once literally real. What we want to
depict is the fact that those peace-loving peoples of our
ancient, matristic past who revered a goddess also accorded
women positions of power and honor. These powerful
women of the past were the same women who bequeathed
to us the first gifts of civilization, the knowledge of
agriculture and of crafts. In creating contemporary images
of women we consciously want to relate ourselves to our
most ancient woman-centered past. By doing so we can
reconstitute a lost tradition artistically. While all artists
employ fantasy, the dream and the imagination, we must
be careful not to mystify our comprehension of the creative
process. Art has both a conscious and an unconscious
dimension." Here I want to emphasize the conscious
component of what we had previously considered to be
purely unconscious—the re-emergence of the goddess
image. The importance to Feminism of stressing how social
change, political action, and consciousness affect the
imaginative capacities of women's creation must not be
underestimated, lest we lapse back into identifying women
artists solely with the "intuitive" aspects of creation alone,
and ignore the evidence of their conscious intellects at work
in making art.

IV. The Political Dimension: My Collaboration with Irene Diamond

The fourth and most recent stage of evolution in my
ideas concerning the Goddess image came as a result of my
encounter with political scientist, Irene Diamond, who is

now at U.C.L.A We have been discussing feminism, culture, and politics for two years now, and our dialogue has proved to be most fruitful. I should add that politicized feminists are usually very wary both about the "goddess" and about "feminist spirituality."

In 1980 when I co-created The First International Festival of Women Artists at the Nye Carlsberg Glyptotek Museum in Copenhagen, women with a political commitment to action claimed that so long as there were women on the planet dying of hunger and living in extreme poverty, the arts were at best a frill, and our energy should rather be spent working in the _real_ political arena. Our response was that artistic images change consciousness; that art has always been a threat to totalitarian governments, which explains why artists are always the first to be banished by those regimes. Thus, we maintained that art is highly political.

Irene explained to me why, as a political scientist, she had originally objected to any talk of art and spirituality, and especially to references to the Goddess, at least before our dialogue had begun.

In the first place it seemed to her that the Goddess was the symbol of all the things which women were trying to flee, such as fertility, resulting in unwanted pregnancy, etc. Secondly, the Goddess represented a spiritual mode of ecstasy, a mode that was not one of control or of reason. The mainstream of Feminism was interested in wresting control away from the patriarchal bastions of power, and giving women control over their lives. To feminist political scientists the goddess seemed to symbolize the old cliches about women and fertility and about women lacking the powers of reason. Yet, at just this time Irene was beginning to formulate a feminist critique of the mode and language of "control," which she saw as part of the scientific discourse of patriarchal "power over." She names this defect "Andro" or "Gynocentrism." Scientism, and its delusion that man can control all of nature leads to the worst nightmares—ultimately to nuclear disaster. The problem with putting men or women at the center of a political vision is that it ignores the webs of connections we have to the cosmos and to the cycles of nature, to the plant and animal worlds, and to the earth. The scientific revolution deluded man into thinking that he could master and control nature, and mainstream Feminism was simply trying to take that control away from men and give it back to women. Yet it was essentially using the same discourse of "control."

Irene Diamond calls for a new discourse which understands the limits and delusions of scientific control, and is sensitive to the contexts, textures, webs, and relationships that sustain life. Some of these textures are artistic and spiritual, and this is where the Goddess comes in.

I have named our joint vision "Embodiment Theory." Although the word "Embodiment" comes from Irene, she is reluctant to give it a single name. Embodiment Theory simply states that we must always be mindful of the fact that we are embodied creatures, that we are interconnected with things greater than ourselves such as the Earth and the Cosmos, and that any damage we do to them, we ultimately do to ourselves as well. Embodiment, in asserting that men and women are a part of nature, refutes the androcentric position of man (or woman) in control of nature. It affirms that the destruction of our planet stems from the delusion that the world can be mastered or controlled by humans.

Together, we call for a new ethics, art, and politics that will be mindful of this critique of andro-gynocentrism. In this new art and politics, the figure of the Goddess emerges as the symbol of creation with female creativity. This new art, in understanding the cycles of nature and the cosmos, often expresses its meaning through rituals which celebrate our embodiment in the cycles of the body and of the body of the great Mother. This new art, of which the Goddess becomes the symbol for the Earth Mother, does not erect monuments which destroy or triumph over nature and time. Instead, it extolls our interconnectedness with the earth and the cosmos, rather than asserting our mastery over them. Thus, it is ecologically and politically self-conscious.

Judy Chicago's Birth Project is one example of the use of the Goddess image to celebrate both female fertility and artistic creativity. It is a fact that with the pollution of our earth and our waters, human fertility has decreased. Thus, artists must become conscious of the earth's fertility if they want humans to continue to be born of humans. If they are not mindful of the Earth's fertility, they will be plunged into a nightmare world from which human fertility is absent. Thus, they must not pollute the Earth, even in the process of making art. Miriam Sharon, in Israel, celebrates the Nomadic Desert Peoples, the Bedouins, whose tents leave no traces which could destroy the sacredness of the pure Earth, their Mother.

Donna Henes and Faith Wilding perform solstice and equinox rituals calling attention to the natural cycles of the cosmos.

Helene Aylon creates an Earth Ambulance, and transports the ailing earth on a stretcher to the U.N. because it is the wounded body of our Earth Mother.

Rachel Rosenthal, in Gaia, Mon Amour, chants, keening against an Amerindian backdrop, calling upon the spirit powers of the universe to save the planet.

Leslie Labowitz raises sprouts as an artwork, commenting on how we must put our art-making energies into the regeneration of the earth.

Christine Oatman spreads her magician's cape on the barren earth, and raises a field of flowers out of the heart of her Earth Mother.

All of these artists see the Earth as our Mother, and conceive of us as parasites feeding off of our host. If we destroy here, we will destroy ourselves, as well.

This vision of interconnectedness, this holistic vision calls for a new politics, and it is this politics that Irene Diamond is now elaborating in the book she is writing. It is a Green Politics, and it is our joint vision that ethics and aesthetics reciprocally inform and reinforce our politics.

Where, then, are we heading after a decade of feminism in the arts?

The evolution of my thinking seems to be leading to the following conclusions: While women artists may still have more of a struggle ahead in the domains of Art History, Art Criticism, Administration of the Institutions, and changing the Images of Women in Art, my perspective is that feminist art is moving in the direction of creating a new mythic vision which ultimately links aesthetics to ethics and politics in very important ways.

In contradistinction to the Great Goddess of "Old Europe" whose rediscovery and reclamation partially inspired the creation of these new feminist art works, the emergence of contemporary goddess images and symbols does not represent a predominant cultural belief nor the actual special cases of personal transformation. Rather, it shows how creativity is directly affected by a combination of social factors such as political activity, the new feminist scholarship, and feminist education—all a part of the contemporary Women's Movement. What we have seen is how profoundly research, education, and politics may affect a transformation in the workings of women's creative imaginations.

We may also observe that contemporary feminist artists are weaving a new Creation Myth. In the old myth woman was born of man, and when she tasted of the apple from the Tree of Knowledge, God the Father expelled her from the Garden of Eden.

In the new myth woman is born of woman, of a female Creatress. In tasting of the apple from The Tree of Knowledge (read here, in doing feminist research) she is learning about her true origins. In a gynocentric world she will not be expelled from the garden by her female Creatress; she will, on the contrary, be called upon to cultivate that garden.

In Leonora Carrington's Women's Liberation poster, Mujeres Concienca we see the new Eve returning the apple to the old Eve and and rejecting the myth of the Fall. This new Eve then experiences illumination as her gynergic energy, the serpent power of kundalini (so Leonora Carrington conceives of it), rises through the Chakras of her body to the third eye of illumination. The poster is green for Green Politics, for when women reclaim their power they will use it to protect and regenerate the natural life that flourishes so bountifully upon our planet.

If indeed, as I have argued, contemporary feminist artists are affecting the thinking of feminist political scientists, then, in view of the threat of planetary

annihilation, nuclear winter, and cosmic pollution, The
Return of the Goddess in Art now takes on a political
dimension. It may even signify the opposite of what it
meant in the early 70's. Whereas the Goddess once
symbolized a reminder of our erased prehistory, of the
witch burnings, of spirituality connected with the practice of
an original Mother goddess religion, or the repression of
female creativity, etc., now, in the mid 1980's the Goddess
has come to signify a fusion of ethics, aesthetics, and
politics in a global, holistic vision of survival for humankind
through feminism in practice both in art and in life.

It is important for us to recognize that in one decade
women in the arts have not only established important new
directions in art history, criticism, exhibitions, and
administration, but that, inspired by the multiple actions of
women in the Women's Movement, they have actually
transformed the content of their creations in ways that
spell out a new mythic meaning for feminists. I would like
to see us acknowledge the profound interrelationship that
exists between women's politics and women's art.
Admittedly, the Goddess is only one of the myriad ways in
which the themes enunciated in the Women's Movement
have influenced the creative visions of contemporary
women. The protest against all forms of personal and
political violence has also come to play an important part in
the arts of contemporary women. However, I believe that
it is important to understand that the re-emergence of the
Goddess today does transform the myth of the Garden of
Eden in two fundamental ways:

1.   It establishes knowledge and truth as liberatory
     processes for the creative mind.

2.   It stresses the importance of an ecological perspective
     so necessary in a world in which all forms of life as we
     know them are threatened with extinction.

These, then, I contend, are two of the more recent
meanings of the re-emergence of the Goddess in
contemporary art. As a symbol for the creative self, for
knowledge and for life, the Goddess today is a potent image

for catalyzing feminist energies of transformation. It gives me personal hope to know that the search for truth that scholars engage in can have such a deep impact on the creative lives of women of our time and of the future.

Footnotes

[1]Joanna Frueh. "The Dangerous Sex: Art Language and Male Power." Paper delivered at The College Art Association, Los Angeles, 1985, p. 10.

[2]Gloria Orenstein. "Reclaiming the Great Mother: A Feminist Journey To Madness and Back in Search of a Goddess Heritage." Symposium, Vol. XXXVI, No. 1, Spring, 1982.

[3]Gloria Orenstein. "Towards a Bifocal Vision in Surrealist Aesthetics." Trivia, No. 3, Fall, 1983.

[4]Gloria Orenstein. "The Re-emergence of The Archetype of the Great Goddess in Art by Contemporary Women." Heresies, Spring, 1978.

[5]Erich Neumann. The Great Mother: An Analysis of an Archetype. Princeton: Princeton University Press, 1955, p. 4.

[6]Sheila Moon. A Magic Dwells. Middletown: Wesleyan University Press, 1950, p. 152.

[7]June Singer. Androgyny: Towards A New Sexuality. New York: Anchor, 1976, p. 71.

[8]Donna Byars. Personal Interview, 1978.

[9]Merlin Stone. When God Was A Woman. New York: The Dial Press, 1976.

[10]Marija Gimbutas. The Goddesses And Gods Of Old Europe: Myths and Cult Images. Berkeley: University of California Press, 1982.

[11]Gloria Orenstein. "Une Vision Gynocentrique Dans La Literature et L'Art Feministes Contemporains." Etudes Litteraires, Vol. 17, No. 1., April, 1984. Translated from the English into French.

[12]Estella Lauter and Carol Schreirer Rupprecht. Feminist Archetypal Theory. Knoxville: University of Tennessee Press, 1985, pp. 11-15.

[13]Naomi Goldenberg. Changing Of The Gods. Boston: Beacon Press, 1979.

A Black Woman Writer Thinks Back through Her Mothers

by Paule Marshall

[The following was extracted by the editors from the transcribed text of Ms. Marshall's extemporaneous remarks at the Conference.]

I am especially pleased that the Conference gave me the opportunity to renew my friendship with one of the prominent writers in America today—a woman who was a feminist in her life and work long before the word "feminist" was coined. I'm referring to none other than the poet, the novelist, the teacher, and the dean of American Black writers, Margaret Walker Alexander. And I would like to dedicate this paper to Margaret Walker.

I'm a novelist, a fiction writer, a storyteller, and I'd love to do that all the time. I'd love to just sit in a study and write my stories and books. Even though I go through these dreadful writer's blocks and I have these terrible self doubts, that's all part of the profession. But I'd like to write all the time. Unfortunately that's not possible. In order to eat and pay the rent I have to do what a lot of writers do, and that is, find other means of employment. Like many other writers, I teach.

In the Spring of '84 I had the good fortune to be invited out to the University of California at Berkeley. They treated me very well there. I taught one course and they provided this nice little house, which was on a hill just a little away from the university grounds, on a hill which afforded me a view of all of San Francisco Bay.

The house was equally impressive. It belonged to someone in the English Department who was on sabbatical, and it was clear, it was obvious, it was unmistakable that she was a Virginia Woolf scholar.

In the study there were all of Virginia Woolf's books, her novels, of course, her diaries, her collections of essays, and so on, and then there were all these books about

Virginia Woolf. And just over my desk there was this large
framed photograph of Virginia Woolf, her smoking a
cigarette in a long holder, which she was holding at this
defiant angle. And then there were those heavy-lidded
Virginia Woolf eyes looking down at me all the time. It
was rather spooky. Who's afraid of Virginia Woolf? Well,
I was, after a time.

So I decided—look here, I'm going to have to make my
peace with you, because we have to live in this house for
these six months together. And so I went and reread A
Room of One's Own —her manifesto, as you all know, for
women who would be artists, who would be writers. And
as you remember, she lists the conditions that a women
needs to get her creative work done. First of all, you have
to have some talent. I mean that goes without saying. But
once that's there, then there are some other things that
have to be in place for the talent to be expressed. You have
to have your own space—that room of your own. And she's
not only talking about the physical room, she's talking
about the kind of environment and surroundings and people
who will help you to get the work done. So you have to
have this space.

She says as a second requirement that you've got to
have what she inherited, which was five hundred English
pounds per year. In other words, you have to have some
money.

She also made another arresting point, which for some
reason, perhaps because I was young, I overlooked the first
time I read A Room of One's Own many many years ago.
She says: "Books are not single and solitary births. They
are the outcome of many years of thinking in common, in
thinking by the body of the people, so that the experience of
the mass is behind the single voice. A woman writer thinks
back through her mothers."

What Virginia Woolf was talking about, of course, is
that there is this tremendous importance of the literary
foremothers for the woman writer. All of those
women—those few women, rather—of an earlier period,
who wrote in the face of the most unimaginable odds, who
forged the way, who set an example, who served as models,
so that each book, novel, play, story, is informed by the

efforts of all those who have gone before.

And so what I'd like to do is to think back through my literary foremothers who were very different from those of Virginia Woolf, and to describe at some length a group of women who, more than all of the books I read and all of the creative writing courses I took and all of the writing workshops I attended, were the ones who were responsible for my becoming a writer. And not only responsible for my becoming a writer, but who, to a large degree, were responsible for the major themes and concerns in my work. They are the ones who constitute the body of the people and the experience of the mass behind my voice.

Now the best way to describe these foremothers is to say that they were poets. Now they didn't look like poets. They were just a group of four or five terribly ordinary-looking women—housewives. One of them happened to be my mother. They didn't look like poets at all. They didn't dress like poets. No berets, no capes, no outrageous attire to startle and to attract. In fact they used to wear, to my acute embarrassment, these plain bargain basement housedresses, and during the winter, these long solemn dark coats, and these dowdy hats that looked like something left over from the Queen Mother of England.

And they didn't do what poets were supposed to do, which in my childish imagination was to sit up in an attic room writing verses. These poets each morning got out an apron and a pair of what they would call their working shoes and put them in a shopping bag—or sometimes, in just a brown paper bag—and they took the bus or the trolley or the train (this is back in the late thirties and forties I'm talking about now) out to the white sections of Brooklyn. I grew up in Brooklyn. And for those of the women who did not have steady jobs, they would wait on certain designated corners in Flatbush, which was the white area of Brooklyn, for the white housewives to come along and offer them a "day's work," as it was called, just a day's work cleaning these people's houses. At that time this was the only kind of work available to Black women who didn't have any particular skills.

So my mother and her friends would do this, maybe

three or four times a week. Then in the afternoon at about 3:30 or 4:00 o'clock they would make their way back to our part of Brooklyn with their little salaries in their purses, and they referred to the salaries as the "few raw-mout pennies." Anyway they had a kind of ritual. Once they got back to our section of Brooklyn, they didn't separate and go their different ways; by way of bringing the day to an end they would stop off, usually at my house, and sit in the kitchen (it was one of these large old-fashioned kitchens in a brownstone house) and they would talk.

I remember them sitting around this large oilcloth-covered table and talking. And it was the responsibility of my sister and myself to keep them supplied with cocoa and tea. And they would sit there and talk while we served them, or when we weren't serving them we would sit over in the corner being seen but not heard. And they talked endlessly, passionately, brilliantly. Now at first I did not understand because I wanted to be outside playing, not sitting up there in the kitchen with them, that this was the best thing that ever happened to me.

Anyway, they would go on sometimes for about three or four hours talking. And I didn't realize it at the time but the talk was highly therapeutic. It was, first of all, a way in which they sort of overcame the day. They recovered from that long wait on the corner. They got the taste of the workday out of their mouths. They reaffirmed their humanity. The talk was also for them a form of intellectual exercise. It helped them to stretch their minds, because they talked about everything, and they had an opinion about everything. And the talk was also a form of entertainment because of course in those days there were no TVs, no Sony Walkmans, no stereos, no video games, no ghetto-blasters. People sat and talked to each other. They entertained each other by talking.

And, as I said, no subject was beyond these women. The first thing that usually came in for discussion in these afternoon talkathons was the people they worked for. They ran them down. And they were shrewd students of psychology. They knew those white housewives for whom they worked far better than those housewives would ever know my mother and her friends. They also talked a lot about the economy because we were still feeling the after shocks of the Depression, and of course, as Black women, they were the ones who felt the brunt of the Depression the hardest. So they talked a lot about the economy.

They also were always bringing up the question of war, or of, as they put it quoting the Bible, "war and the rumors of war." They talked a lot about the First World War when they were young women— 18, 19, 20—still living on this little tiny island from which they came in the West Indies called Barbados. They were all immigrant women. I should have mentioned that before. They were there on this island waiting for the chance to emigrate to the United States, waiting for this war to be over. So they talked about World War I.

They also discussed, and with great outrage, a war that goes unremarked in the history books, the 1935 war in which Italy invaded Ethiopia. That filled them with fury. The thought that the nice little small emperor, Haile Selassie, had to go into exile in England, and the fact that Ethiopia was overrun by the Italians just enraged them. Enraged them to the point that they took one of the old folk songs that they had been taught as girls growing up in Barbados and put new lyrics to it. It was called, when they were young, "Come 'Round Alice," and they changed it to express what they felt about Mussolini going into Ethiopia:

If I was a grasshopper
I would hop about in the grass
And when Mussolini pass along
I would dash a lash in his...
Come 'round Alice.

They also talked about the Second World War which was just heating up at that time. Hitler had already invaded Poland and the Holocaust was underway. They discussed national politics, FDR—Franklin Roosevelt was their great hero— because, as they perceived it, he was the one who had rescued the country from the great Depression. He was the one who had made it possible for them to find jobs in defense factories. They also liked some other things about FDR. They liked the way he dressed and carried himself. There is a picture of Roosevelt at Yalta with Churchill and Stalin, and Roosevelt is there wearing his battered fedora at a rakish angle and he's got this long cigarette holder, a' la Virginia Woolf, and this long flowing black cape—the man had style. And my mother and her friends appreciated style. So they liked Roosevelt. They liked him up until the point when he interned the Japanese, and then they were finished with FDR.

But the man who was their political god was an early freedom fighter in the twenties by the name of Marcus Garvey. He was the one who spoke for working class Blacks like my mother and her friends. In terms of popularity he was on the scale of a Jesse Jackson, a Martin Luther King, a Malcom X. And so when they first came to this country in the early twenties they contributed to the Garvey Movement out of their meager salaries as domestics. They joined his Nurses Brigade, though, of course, they weren't trained as nurses; and they would march in their white nurses uniforms up Seventh Avenue during the great Garvey Day parades. And they also bought shares in his ill-fated Black Star Line. These were the ships that were going to take Blacks back to Africa. They contributed to buying the ships. Now, I'm sure, the women would not have gone if Marcus had realized his dream, but it did say something about them. First of all, that they thought politically and that they had an identification with that larger world of Black people.

And so there they were, these women, talking about all of these things; and it wasn't only the wide range of topics, but also the way they put things—their style, their use of language. They had taken the King's English, and I make emphasis on <u>King</u> —it was not the Queen's English—they had taken the King's English, white male language, which had been taught them in the primary school of Barbados and they turned it around. They transformed it. They made it into an instrument which expressed them. They brought to bear their own stinging rhythms and accents. They played around with the syntax, with the arrangement of the words in the sentences so they sounded better to their ears. They introduced the few African-derived sounds and words that had been passed down, that had survived the diaspora, such as the word "yam." Now "yam" is not our southern yam, but the West African staple which is a sort of starchy vegetable which looks like potatoes. But yam is also in West Africa the synonym for "eat," so my mother would always say to me: "Don't yam up everything on your plate so quickly."

They enriched English with a raft of Biblical quotes, colorful metaphors, proverbs, sayings and the like, all drawn from their experience as women. They would say, for example, when there was trouble—if someone had had some personal calamity, the loss of a job or some discrimination they had suffered, or a marriage broken up—they would say: "Soully-gal, you got to tie up your belly." What they were doing was referring to the old-fashioned practice of wrapping the belly band around the navel of a newborn baby to hold that stomach in; they took that and used it as a metaphor for being able to withstand personal tragedy, of surviving, of being able to go on. They would say, drawing from their experience growing up in these little islands in the West Indies: "The sea ain't got no back door," meaning that the sea was not like a house where, if there was a problem, you could run out the back; meaning that one had to be respectful and cautious, not only of the sea, but of nature in general. They would be appalled at what we are doing to the environment today.

They also joked a lot in their language. They would say about someone who wasn't particularly attractive: "Oh, poor soul, he got a face like an accident before it happened." And as for those women in the community who were somewhat free, a little too free, with their sexual favors, they were known in the lexicon of my mother and her friends as "thoroughfares," in the sense of men like a steady stream of cars going up and down the road of their lives.

And their favorite adjective for everything in the world, it seemed to me, was a rather contradictory compound—"beautiful-ugly." They would go downtown Brooklyn and buy a dress or a pair of shoes or a coat or what-have-you, or they would buy a house, and they would refer to it as this beautiful-ugly house, the beautiful-ugly pair of shoes I got, this beautiful-ugly coat I just bought. And I would wonder, why the "beautiful-ugly" when they know and I know the thing is beautiful. Why do they introduce the "ugly?" Well, part of it, I suspect, is sort of analogous to knocking on wood. You introduce "ugly" so that nothing will happen to this prize thing which you have just come into possession of.

But something else was operating. There is a theory in linguistics that what a people do with an idiom, what they do with language, reflects the way they see the world and their place in it, that it expresses their concept of reality. So the use of the term "beautiful-ugly" suggests that the mother-poets, as I call them, saw life in terms of a basic duality. They understood the complexity of experience, so that each thing to them contained its opposite, and that these opposites weren't in conflict, weren't in contradiction, but these opposites were equal and complementary and necessary to the whole. So that for them, for example, there wasn't the Western preoccupation with the mind-body split. They saw the mind and body as making up the whole. To give you an example of how they expressed that whole concept, they referred to each other as "soully-gal." "Soul" meaning soul, spirit, mind, intellect; "gal" meaning body, woman, physical self; and they linked those two. They were always saying "soully-gal" this and "soully-gal" that. They saw no split between the two, so that what they were doing with language was, first of all, using it as an art form, an art form that was most readily available to them.

They were not women who were able to go out and paint pictures or learn to dance and so on, so they took what was there—language—and they treated it as an artform. They invented it. They bent it and shaped it, manipulated it to express them because they were women with a tremendous need for creative expression. They also used language as a means of exercising control over their lives because, of course, given the society, they were women who were absolutely powerless. But because they were special kinds of women they couldn't bear the thought of their invisibility. Nobody knew them, these immigrant Black women there in Brooklyn, and so they would use

language as a way of attesting to the fact that they were
there, and that they could at least, for the time they were
sitting there around the table, exercise some measure of
control over their lives.

They also used language as a weapon in that they
used it to criticize, to question, to reject, and to use
Elizabeth Janeway's term, to "deconstruct" white male
institutions, such as war, the church and the political and
economic world that oppressed them, a world constructed
by men, white men. They fought back with the only
weapon at their disposal—the word.

They were my first teachers. They taught me, for
example, the basics of characterization, because I had never
met any of those women they worked for, by the time they
got through describing them, I saw them clearly in my
mind's eye. They taught me how to make people come
alive on the page. They also gave me my first lessons in
the narrative art because they were simply born
storytellers, storytellers in the oral tradition. They taught
me how to shape and construct a story, and above all they
trained my ear to the power and beauty of common speech.

I think it was Ralph Ellison who said that writers
begin their conditioning as manipulators of words long
before they become aware of literature, and that was
certainly my case. Long before I could make out the first
word in "Dick and Jane" or before I could write my name in
big block letters, I was already attuned to the folk voice, to
the oral art.

But in addition to the lessons in craft and technique
that the women were giving me, they also passed on two
other gifts which have profoundly influenced my life and
my work. All that talk that went on in the afternoon
around the table, all that imagery that had to do with the
mouth—"I ain't got no cover for my mouth," they were
always saying; or they were always giving somebody a
tongue lashing and the really superlative talkers like my
mother were known as "mout-kings"—and what all that
verbal assertiveness did for me, conveyed to me, at a level
beyond words, was the fact that I was no less for being
female, and that I was no less for being Black. And that
even though I would grow into a world which would try to

deny my worth and my humanity that I had a
responsibility to them and to myself to be my own person,
to insist upon my right to be in the world, and to find work,
not the kind of work, of course, that they were forced to do
but to find meaningful work. The message was clear from
very early—do something, and be good at it.

Unfortunately the mother-poets gave out mixed
messages, because all of the time that they were insisting
that I be this independent self-sufficient, work-oriented
person, they were also programming me very carefully to
take the conventional route—marriage—and the traditional
kind of marriage, not the kind of interesting arrangements
that young people now go in for. They meant no living
together, marriage, church, children and houses and so on,
because the one thing that the mother-poets loved above
everything else was a wedding. The bigger the wedding,
the better. Every Saturday I remember my sister and I
were being dragged off to some wedding. It got so that I
detested that song, "Because God Made Thee Mine," which
was always sung —no, not sung, rendered by some local
soprano who couldn't sing.

And so they created a dilemma for me, a dilemma
that has plagued my life, and it's the dilemma of many of
the women in my stories. I've tried to work out that
dilemma through my characters. Some of them win, some
of them don't, which is the story of my life. Anyway, my
women are always questioning these roles that have been
imposed upon them by the society. They are always trying
to define themselves on their own terms. They are always
sort of struggling with this triple-headed hydra of
racism—the kind of racism that you get in the North, that
kind of subtle brand of racism, that condescension and
patronizing brand of it. So they have that to deal with.
And sexism, and of course, class bias.

But I'm also trying to do something else with my
characters. I mean, aside from their quest for personal
freedom, I am also trying to push them somewhere else in
the literature. And that is, it's not enough for me any more
for women to be trying to realize themselves. I mean that's
our God-given right and we have got to do that, but I think

we also need to do something else, and that is to be more involved in the social and political issues.

Women in the Performing Arts: Whither the Year 2001 - A Catalytic Force in the Artistic Firmament, or Still Riding "in the Back of the Bus?"

by Ruth C. Dean

Marian Anderson once told an interviewer: "My mother taught me you can't do anything by yourself. There's always somebody to make the stone flat for you to stand on."

And indeed, this great contralto, now living in retirement in Connecticut, did flatten the stone for countless generations of Black singers to follow. She is best remembered for the concert she gave in 1939 on the steps of the Lincoln Memorial after the Daughters of the American Revolution refused her request to sing in their hall. She was also the first Black singer to break the race barrier at the Metropolitan Opera.

In later years, Miss Anderson philosophically observed: "We are past the day when people think in terms of racial stereotypes."

Indeed, we have progressed to such a point, wrote New York Times cultural correspondent Harold C. Schonberg in a 1982 article, that a new generation of Black opera stars, while acknowledging its debt to Miss Anderson, feels it is established enough to be irritated when referred to as "a Black singer." Said Leona Mitchell, "I just want to be judged as an artist." Added the writer, "Others, among them Leontyne Price and Kathleen Battle, simply refuse to talk on the subject."

How like the sentiments I encountered in interviews with a group of the nation's top women artists which I obtained for this paper. Almost every one I talked with, be she composer, playwright, dancer, actress, opera conductor or broadcaster indicated in her own way that she would like to see the day—to paraphrase Miss Anderson—when people will no longer think in terms of sexual stereotypes.

You may wonder why I chose such a fancy title for this paper. I felt it illustrated in a dramatic way that the cause of women in the arts is not unlike the situation that faced Rosa Parks, the Black woman who inspired the civil rights movement in the 1960s when she resolutely refused a bus driver's order "to move to the back of the bus." Of course, the women's movement and the civil rights movements have for years shared sympathetic goals. So I thought the "bus" metaphor might serve as a barometer of how far women in the arts have come since the last conference convened by this body twelve years ago. Are they still "in the back of the bus," silently swallowing the indignities that bar them from equal opportunity, or have they moved further to the front, assured of some victories won and still hoping for the dawn of a real equality when talent and ability will enjoy mutual acceptance and respect?

A late night call from composer Ellen Zwillich cinched my choice. "I love your title," she exclaimed. I should explain, Ellen was on a list of fifteen women prominent in the performing arts suggested by this conference's planners, which I queried by letter for their views on the status—and progress—of women in their respective art fields. The response was warm, perceptive, revealing and hopeful that the conference would address itself to the many inequities that still exist despite the higher level of expectations and opportunities the women feel now prevail; in comparison to 1973.

Yes, there is still discrimination, overt and subtle, on Broadway, in Hollywood, on the orchestra podium, and in the board rooms of television networks and movie studios.

Before I go into a more detailed exposition of my conversations with these women artists, a few of whom were of my own choosing in addition to the suggested artists' list, I would like to briefly comment on the broad general areas in which they appeared to share common opinions and experiences. High up on the list were the subjects of family and child care, employer sexist attitudes, and mistrust that a woman can do as good a job as a man, even with better training. Surprisingly, a younger generation of artists, seemingly umindful that networking has been around along time, have made a fresh discovery of it and are surprised to discover how many grievances they share, and how expeditious mutual problem-solving is when they interrelate with one another. They also lamented that women "aren't taken seriously enough" by their male colleagues, and that to get anywhere, "a woman has to be twice as good as a man."

Unquestionably, the economy and federal cutbacks in support for arts institutions have reinforced these attitudes. If an artist is worried about keeping his or her job, everything else becomes pretty irrelevant including what I detected was a more muted voice in pressing grievances.

Indeed the arts world is looking at its bottom line too. On Broadway, the commercial theatre favors money-making musicals over experimental plays, while high ticket prices and poor reviews are driving audiences away. Smaller ballet companies and regional theaters are spending more time on fund-raising than play scouting and dance touring, and the red ink is appearing more frequently on smaller arts organizations' ledgers.

Yet, despite these "danger" flags, there has been a veritable explosion of women's talent everywhere: plays, movies and television dramas about women and women's issues and lifestyles, and Pulitzers, Oscars, Emmys, Obies and Tonys to women artists for outstanding work and extraordinary performances.

Who can forget Jane Fonda's monumental portrait of The Dollmaker? Or, Sissy Spacek in The Coal Miner's Daughter. Or Jessica Lange, as Jewell Ivy, the Iowa farm wife saving her farm from foreclosure?—"the new hero-woman," one male reviewer dubbed her. When I asked stage and screen actress Celeste Holm if she had encountered bias in her career, she exclaimed: "never in my life have I had a problem like that, except in Hollywood. The attitude in Hollywood is that girls are adorable, but women are a pain."

Miss Holm, who is a member of the National Council of the Arts and vice president of the Business Council on the Arts, in New York, said discussion is out of the question in Hollywood. "They do not want to hear you. They do not want a woman to think," she said. "They cannot deal with it." Miss Holm added that she has never seen this attitude in the theater, "never seen it in any of the arts." An actress she knows told her, "I keep my anger hot in order to keep my talent strong," on which Miss Holm comments,"I don't think anger is a good motivation for any kind of creativity. I mean anger is for smashing things."

Mexican-born Margo Albert, another actress member of the National Council on the Arts, who died a month after conclusion of this arts conference, told me in an earlier interview that she made a conscious decision to give up her acting career when she married actor Eddie Albert. As she explained it in her own inimitable, expansive way: "I was not the kind of woman who could be a really good actress—the kind of actress I was—and a very good wife." She never regretted it, she said, because she continued to live her life "creatively in other ways." She believed women artists have "got some serious decisions to make within ourselves about what matters. For example, it matters to me to have a good marriage."

Mrs. Albert, who founded the Plaza de la Raza in Los Angeles, a multi-racial and multi-cultural community center, said she believed "minority women have just as hard a time as ever. I don't think it's moved at all. I think Black women have made more progress than Hispanics." In fact, she said she felt Hispanics have suffered from stereotyping, particularly in movies and TV sitcoms, and that it's about time there was an awakening to their worth "as human beings like everybody else." And nowhere more evident than in Hollywood, the late actress believed. "Because men control so much of the actual production (of films), the selection of material and the possibilities and the potential for roles for women is limited by that—more so than if women were truly a little more into that entrepreneurial decision-making level." In our interview, she added, "there are the exceptions of a Jane Fonda," for example, "but a Jane Fonda who has had an immense struggle, concocting her own productions, putting them on. It was a big, big effort for her to do Coming

Home and On Golden Pond. They didn't come easy."
Women are moving up in the movie industry, albeit
slowly. It still makes headlines when we read of the
ascendancy of one woman into one of the power slots.
Early in 1985, Paramount Pictures announced the
promotion of a 38-year old production executive, Dawn
Steel, to president for production. Her new title boosted her
to the super strata where she reigned as the top female
executive at any major studio. Yet her new title still placed
her one level below the presidency at 20th Century Fox
that Sherry Lansing held from 1980 to 1983.

If opportunity comes slow in Hollywood and on
Broadway, the 1980 Census figures for women and
minorities in the American artist labor force look a lot
better. Women had the most spectacular increase of 162
percent over the number of women artists in 1970, while
men increased 53 percent. About 38 percent of artists are
now women.

In 1980, there were 411,066 women artists out of a
total artists' working force of 1.08 million, as compared to
157,165 out of a little over half a million in 1970.

Certainly women seem to have come into their own on
our living room television screens, what with older
actresses like Angela Lansbury, and the venerable Judith
Anderson, of Medea stage fame, playing in series films
while a younger crop entertain us with the doings of
parents singles Kate and Allie and lady cops Cagney and
Lacey. Forsaking glamour, Farrah Fawcett dramatized in
horrific detail the plight of battered wives in The Burning
Bed while Marlo Thomas and her screen husband coped
with bringing a homosexual son out of the closet.

In the theater, these are golden years for women
playwrights, but in other areas like scenic design the
women are bucking sexist attitudes and job barriers.
Clouding the issue is the generally poor economic state of
Broadway, with so may theaters dark, and plays opening
and closing like elevator doors.

Emily Mann, playwright and director, whose
Execution of Justice was the third of three plays, all
written by women, that were mounted in the 1985 season
by Washington's Arena Stage, made a happy discovery at

Arena.

When she told artistic director Doug Wager that she couldn't help but notice the coincidence of the three women playwrights on his main stage while theatre writer John Guare was in the basement Playlab, "where they used to put the women," she said he looked surprised and simply said, "you know, I hadn't noticed." Nor had he noticed the coincidence of two women directors on his staff which Mann said "simply were the best directors for the plays he was doing. That's how far we've come."

In fact, she feels this incident "perfectly encapsulates the difference in the profession between now and five years ago."

Miss Mann said she'd worked "very, very hard in the women's movement" to help women break down the barriers "that have been very clearly erected in the profession," and thinks they are coming down.

Her latest play, Execution of Justice, is a socio-political drama inspired by the public outcry that followed the light sentencing of Daniel James White for the 1978 slaying of two political rivals, San Francisco mayor George Moscone and Supervisor Harvey Milk, the city's first openly gay elected politician. "And here he (White) was let out (paroled) five years after confessing to murdering them," said Mann. So her play, she explained, is "about the criminal justice system, about America, and America's value system."

Mann, and her sister playwrights like Marsha Norman, whose 'night, Mother won the 1983 Pulitzer Prize for drama, got their starts in regional theaters, which Mann feels comprise this country's "real national theater." Norman's play made it to Broadway, but not many other women-authored plays have. Mann thinks in time this final barrier will come down, because "most of the first rate stuff is coming out of the regional theaters and will eventually go to Broadway." Right not, she said, theater in New York is "crass."

"If you bring the producers the next Chorus Line, they don't care whether you're gay, straight, male, female, Black or green—they'll take it," she said. "They want money. But if they see a talent and a beautiful new play that has something important and risky to say, they're not going to touch it."

The prospects for women directors, she believes, are even worse in the commercial theater. "Women will have to prove they can handle a big budget and make money when the pressure's on," she said. In the present climate, she doesn't think the producers "can handle women in that position of authority."

Marjorie Bradley Kellogg, one of the few women scenic designers working regularly on Broadway, agrees with Mann's view. She doesn't think producers are ready for women directors yet, but believes both female directors and their female auxiliary staff who've started with a play in one of the regional theaters, will follow it to Broadway and make their debut that way. All women will need, she maintains, "is a chance to prove they can handle it" in this essentially male-dominated industry.

Miss Kellogg, who's done sets for Joe Egg, The American Buffalo, Requiem for a Heavyweight and Best Little Whorehouse in Texas said, "I've been lucky (having steady employment), but there aren't enough of us working on Broadway. I could easily name a dozen women who'd be capable of doing Broadway shows. If there are a dozen shows on Broadway, if one of them is designed by a woman, it is notable. "No," she said, she has never won, or been nominated for a Tony. "No woman ever has." I'm glad to amend that. As all of you who viewed the 1985 Tony Awards—telecast since that interview—know now, Heidi Landisman got a Tony for Big River —the first woman scenic designer to get a Tony, she happily announced.

Women playwrights are definitely in the ascendancy, according to Kellogg. There are a lot of them writing, and they're writing good plays. "And if the play works," she said, "people are going to leap for it. There's such a shortage of the product that it really doesn't matter who wrote it."

Two years ago, Ms. Kellogg co-chaired a committee of theater women who put together a survey questionnaire which they sent to 25 of their designer colleagues, simply asking: "Is there discrimination in the theater?" They got

17 replies. They learned that many of their problems were shared problems. One question asked: "Are there any old-boy networks from which you feel excluded?" Ninety-three percent answering a resounding "yes." In a variety of questions, the women were asked to pinpoint actual instances of discrimination in training, hiring, on the job, and level of pay.

Some of the answers speak for themselves. In training, some were told, "women would just get married and become Sunday painters," and they "ought to go into costume design if they wanted to earn a living," and finally one was told she would "never get work (as a set designer) unless she wore low-cut dresses."

When it came to on-the-job discrimination, one replied: "Producers in regional situations don't take my evaluation of progress (in the shop) seriously. I have learned to employ a male assistant to get the job done." Wrote another: "When a lot of money is at stake, not a set budget of $3,000 or $20,000, but several hundred thousand dollars, producers and shops feel more comfortable with a male designer. It may be so far that male designers have had experience on that level, so that producers (will) not bet on a dark horse." But the more optimistic of the respondents felt that things were simmering down to a simple "show-me" attitude, with just occasional cracks from the less liberated stagehands.

In fact, Ms. Kellogg stressed the economic crunch has brought the male and female designers together in a common cause for survival, and that "deplorable but true," her sister designers feel "it is no longer terribly popular to be a strident feminist. I mean it's not chic anymore. And what is chic is very powerful. People find it unattractive; therefore not something that one would want to be, as opposed to thinking about the real reason for being a feminist. We're living in an age that is very concerned about appearance in a way that the last couple of decades were not so concerned."

This kind of thinking, Ms. Kellogg conceded, " is not good for the forward progress of the women's movement, and I hope it won't be a set back. I hope it's just a slowing of the progress. She hopes one of the issues that will get ironed out during the slowdown is child care," because it is difficult being a free lance working woman with a child."

A working mother with a child poses even greater professional hazards in the world of the dance. Margaret Jenkins, a former associate of Merce Cunningham who founded her own ballet company in San Francisco in 1972, thinks, "it is not an accident that there are hardly any women choreographers. In fact I've never had one role model of a woman who has a family and also does what I do." Ms. Jenkins is married to an attorney "who's very cooperative...so I'm not completely dependent on my income," and has a 5-year old daughter, she says she "decided to have fairly late in my career as a performer."

Ms. Jenkins, who is a central figure in the development of contemporary dance on the West Coast, said she thinks "the nature of this career is very complex in relation to being a fulltime mother, and so the choices you make are very complicated along the way. Recalling her conversation with a colleague who'd guest-performed with her company, she said her colleague told her of her acceptance into a very famous dance company. Then she got pregnant, and the company's choreographer told her: "Sorry, I don't want anybody with kids."

The basic problem as Jenkins sees it, is that "you perform as a dancer the same years you can have a kid, so it's complicated. Factories provide day care centers, she reasons, "so why is there no system within the arts community for a day care center?"

Margie Jenkins backs up her dances, which the New York Times once described as "resembling a puzzle without solution," with set designs done in collaboration with gifted women artists. "The work that I do," she explained, "uses the modern dance vocabulary, and by working with individual artists, it's like you add another layer of meaning to the work by what they create in the environment."

Another ballet pioneer, Barbara Weisberger, founder of the prestigious Pennsylvania Ballet which she left in 1982 during one of its most troubled periods, described the problems she sees facing classical ballet companies as they grow into multi-million dollar institutions.

She feels "these companies have become mere

presenting organizations, and some of the aspirations of those who founded them have gotten lost in the shuffle."

Three founders, she said, "had a very humane understanding of what it took to get something going—and on a shoe-string. We held on with bloody fingernails! You hold on until you're dead!" Recalling those earlier days, she said the Pennsylvania Ballet was in the forefront of de-centralizing ballet from New York. It had munificent grants from the Ford Foundation and grants from the National Endowment for the Arts. "That's what gave it impetus, the luxury to indulge in a vision," she recalled. But the whole picture changed with "de-funding of the arts," she said of the Reagan administration cutbacks.

"Now what I feel is happening," she said, "is what I call the Eskimo grandmother syndrome—you know the legend about the grandmother who's put on a ice floe to drift out to sea and die after she's outlived her usefulness."

Weisberger said she was "replaced by a managerial type, a man," a trend which she noted reflects not only what happened to her but to her sister founders of other ballet companies. "In every case a man replaced a woman," she said. "None of it was pretty. It was done with very little humanity. But instead of asking how, we must ask why it was done? Our strengths, capabilities, sense of vision and motivation meant one thing that was being reacted against."

Ballet has now become highly commercial, a fact she fears may upset the balance that should prevail between artistic direction and motivation. "It means the sense of mission is lost," she concluded. "Now I feel the prevailing attitude is that women are dispensable, that they get in the way."

Echoing Emily Mann's sentiments about how crass the commercial theater has become, Weisberger said she felt the same thing has happened in ballet because the new managers were also becoming overly concerned about the bottom line at the sacrifice of the art itself. "There has to be some compromise; you have to know how far to go without destroying what you have," she said. "Those who are responsible for the fiscal health of the organization do not see it that way. They feel artists are unrealistic. And when you lose sight of the true sense of purpose, anything can happen."

That's why Weisberger is embarked on a new project of her own design, financed by a Ford Foundation grant. It is called the Central Pennsylvania Youth Ballet, a training and support center for promising young talent, which will also serve as a feed into professional companies. She hopes it is a place "where all the things that can no longer happen in large companies will happen. I'm building another nest," she said. "That's what women do."

In the world of music, women's chances of success are as diverse as they are in the theater. Women composers and orchestra players are faring better than they did ten or twelve years ago, but women conductors pursue a lonely course toward full acceptance, at least in the major orchestras. The same is true of orchestral managers; there are more opportunities for women in the smaller orchestras than in the larger ones.

When Catherine French, now the chief executive officer of the American Symphony Orchestra League, was just starting out, she got a job as a girl Friday at the American Symphony Orchestra when it was under the baton of the fabled Leopold Stokowski. In a few years she was running the orchestra. She thinks she was the youngest general manager of a major orchestra in the country. But you won't find a women general manager with a major orchestra today, she says. Why?

"I think that what's happened," she explained, "is that, as orchestras became bigger, as seasons became longer, union contracts more complicated, the financial stakes got higher. They had to be run as a business. And no longer was there someone sitting around in a board back room, writing checks to cover these deficits. That was the era of the grande dame. But now a broader base of funding is necessary, and therefore the demand for business skills is greater."

French also thinks it has a lot to do with the "point of view" of the orchestra board which she paraphrased: "You know, it's all right if you can manage something with a budget of $1 million, but can you really handle $15 million?"

Added French: "I have certainly witnessed situations where in examining the pool of people who should be considered for a particular job, women who are as qualified as their male counterparts are not called. And I think there is still somewhat of a sense on orchestra boards that it's a man's job."

She thinks there's still "subtle discrimination in the area of power—an almost unconscious, sort of subliminal, resistance to vesting women with the amount of power that is part and parcel of the job of music director/conductor, or general manager."

But if "breaking through at the top" is hard for orchestra managers, consider what the odds are for women to become musical director/conductor. For women, the chances are practically nil. "So much of the image that surrounds the conductor is a male image," said French. "It's a male concept, a male picture that one has when one says conductor." "And even if the fates are kind, she points out, the woman conductor still has to overcome the resistance of the board that is looking for the great, charismatic male conductor."

However, women ARE beginning to make it into the upper echelons, both as conductors and managers, but almost imperceptively, said French, "because there is a heightened sensitivity, a heightened awareness and much more attention placed on quality and ability and much less attention paid on sex." However, she thinks women have to be better than their male counterparts. "It's somewhat the same in any minority," she said. "They've got to be outstanding."

To name a few, she cited veteran conductor Antonia Brica, Eve Queler, of the Opera Orchestra of New York, Judith Somogi, who was with the New York City Opera and now is conducting in Europe; Victoria Bond, who was a product of the Exxon Youth Conductors program, and Catherine Comet, associate conductor of the Baltimore Symphony.

A comparative few perhaps. "But they're coming," she said. "They're already in the second tier of management in the big orchestras, in the first tier in the smaller orchestras. And as the jobs open up at the top, those women are going to be in the pool. And sooner or later someone's going to break through. My guess is sooner than later. Someone's going to break through in one of the top-ranked orchestras, and then from there it's going to be easy."

But the view from the podium doesn't look this rosy to a woman who's established herself as one of the country's outstanding conductors. Eve Queler, music director of the Opera Orchestra of New York, answered my letter to her with a cry of anger.

"I am disgusted at the situation regarding women in the field of conducting," she wrote in her letter which I will quote in most of its entirety. "Most orchestras and opera companies hesitate to take what they think is a chance. The most frustrating thing is that women do nothing to help other women. I don't know how we can expect men to give us recognition if women will not. It does not suffice to invite a woman to conduct a program of all women's compositions. That will only tighten the ghetto and I never participate in such concerts.

"Many groups of artists, such as composers, protest that they are discriminated against because they are women. However, the outstanding American composer today is Ellen Zwillich, whose music is played everywhere. There is no comparable women conductor."

Her letter continues: "So, my field is lagging behind some others and I feel frustrated and deserted. There are numerous women in positions of power in the musical world who could do something and do not. There are several women in charge of major opera companies in the USA as well as numerous women who are very influential on boards of symphonies.

"I am kept busy accepting all sorts of lovely honors, Woman of the Year, etc., but in my opinion, my career is no further along than it was ten years ago."

Ellen Zwillich, the first woman to be awarded the Pulitzer Prize in music, in 1983, certainly deserves Eve Queler's praise, but she is also a sensitive professional who's also well aware of the barriers that still hold back her fellow musicians and the performance of the works. But she is very hopeful.

"Things have changed so unbelievably in the last
twelve years," she told me, "it is almost frightening to
remember what it was like." One of the problems she sees
for women in music is that "it is not possible to write music
in isolation. Women traditionally have been isolated as
performers. In Europe, orchestras still do not have women
members." She said that was noticeable when the Vienna
Philharmonic visited San Francisco a year ago, especially in
contrast to the San Francisco Symphony, which has many
young women players of several nationalities—Black,
Hispanic, Oriental. But she thinks things "have improved
in recent years." The pattern in professional music, she
said, is that "more and more women are being
represented." So compared to what it used to be, she
thinks discrimination is "relatively minor."

However, prejudice is still there, she conceded. "If
people think you should sit in the back of the bus, it's their
problem if the law says you can sit wherever you like, and
they can't prevent you from doing so," she maintained.
Just as there are laws to protect Blacks from being
deprived of their rights, so she believes there should be
legislation to protect the rights of women through passage
of the Equal Rights Amendment.

Ellen Zwilich sees a new day dawning for women in
music. "Dramatic strides have been made in the last 20
years," she maintains. "There are no barriers to
performances today. You can find champions of your work
both male and female. There's been a great effort by
women who organize music. There are several formal and
informal networks among women," including the
International League of Women Composers, of which she is
a member, and the American Women Composers in
Washington, D.C.

Where she sees a real need to be fulfilled is education
of the public to an appreciation of all forms of music. "The
major problem we face today is that we are virtually an
illiterate people so far as awareness of the fine arts is
concerned," she said. "In the order or priorities our society
sets, the arts aren't important. Pop art reigns, because
they don't have any contact with serious music." She sees
it as an education and media problem, even she surmises,

"an inherently anti-intellectual thing we may have to deal with, which is the inability to understand."

Zwillich predicts that by the year 2001, "women will have made a tremendous impact (by bringing) something very, very fresh to the arts. I don't know any one woman composer," she said, "who doesn't ask herself, why am I doing this?" She feels that art is a strengthening and clarifying experience, because "it gives you a sense of control of your own destiny. When you define (your art), you are less vulnerable to fashion and fad, less vulnerable to criticism, more focused on your own values."

However, she doesn't like being called a "woman composer." To her it's like saying a "lady doctor." She said she feels very good about the things that have happened to her in the last few years. "I haven't had to sacrifice being a woman, and I don't want to act like a man."

She said she sees this conference as "a very stimulating exchange of knowledge and information about the arts by a society that doesn't recognize the arts although I'd love to live in a world where that was not necessary."

Scottish-born operatic composer Thea Musgrave echoed Ellen Zwillich's concern about finding audiences for new music. In fact she doesn't believe that the barriers to acceptance in composing are so much sexual barriers, as the difficulty both sexes have in "getting started and getting their work performed." Quite often the schools where they've received their training will give them a good boost, but it's the lack of response they encounter in the outside world, she feels, that blunts their professional hopes. The problem, Musgrave said, "is how to get funding and get people to go and hear new music."

Musgrave's latest opera, <u>Harriet: The Woman Called Moses</u>, created a local sensation, when the Virginia Opera Association debuted it in March in Norfolk, VA. Its ten performances were sold out, and there was a waiting list of hundreds who could not get in. "That is one of the most wonderful responses; that really was fabulous," explained the composer.

Musgrave, who grew up on Negro spirituals she

learned in school and heard sung on the radio by Paul
Robeson in her native Edinburgh, has been a U.S. resident
for the last ten years. She is married to Peter Mark,
artistic director of the 10-year old Virginia Opera
Association, considered the most daring and successful in
America's growing network of regional opera companies.

Harriet, which is her tenth opera and her first on an
America subject, has a special appeal to women, as it is
based on the life of Harriet Tubman, the 19th century slave
who followed the North Star to freedom from Maryland's
Eastern Shore, and then returned 19 times to slave country
to lead her people to freedom along the Underground
Railroad.

As Musgrave describes it, her inspiration to do the
opera came in "a flash," as the result of several
impressions coming together. When her husband was doing
Porgy and Bess for the Virginia Opera several years ago,
she said she went along for the auditions in New York.
"And I was just absolutely amazed by the wealth of black
talent," she recalled, "and the thought crossed my mind,
Gee, it would be nice to write an opera for these singers one
day." Then a little later, she came across the story of
Harriet Tubman, and thought this is fabulous; what a
wonderful story. Thus, the opera, which took her four
years to complete, was born. The opera, which received
mixed reviews, was commissioned by the Virginia Opera
and the Royal Opera in England, "so we can tell the story
in Europe," said Musgrave, who wrote the opera's libretto
as well as the music.

She was looking for a woman heroine to write an
opera about, she told the Washington Post in an interview ,
for to her, "Harriet is every woman who dared to defy
injustice and tyranny—she is Joan of Arc, she is Susan
B. Anthony, she is Anne Frank, she is Mother Teresa."

In the brief interview I had with her, she told me "the
support we had in Norfolk for the opera was absolutely
fabulous, both in the white community and the Black
community, and (embodied) all my hopes that together we
must fight against these evil things like
slavery—discrimination in any form. But we all have to do
it together."

That sentiment is a fitting end to this paper, which began with a memory of the great 20th century Black singer Marian Anderson. For, in a spiritual sense, in writing this operatic tribute to a 19th century Black heroine, Thea Musgrave has stood on the stone Marian Anderson has smoothed for her.

DISCUSSIONS—WHERE WE ARE NOW

The second set of discussion sessions were constituted along arts discipline lines to consider such questions as: the current impact of women artists; the unique problems still faced by them in the launching and building of careers; the effectiveness of the support systems now available, and what new efforts might be needed.

The following arts areas were examined:

Literary Arts
Visual Arts (and Crafts)
Performing Arts
Arts in the Mass Media
Arts of the New Technologies

Literary Arts

Leader: Rhoda Lerman

Rapporteur: Nellie McKay

<u>Excerpts from the Discussion</u>

<u>Margaret Walker Alexander</u>: A published author for fifty years, I've been writing about being a Black woman in America for all of my life. And I've always been a feminist, always been a nationalist. As a Black woman I've had a constant fight against racism, against fascism, against sexism. I look back on my life and realize that in academia I met great opposition as a woman, but I learned that Black women in the deep South do not undergo as much discrimination as white women in big white co-ed universities. If you are Black and prepared with degrees—the union card—you can head a department in the South. Most white women in white universities don't have these same positions. That's the strange thing.

* * * * * * *

<u>Robin Morgan</u>: The underclass always knows more about the power class than the other way around. It has to. Its antenna are always out. Women can write male characters with more complexity, and even more compassion, and more severity and fairness and balance than men can write about women. Few men write about women with any validity. Especially today. It's getting worse.

<u>Elizabeth Janeway</u>: Anton Chekov was an exception. His interior knowledge of inferior positions could very well have illuminated his understanding of women.

<u>Margaret W. Alexander</u>: I've just completed a book on a Black male writer, Richard Wright. He always had negative treatment of women. He seemed to hate Black women even more than he hated white women. I've

wondered why the average male writer was so unsympathetic to women and why the average male critic either ignored or decried women. Anthologies omit great women writers of all nationalities. Men editors and authors left women out. We've had two hundred years of Black writers. Many of these are not in anthologies either. When they are there, they are Black <u>males</u>, not women. Women do a better job with male characters than men do with female characters.

<u>Rhoda Lerman</u>: Have you read Bernice Kert's <u>Hemingway's Women</u>? Hemingway's attitude toward women was dreadful. My male graduate students were all trying to write like Hemingway. It was that sharp, fast dialogue, not internal, good plot, no interior examination of things, no feeling. Have you seen this as a basic difference between male writing and female writing? Look at the subject matter of women writers. Our choice of subject may affect our success in publishing. For a time erotic and neurotic fiction was popular with men. Are women now writing books about subjects other than home and hearth? Has a woman written a war book? A book on politics by a woman? As our experience broadens, are we going to be writing different novels, to gain a wider readership?

<u>Margaret W. Alexander</u>: Have you ever read Bessie Head? She has written three great political novels. I consider her the greatest Black woman writer in the world. She writes about politics and the system of oppression under which she has lived in South Africa. She defines what the human spirit is like under that oppression. You relate to her characters, whether they are male or female. You understand who the enemy is: the enemy is that political system.

<u>Robin Morgan</u>: Bessie Head is widely published elsewhere, not in the United States. This is an American problem, not helped by our educational system.

<u>Margaret W. Alexander</u>: This is a decade of women writers. Women write fables and use women's language that comes out of our living.

<u>Elizabeth Janeway</u>: The prism of vision that lies between
the world and the writer has reflected all it can of male
vision. It has run out for men.

Summary

Nearly all of the twenty participants in the Literary
Arts discussion were published authors whose combined
work covers the range of literature: poetry, fiction,
non-fiction, novels, biography, criticism, feminist theory,
plays, musicals, scholarly articles, essays, editing.
Experience in years and in volumes published varied
widely, from those hoping soon to enter the ranks of the
published to others with more than a dozen books.
Interestingly, a majority support their creative habit
through academic appointments.

Where to publish was an early question. Agents often
advise against patronizing Women's Presses if an author
hopes for a wide audience. Just as promotional descriptions
that portray material as "feminist" are viewed negatively
in many quarters, so, too, identification with a Woman's
Press carries a stigma. There are considerable economic
disadvantages for an author to publish with a small firm
where advances and royalties are minimal if not
non-existent, and where promotion is limited. The
dilemma, then, for this group of women writers was how to
reach a large audience and enjoy financial rewards without
somehow betraying their literary sisters.

Women's publishing houses, of course, appeal to many
women writers, as they exist to give visibility to products
by and about women. The reality, particularly for less
well-known authors, is a far greater likelihood of acceptance
by a Woman's Press, where "feminist" is not a forbidden
word, than by larger, more prestigious firms. Ironically,
Carolyn Kizer's Pulitzer Prize winning volume of poetry
this year was published by a small press after being turned
down by four trade houses.

Even the solicitation of individuals to write blurbs for
book jackets or other publicity poses a problem. Does one
choose men? known feminists? Someone who is an

authority on the subject and has prestige certainly is desirable, but within that category is there a preference?

Both the language used to communicate and the thematic substance of the material were also considered. While no one contested the notion that women writers try to say what they believe to be true as clearly as possible, there remained the questions: Do we talk for ourselves or for our audience? Is a male writer's perception of another human being different than that of a female writer? Are women writers more sensitive and sympathetic to their men characters than male writers are to their female characters? Is it easier for a woman writer to portray the female experience than the male experience? Creating characters, female or male, that become so real that there is no danger of the author substituting rhetoric for conversation is not only an imperative and a challenge, it is part of the pleasure of writing.

In reviewing both the choice of subject matter, which too often influences the "success" of a book, and the new symbols and language that women are bringing out of their own experience, the assertion was made that the male vision is sated because men have done it so long they've used up their capacity to name and this naming must now be done by people who can bring a sense of fresh discovery.

The stigma still attached to being a feminist persists because feminists have different values and the dominant culture doesn't want opposition. Women must not apologize. Rather, in the process of writing to an ever widening audience, women must create language that persuades, or, at minimum, successfully counters the establishment values.

Visual Arts

Leader: Cynthia Navaretta

Rapporteur: Leslee Corpier

Excerpts from the discussion

Cynthia Navaretta: I think one of the most serious
problems is the new painting of the eighties, with its macho
elements and misogynic imagery of violence which implies
authoritarianism. It's largely ironic that it was the early
efforts of women artists who opened the way for this
Neo-Expressionist painting, for it's now imposing a style of
painting that's really alien to women's concerns.

Kristine Cottam: There was a show in an East Village
gallery in New York this past spring. The title was
Feminists and Misogynists Together At Last. It was
amazing. I came to find out that they legitimately had
feminists and blatant misogynists in the same show.
     The work that I saw there was violent beyond belief.
Misogynic to the point that the art work should have been
thrown out in the first place. And slick. Very slick. Very
professional. Very carefully crafted—to the degree that if
you could ignore the content the work was aesthetically
pleasing. But I couldn't get past the content.
     I found this kind of painting repeated all over New
York, all over the east Village, all over Soho. Images of
men fondling children, women's bodies being torn into
pieces, decapitation, forced sexual encounters. All
graphically depicted. For sale for thousands of dollars on
those pristine walls in Soho. The work was legitimized by
its placement in these galleries. I found myself just
absolutely appalled.

Elaine Perret: What bothers me is that our youth is
picking up on this, and it's not just in high school where I
find a lot of it, but also down in the grades—little kids from
about the third grade up are cutting off heads. It used to be

when we found children doing this in their art work we'd
send them to the psychologist. But now it seems to be a
cultural thing.

* * * * * * * * * *

<u>Ellouise Schoettler</u>: I think if you examine the alternative
gallery systems, you will find a lot of life and a lot of
freedom. You can do a lot of things and the market is not a
consideration. Many people I know operate both within the
commercial system and the alternative system.

<u>Unidentified</u>: I just have the sense that the women's
support organizations that were there maybe five years ago
aren't as vital—or don't exist any more. And I find that
kind of discouraging. But maybe other people don't have
that same perception.

<u>Cynthia Navaretta</u>: Well, many of the organizations still
exist, but they are becoming increasingly difficult to
maintain. Funding has been reduced for the women's
organizations and galleries. They were very safe places to
be, and in some cases during the seventies they almost
became ghettos. Do you mind if I say that?
     I just want to mention something else which may be
endemic to the women's artists movement. Recently a
group in New York that call themselves the Guerrilla Girls
have been plastering copies of a poster all over Soho on
buildings and on telephone booths. It aroused my curiosity,
because it was almost identical to something we had done
thirteen years before. So I made a xerox of one of my
historic documents and I wrote the group a note and said:
"Had you ever seen this before? Did you know that we
were active many years ago—we who are now aged and no
longer go around pasting things up on walls?" Then this
young woman called me the other morning and said," I
couldn't believe it. You mean you really did that?" And I
said, "Have you never heard of anything that women did
during the—you know—the first wave?"
     It was so incredible. Their poster was almost
identical. It names almost the same galleries. It's

shocking, appalling, incredible, unbelievable.

I sent the group a description of what we had done, all the demonstrations we conducted in 1972. These young women were so astonished, "<u>You</u> <u>did</u> <u>all</u> <u>that</u>?!"

That's the reality of it, that after all that work—the ferment of the seventies was very encouraging and we thought we had made great progress—here we are back at the same point. These young women are starting it all over again. They're reinventing the wheel.

Summary

Everyone spoke of their concern and distress about the NEW PAINTING of the 80's.

This Neo-Expressionism is violent and misogynic in context. Subject matter includes forced sex and mutilation. The style is slick and well crafted. The prices are in the thousands of dollars. The new painting is now in all the museums, galleries and magazines. Individuals spoke of their reactions—nausea, physical illness, nightmares, and anger.

Speculations as to why this type of art is so popular now:

- male backlash to women's movement
- men's feelings of powerlessness
- male anger
- desire for profit

Stereotypes peak during social turmoil as shown by the way Blacks were portrayed during the post Civil War period, particularly in the 1890's, and also during the Civil Rights period of the 1960's.

We need to protest these exhibits. We need to speak/describe ourselves. We need to educate the young to value women's art.

It is important that women become collectors of art, for this can be a vital way of asserting cultural leadership, and of encouraging women artists.

Alternative galleries have been a major networking and support structure for women artists.

There was a concern expressed about today's highly speculative art market and about SELLING OUT and losing the spirit/the essence of art.

Recently a group of "Guerrilla Girls" put up posters around New York City naming the top galleries that show less than 10% women artists' work. The poster was nearly identical to one put up 13 years ago which named virtually the same galleries. The Guerrilla Girls had never heard of the earlier protest movement, and the galleries themselves had not changed in 13 years.

Performing Arts

Leader: Joan Woodbury

Rapporteur: Rhoda-Gale Pollack

Excerpts from the Discussion

<u>Barbara Colton</u>: Actors Equity as well as the Screen
Actors Guild and the American Federation of Television and
Radio Artists have been engaged in statistical analyses in
recent years about acting roles for women—the kind of roles
women are playing and the percentages of roles that are
available for them as opposed to men.

In the legitimate theatre when you go to see a play
you will find that regardless of the play's style or when it
was written that almost without exception there are many
more roles for men than there are for women. A slightly
different statistic, but in the same vein, is that as few roles
as there are for women in general there are that many
fewer roles for Black, Hispanic or Asian-American women
in particular.

For several decades now Actors Equity has
encouraged management—directors, casting directors, and
agents—to open up their imaginations with respect to how
they might cast a particular role. The Union is promoting
what we call non-traditional casting—and this is specifically
being advanced on behalf of women over forty and Black
men and women. In casting the role of the teacher, the
lawyer, the accountant, the cop on the beat, the roommate,
or whatever, we urge that consideration be given to a
woman or a man of color. Why not choose women to play
many of the roles that traditionally were written for men,
or that had originally been played by men, and in the
process give the play a slightly different slant?

This was done quite successfully with the play <u>Whose
Life Is It, Anyway</u>? When it was first done in this
country—it came originally from England—the producers
argued that the lead role could only be played by a British
man, and they petitioned Actors Equity to allow them to

cast Tom Conti who had played it on London's West
End—"because there is simply no American male who can
play this role." Of course, two seasons later on Broadway
the role was not only played by an American but by an
American woman—Mary Tyler Moore—with certain minor
script revisions.

It's that kind of imagination expansion that the Union
is urging. An actor is an actor is an actor. Physical
appearance doesn't really matter as much as people think.
In most cases the audience will accept any color, or, indeed,
any gender.

I would like to ask the representative of Local 802 if
there is any thrust on behalf of women by the Musicians
Union—especially for jobs in the orchestra pits of Broadway
shows or in symphonic orchestras?

Libby Shapiro: The only thing that exists in the way of
guidelines or criteria in 802 is the agreement with the
theatre owners about the make-up of the pit orchestras on
Broadway. For about ten years we've had guidelines that
require that twenty percent of the musicians in the pit be
minority. Now, that means Hispanic, Asian, Black, or
women.

Unidentified: Women are not considered a minority!

Libby Shapiro: 802 does consider women to be a minority.
That makes Asian and Black males very upset.
Interestingly enough, for the most part the Blacks in the
orchestra pits are women. They're women string players.
Because these Blacks are women rather than men, the
white guys in the orchestra feel less threatened. So the
theatre owners are taking care of a double quota—although
there is no quota for women. And there won't be any
quota. Our union does not support quotas for women.
We've been told that very straight-forwardly.

Unidentified: Are there more women in orchestras now
than there were ten years ago?

Libby Shapiro: There are, and there have been for some

time. But they're string players. They're non-traditional instrument players. Not trumpet players. Not reeds. Not woodwinds. Not drummers.

<u>Margie Adam</u>: During the last ten years or so, there were some women performers who decided not to spend a lot of energy trying to get into those male domains but rather to develop alternatives of their own. Out of that effort they created women-run record companies, women's distribution companies, women's production companies, as well as a kind of wild band of women musicians and singers who have performed around the United States. We started out in, you know, not the most hip venues—church basements, and multi-purpose rooms. But within the past four or five years we've performed in Carnegie Hall and in many of the major and legitimate halls in the United States.

Our sense was that we really could not afford to wait to get the kind of support that we might hope for from unions or from any other male-identified sources in the entertainment industry, but instead that it was necessary to develop our own industry and to support our own. It's now become clear that there are limitations to how far we can go with this effort. However, it has allowed for a whole set of women who otherwise wouldn't be involved in the music business and in music as an art—in popular music, in particular—to <u>get</u> <u>involved</u>. Not only as performers but also as the technicians, as the producers. There are lots of areas that women just wouldn't have been engaged in otherwise.

<u>Unidentified</u>: You formed the women's groups to get work? Or is it the opposite, that you wanted to be in women's groups and nobody would hire you?

<u>Margie Adam</u>: We came from many different experiences. There were women who were already working in the industry and decided they liked playing with women, so they focussed energy toward coming together in an all-women's group. It's not that they couldn't get men to play with them, but instead that they chose to see what would happen if all women played together. There were

women who had lots of experience in the industry and decided they didn't like how they were treated there, so they wanted to try an alternative network. And there were women who began their careers in music with a kind of outlaw perspective which said: Let's build our own industry. That's what we were developing at the same time—a kind of alternative performance and recording network around the United States.

Unidentified: How does that work out for you?

Margie Adam: It's very interesting, for I as a performer and a recording artist with my own women's recording label have found over and over that I would meet women who were signed to major recording labels and felt very proud because they considered themselves to be embraced by that so-called mainstream music industry, but the fact was that as an independent I sold many more records, had a much larger audience, and played many more places around the United States. However, in this society unless your particular artistic statement is validated by male cultural institutions, in lots of ways you don't exist. So it didn't matter that I was selling all these records.

I use myself as an example of a number of women who have been very successful doing music controlled and produced by women, who are not always seen as legitimate—chiefly because we have developed women's alternative institutions to put that music out.

Unidentified: Are you not hurting yourself, or is it better for you that way?

Margie Adam: Well, it's an alternative. It's not better one way or the other. Ultimately I think it's important to give women as much access as possible to the means of putting music out into the world. In the early seventies there were many women who wanted to be a part of the musical experience but did not see the ways to become sound engineers, to become lighting designers, or producers, or performers. The fact that some of us had the audacity to start an alternative network has created a study place, a work place, and a practice place, which now helps women in all the areas of music to move right over into the so-called mainstream industry. Some of us have decided to stay and continue to build these alternatives. I think both routes have to go together. It's not one or the other.

Summary

Discussion clustered around two major issues: 1) current impact of women performing artists and, 2) creating more effective support systems.

The importance of role models and foremothers was a motif throughout the entire discussion.

There was considerable exploration of women's alternative networks/institutions—performance organizations, private recording companies, festivals, etc. It was noted that such efforts have provided a study place, a workplace, and a research place for women artists; further, that they have led to the following: the growth and advancement of an independent women's music industry; the realization by women artists of the need to expand opportunities by learning to play dual roles in the performing arts—composer/performer, performer/technician, producer/designer, etc.; new means of accessing performance opportunities. However, despite expertise/quality, women's music projects often are not exposed to mass culture audiences.

There was a description of the efforts of theatre and music unions to increase professional opportunities for women and minorities. As a result, there are now more women participating with symphony and pit orchestras. Because of the growing acceptance of the concept of non-traditional casting, more women and minorities now have opportunity to play roles in professional theatre.

Thoughts for moving into the future:

- women performing artists must continue to become more resourceful, resilient and reliant on using their own skills and talents for forging professional opportunities for themselves

- women must continue to think on larger scale than in the past regarding programming for events

There is need for more conferences of this type in order to give women performers the chance to enrich and broaden their understanding of their institutional settings and to develop effective strategies for survival and growth

Arts in the Mass Media

Leader: Kirsten Beck

Rapporteur: Gloria Link

Excerpts from the Discussion

<u>Kirsten Beck</u>: Across the board the one thing that has stood out for me in this conference—perhaps because I'm listening for it—is that there's been apparent progress for women in every field, but there's been relatively little progress for women in radio, television, and commercial mass market feature films.

I'm a member of a professional organization in New York called Women in Cable. Women in Cable refused to endorse the E.R.A., and is considering removing "women" from its name so that it can attract some men. I am absolutely aware that the consciousness of the young women coming behind me in this field is below floor level. I'm terrified because they're anti-feminist. We have tremendous problems with respect to women helping each other—not to mention cracking the power structures.

<u>Gloria Link</u>: The women now in training in universities that the media are going to inherit will, indeed, frighten you with their retroactive concepts.

<u>Margot Lewitin</u>: Those of us working professionally in the media are going to have to interconnect with university campuses. It's clear to me from the small opportunity I have had to meet young women on the campuses that role-modeling is not happening.

There is no question but that women activists are the jokes of the eighties. Those of us who were involved in the late sixties and early seventies are being characterized as "women libbers," with all of the negative connotations. I mean, it's hard to believe that young women who are going to the military academies aren't even aware that the women's movement had anything to do with their ability to attend those academies. I think this is something that we can't pretend isn't happening.

There has been a growing back lash against women's organizations. But it momentarily ceased with the candidacy of Geraldine Ferraro. It was very interesting to me that when she was selected as the vice presidential candidate that briefly all the men in the world who had daughters suddenly came to realize that their daughters could now become president, which led them to the revelation that their daughters had been victims of extraordinary discrimination. So there was a moment there last summer when it was all right again to be involved in activities that were focussing on women's issues.

I don't think it's going to be all right much longer. I mean, maybe another two minutes. I think we really have to hit it head on.

Women in authority make all the difference. All the difference. Really, what has to happen is that women have to become the producers and managers of stations. That has to happen, because when it does happen, with but a few exceptions, the whole context of the work shifts. Women become central to the work. We don't even have to talk about politics. All we have to talk about is the centrality of women in a given program, whether it be that wonderful Linda Ellerbe on the overnight news show that went off the air, or Cagney and Lacy. Women write Cagney and Lacy. Women direct Cagney and Lacy. And women produce Cagney and Lacy. Until that happens more widely we're not going to have a chance.

Summary

- Within the past decade there appears to have been progress for women in all areas except mass media.
- The public consciousness needs to be raised regarding the paucity of women in the media and their limited role in it.
- The public consciousness needs to be focussed on visual literacy—i.e. the development of the ability to be critical of the images presented in mass media.

- There is a need for women to deal with the current failure of those in mass media to fully recognize the potential educational and creative role of television and film in the life of the individual.
- Because women in positions of authority make all the difference in mass media, women must aspire to and take power.
- There is a need for women in the media to interact with the colleges and universities which train people for the media in order to provide role models for the young women.
- Younger women in the media now appear to be anti-feminist—a blacklash that makes it very difficult to crack the power structures.
- There must be an interlocking strategy of women in all of the arts to deal with the concerns of women in the mass media.
- There is need to compile statistics to counteract such surveys as the Annenberg Study which does not accurately present the roles of women in mass media.
- The reluctance of women artists to use the media to get the message out should be overcome. They have to be taught and encouraged to use the tools and the techniques of the media.

Arts of the New Technologies

The discussion was group led.

Rapporteur: Ariel Dougherty

<u>Excerpts from the Discussion</u>

<u>Maria Mazzara</u>: Home video is a way to get to people!

<u>Margot Kernan</u>: Home video is a big territory waiting to be developed. Its potential excites me. I'm interested in video as a new form of writing.

A group in Washington is working on a video magazine—a video tape distributed on cassette. Six of us are going to make the magazine's first issue. We will distribute it through the Washington Project for the Arts, with rental and sales to schools, colleges, and libraries. We use our own equipment.

<u>Ariel Dougherty</u>: Another approach that we've seen is video serving as letters. I'm referring to the <u>International Videoletters</u>, which evolved out of the Feminist Film and Video conferences in 1975 and 1976. Women's communities in 14 cities prepared video tapes—reel to reel tapes, one half inch, half-hour each, unedited—and exchanged them monthly. This project was unfunded and very inexpensive. The tapes should be archived, because for two and a half years they provided a rich and valuable communication.

<u>Summary</u>

The discussion highlighted the importance of women artists working in and developing the technological forms, since they have the potential of moving the arts into new dynamic roles.

The group felt that the promise of cable access had been stymied, that its time had perhaps passed, and that the future likely belonged to the growing home video market. Home video was, in fact, seen as a prime way in which culture might be transmitted by the women's movement, particularly as women artists evolve the techniques and models for creative video use.

A women's group in Washington, D.C., is currently developing a "Video Magazine." Another approach, that of the "video letter," has already demonstrated its usefulness, namely, via <u>International Videoletters</u>, which represented a bi-monthly sharing of video communications among 14 women's communities during 1975 and 1976. The scores of media women who worked on the <u>International Videoletters</u> referred to them as our "tribal notebooks."

Due to the newness of the computer, its possible creative uses are still largely uncharted. Telecommunications via modems was projected as an important way to share ideas, program plans, fund-raising strategies and travel schedules.

While the use of these technologies holds the potential danger of increasing isolation, that is balanced by the hope that they will save time that can better be spent with other women and in making art. As Maryo Ewell so eloquently stated in her address, technology is an appropriate resource for feminist artists, and we must seize it to insure our future and the survival of the planet.

The Beloved Community:
Toward a Feminist Definition
of Community Arts

by Maryo G. Ewell

> I believe in the beloved community and in the spirit
> which makes it beloved, and in the communion of all
> who are, in will and deed, its members. I see no such
> community as yet, but nonetheless my rule of life is:
> Act so as to hasten its coming.
> —Josiah Royce

My perspective on women and the arts is focused on
community arts. For purposes of this paper, "community"
refers to a community of place, of geography, not a
community of artists, or of people who pursue a particular
art form, or a community of ethnicity or heritage of
experience.

What's odd about the community arts arena, in my
view, is that it has traditionally been a woman's field. I
believe that more women are running community arts
organizations, or undertaking community arts projects,
than there are men who can even define the term. So what
can we say about the state of community arts in the past
ten years? Some things appear to be no different. It is still
said that community arts are synonymous with "amateur"
art, with "recreational" art, with art as therapy, with art
as hobby.

But our champions, the defenders of the little guy, will
point out that community arts is indeed changing. The field
is "professionalizing." More events are attracting more
audiences in more communities than ever before. More
money is being raised for more arts organizations.
Management of local arts activities is better, books are
better kept, "marketing" is no longer a terrifying concept.
Indeed, they say, more men are being attracted to the field.

I must ask, is this success, that the field is becoming

more professional? Is this the appropriate measure of
change over the past ten years? My fear is that, in
focusing upon "professionalizing" as synonymous with
"success," we are in danger of losing our field altogether, or
at least endangering the real gains I believe that we have
made in terms of people participating in the arts, and in the
arts being meaningful in people's lives.

Look at how we talk about our field. We are still
pleading to be considered valid in the arts world...there is
no spectrum of excellence in the arts that includes
community arts. We still are defensive in the "real" arts
world and we long for the respect of the major arts
institutions. We frankly have not attained the "broad base
of community support" that we believe should be
characteristic of a community arts program. At the
National Endowment for the Arts "community arts" is
synonymous with the Local Arts Agencies Test Program,
which defines community arts organizations in terms of
their regranting or consulting activities—not in terms of
what changes they have caused in their communities. And
at the NEA, the Expansion Arts Program, which deals with
issues of change and of the arts of traditionally
disenfranchised artists, organizations and audiences, is not
considered a community arts program at all.

In short, there is confusion and frustration on the part
of community artists, organizations and administrators as
to what is happening to us. We don't know how to define
community arts, much less evaluate its impact. Much of
the problem lies in our language and in the values which we
have believed that we "should" have, in the world of arts
administration. I believe that community arts is a feminine
endeavor in much more than a demographic sense. It is
transformative, essentially, and yet we have tried to define
ourselves in terms which are masculine, and to measure
our success in terms which are masculine.

I recall any number of studies which examined the
problems faced by left-handed children whose teachers
insisted that they use their right hands. It simply didn't
work. They tended to be poorly adjusted, confused kids. I
think that this is what we may have inadvertently done to
our field.

I've alluded to the problem of defining community

arts, and I realize that this is what I must try to do before I go any further. I got a definite clue as to why this field may be in trouble when I jotted down all of the definitions that I and my colleagues at both the state and community levels use, interchangeably. There were eleven of them. I had always felt that, fundamentally, they were all the same, that one should use whatever language works to get the attention of an audience, to communicate concepts in particular situations. Now I'm not so sure. I believe that we have been using radically different meanings under the same rubric.

Eleven is a lot of definitions, and I searched for some organizing principles, something which could better focus these replies to the question, "What is community arts?" I found four distinct paradigms which encompassed all of the definitions; and within each paradigm, one of the definitions was qualitatively different from the others.

It was "feminine," according to Carol Gilligan's use of the term in her book In a Different Voice. After considerable research on differential male/ female responses to various situations and to their basic concerns, Gilligan concluded that women tend to value cooperation, process orientation, interpersonal affiliation and caring, and an absence of traditional hierarchy. I use the term "feminine" accordingly here.

In each of the community arts paradigms, the feminine definition is the one least commonly used, but together the four feminine replies hang together, make sense, and paint, at last, a coherent, directed picture of a field with a tradition and with a strong ethic. I felt, frankly, at the end of this exercise as though I had come home.

Let me recreate with you my attempts to sort out the various definitions of community arts, and, I hope, take you with me as I found that I was arriving home.

1.   "COMMUNITY ARTS IS A PROCESS FOR MAKING ART A PART OF EVERYDAY LIFE."

a.   The most common way to discuss this answer is to focus upon the community arts council as a delivery system for the arts. Community arts councils are organized to promote or assist local artists and arts organizations, or to create new opportunities for artists and audiences. As an institution, the community arts council has its roots in the Junior League's Cultural Committees in the 1930's. The first formal community arts council was begun in 1947 in either Winston-Salem, North Carolina; Quincy, Illinois; or Canon City, Colorado.

The numbers of community arts councils—sometimes private, sometimes publicly appointed—have grown to the point where the National Assembly of Local Arts Agencies estimates the existence of some 2,500 organizations. They employ artists, print community-wide coordinating calendars, assist arts organizations with fundraising, ticket-selling, bookkeeping, marketing, even staffing. They sponsor community-wide festivals and touring arts events; work with local businesses to establish downtown art projects; work with downtown revitalization efforts. They buy, renovate, or build facilities for the arts. They sponsor classes and art trips. They put local artists in the schools. And they are tremendous forces for local, state and federal arts advocacy.

The National Assembly of Local Arts Agencies provides them services and a national forum; the National Endowment for the Arts and state arts agencies recognize them as the local partner in the federal/state/local delivery system. Programs in many graduate schools offer training in this field—for field it has become—focusing upon management and organizational structure.

b. A second way of illustrating the delivery system concept focuses on the outreach activity of many arts centers and universities. Perhaps the most extensive example is that of the University of Wisconsin. At the turn of the century, the University was closely associated with Governor Robert La Follette, a social reform-oriented Populist to whom the state owes a great deal of its tradition in government. Lafollette believed that the purpose of a great university is to serve the state through courses statewide as well as on campus, and through the accessibility of the faculty to all of the people of the state. He believed the goal of a university to be a wise and a fulfilled citizenry.

The Governor's orientation was echoed by the various presidents of the University through the years. President Frank, in 1925, said:

> There's a gap somewhere in the soul of the people that troops into the theatre but never produces a folk drama, that crowds into the concert hall but never throws off the spark from a folk song like the spark from a glowing iron. The arts are vital, if in the years ahead we are to master instead of being mastered by the vast complex and swiftly moving technical civilization born of science... (Gard, p. 95).

Presidents hire deans, and in 1931 Chris Christensen became Dean of the College of Agriculture, "bringing his belief that it was just as important, if not more important, to have books, pictures, and music in the home as it was to buy the adjoining 80" (Gard, p. 99).

He wanted poetry and art to become as important to Wisconsin people as dairying: so he hired artists. Christensen enhanced the already flourishing Extension-Outreach arts program at the University by hiring visual artists, playwrights, even a string quartet—as part of the faculty of the College of Agriculture. In the 1970's the staff of the Arts Extension Department numbered 28, many of whose working lives were spent in state cars, helping people across the state realize La Follette's dream. They still conduct classes and offer advice to artists, organizations, and communities; their impact continues to be enormous.

This example is indicative, I think, of an important institutional outreach tradition: a credible institution makes its staff available so that its resources may be used locally. It is primarily a service of the institution, motivated by the immediate need to execute its mission, and by the longer-range need to develop a clientele or political support.

c. "Cultural animation" is a third way of illustrating a delivery system which makes the arts a part of everyday life. "Cultural animation" is a term beginning to appear in

American community/arts literature, though it is already a tradition in many European countries, notably Great Britain. In brief, cultural animation sees the artist as catalyst. The artist lives in a community over time, working collaboratively with local residents to fashion works of art which express shared history, values, aspirations and frustrations. The work may include a component of social criticism, raising the community's consciousness to what life in that community could be; to the barriers preventing that vision from being realized; to the social action that may be necessary to realize the vision. Both the process and product build community self-awareness and pride; create a sense of community cohesion; create community symbols and a sense of the possible.

Naj Wykoff, a cultural animation artist, described to me the process he used as he worked with citizens in a Utah town. First, each individual revealed the image that first came to mind when he thought about his community. For one person, it was the bald eagles clustering at a particular bluff. For another, it was an incident in Mormon history. For another, it was the children playing in a particular playground. Subsequent meetings focused on each person's image. They took a trip together to the bluffs. They researched Morman history. They visited the playground. And from their new understanding of one another's images they together formulated a sculpture for their community which spoke to this new, collective vision.

Of these three ways of discussing the role of the arts in everyday life, the most common "language" is that of the community arts council. And I find that language, in Gilligan's terms, to be aggregate and impersonal. A "good" community arts council tends to be defined by board makeup, by committee structures yielding "effective" programs, by "sound management practices," by programs which "increase audience attendance," by the creation of projects. One hears Gilligan saying, "great ideas or distinctive activity define the standards of self-assessment and success" (Gilligan, p. 163).

A community arts council is also often defined in relation to a "big picture" of a society or an economy; the "economic impact study," undertaken by many, is a fine example of instrumental values justifying the arts. Community arts council case studies are full of examples of groups celebrating their community's life at festivals or in a collective planning process; but the emphasis tends to be placed upon the group itself—not on the interrelation of individuals.

If we allow affiliation, rather than separation, to be our organizing principle, however, we turn to cultural animation as the more appropriate language. An individual works with other individuals who come together to discuss their place and their traditions and ways to symbolize their attachment to these things and to one another through the arts. A common slogan of community arts councils has been, "Our community is creating a climate in which the arts can thrive." This shift enables us to say, "The arts create a climate in which our community can thrive." The arts take their rightful place—they are a given, they need not be defended—and we may focus upon the relationships among people, among neighbors, which may flourish as a result.

If we take this approach, we will no longer need to measure the amount of art that is created, nor audience size. Evaluation will examine people's changing perceptions of the place they live; community pride; neighborhood interaction; the "spilling over" of collective creative endeavors into other facets of community life; people's increasing willingness to try new artistic experiences, to be open to a variety of artistic products, and to see how what they do fits into a spectrum of "art." Programming will emphasize the collective activity, the creative use of shared spaces, the providing of opportunities for people to participate, not merely to observe. And the evaluative "test" of community programs will be the questions, "Did that program teach us something about ourselves?"—"success" will be "Yes"; "Did that program leave something for the people who will live here after us?"—"Yes"; "Could that program have been done identically anywhere else?"—"No."

2. "COMMUNITY ARTS REFERS TO A PARTICULAR

TYPE OF ARTS ACTIVITY."

a. Here the dominant discussion centers around "quality" and "access." Local community theatres strive to be all that they can be by improving management, by offering better plays more professionally, or by taking artistic risks. People are provided with "access" to the best. Often this takes the form of organized trips to Denver to view a major touring show. Or a Spanish-language children's theatre touring in a Mexican-American region. Or the North Carolina Dance Theatre offering a performance plus school lecture-demonstrations in Alamosa, Colorado. Or the opportunity for people to take classes from outstanding artists. Or a major symphony's annual tour of the state.

b. Under this heading I also talk about the folk arts, especially the women's arts. Rarely, it seems, did women folk artists offer social commentary in their art; rather, they tended to focus on their personal world, especially the people in that world (Dewhurst et al, p. 109). Generally, women were unable to receive formal training in the arts, either because art schools were closed to them, or because they were too tied to their homes and to family tasks. They found their creative outlet, often, in "home arts"—in quilts and needlework, in clothing, or in furniture painting. Their work was precious to them, for it was personal.

The following is typical:

It took me more than twenty years, nearly twenty-five, I reckon, in the evening after supper when the children were all put to bed. My whole life is in that quilt. It scares me sometimes when I look at it. All my joys and all my sorrows are stitched into those little pieces. When I was proud of the boys, and when I was downright provoked and angry with them. When the girls annoyed me or when they gave me a warm feeling around my heart. And John too. He was stitched into that quilt and all the 30 years we were married. Sometimes I loved him and sometimes I sat there hating him as I pieced the patches together. So they are all in that quilt, my hopes and fears, my joys and sorrow, my loves and hates. I tremble sometimes when I remember what that quilt knows about me (Dewhurst et al, p. 53).

There is no question but that the first "language"—community arts is about "quality" and "access"—is currently dominant in the discussions I hear. Funding source guidelines for community arts grants usually stress "increased quality of activity" as their primary criterion for awarding funds. Yet "quality" is an abstract, referring to an often academic interpretation of "good" or "contemporary" art—generally unrelated to people's lives. The results, for example, are the all-too-familiar controversies over public sculpture or over "elitist" exhibits and performances; and frustrating attempts at the community level to "educate the public" and to "upgrade standards." "Access," too, is a product-oriented term, involving either "taking people to art" or "putting art where people live." The arts are seen as ends, not means, and the success of an "access" or "outreach" program is measured in terms of increasing attendance. This may be appropriate for arts institutions' audience development programs; but I suggest that community arts has nothing to do with audience development.

If we allow the personal, the sense of affiliation, to organize our thinking, then the dominant "language" shifts to the folk arts— activities in which individuals are given permission to value their own lives and to recognize "quality" in their own experiences and in the ordinary experiences they share with their neighbors.

For example, I've found that it's remarkable what a quilt evokes in people. Recently, I attended a play, Quilters, written by Coloradans Molly Newman and Barbara Damashek, based upon frontier women's diaries. As the women stitch, vignettes of their lives are acted out, and returned to their quilt. At the intermission, I eavesdropped on people's conversations. As far as I could tell, every one was a reminiscence of a piece of handiwork, and what it meant to them. We were with two other couples. Bob, in perhaps his late fifties, confessed to his wife that he still had the first pair of socks she had knitted for him when they were high school sweethearts. She hadn't known. Charles, the only boy in a large family, recalled how his mother required that his sisters quilt and said that just because he was a boy, he should be no exception. He was a better quilter than his sisters—to his wife's surprise: this was the first she'd heard of it. The point is, a lot of people were brought together with a good deal of tenderness that night.

In this context a definition of "quality" which I once heard— "quality is respect for the people"—becomes a meaningful organizing principle. Here "quality" bears no relationship whatever to a major symphony's often disrespectful "light classical" tour of the state in the name of "access." Baker Brownell, a philosopher/community developer in the 1940's and '50's, went so far as to suggest that the folk arts are the only true arts, for they arise as an expression of who people are. If people are allowed to value their own stories and to express them publicly, if people respect one another's stories and personal truths, then the arts assume their rightful place as "givens"—no longer frills for the educated or spectator sports of ethnicity. The work of the University of Wisconsin, in executing La Follette's vision, takes its rightful place in the folk tradition, as groups of people tell their collective tale in drama, oral tradition, dance, literature, architecture and public art.

3. "COMMUNITY ARTS IS A MEANS OF BRINGING ABOUT COMMUNITY CHANGE."

a. The dominant version of the community change paradigm has been called the "professional-technical perspective," and I work with it all the time. This concept of change assumes that society is composed of organizational structures, made interdependent "by social and economic relations and moral obligations and their construction of a consensual ideology" (Crowfoot & Chesler, p. 190). The organization is the unit of analysis; the theory assumes that, in organizations, people are constrained by the roles they play, the information they possess, the values they share, and the operating procedures they have in common.

In order to change organizations, then, roles, information, values, and procedures need to be changed, incrementally, through sound planning and group process. People are encouraged to interact more informally; to mix status levels; to engage in collective problem-solving. A facilitator is often employed by organizations to guide this process. In this perspective, the change agent is often a specially trained, "elite" individual, whose work stimulates a group process in which every member of the organization ultimately shares.

Following this paradigm, community arts councils often try to facilitate networking among community organizations. Well-planned and well-managed internally, the community arts council interacts rationally with other community organizations to achieve joint goals.

b. A second community change tradition focuses upon the dynamic relationships among interest groups. The community development literature suggests that a community must empower itself, both in order to make sound collective decisions and to cope successfully with forces which thrive upon an unequal distribution of resources.

Community arts, in this context, can be illustrated by "The Montana Project." In the 1940's the University of Montana reflected a tradition similar to the University of Wisconsin's, described earlier. When Ernest Melby became Chancellor in 1943 he said:

> Technology has given us the tools to meet the needs of all humanity, but it has given human beings neither the disposition toward each other, nor the social direction by which these goals can be reached. We have given nurture to a science which has remade the productive world, but we have not equipped men to live in that world. We have given wings to the mind of man without putting beauty and love in his heart (Posten, p. 16).

Melby hired Baker Brownell whose mission was to help small Montana communities address questions of community competency and develop a plan by which they could progress through the century with strength, in a spirit of self-determination. Often the findings of the local Study Groups led to a community pageant, a drama in which people recreated their history and set the stage for their future.

> We can build culture into our organizing in many ways. We can begin recommunicating to the members of the group the history that we're in the process of rediscovering....We can help people re-learn the songs that came out of historical struggles, from organizing campaigns, about individual heroes, about strikes, about people's hard times, about people fighting back. We can make our own songs... (Cahn, p. 334-5).

c. A third view is provided by the "counterculture" perspective, which assumes that "the individual is innately good, and it defines goodness in terms of internal unity, primitive union with nature, a capacity for ecstacy and joy as well as cultural creativity and a potential for loving and fulfilling relationships" (Crowfoot & Chesler, p. 194). From this perspective, institutions, as they presently exist, tend to confine individual self-expression and interfere with self-fulfillment and the development of meaningful relationships both with other people and with the natural environment.

"Change," therefore, concentrates upon the individual's search for personal meaning, often outside the framework of existing organizations. The individual may experiment with alternative living communities or alternative approaches to education; may experiment with alternative, "small scale" methods of farming or producing. "Community arts," here, involves the arts as a means of self- fulfillment and assertion of one's humanity. They provide an important way to explore the meaning of a community's collective life, to create community symbols, and to celebrate shared life and place and history.

The dominant "technical" language of the community change approach is, once again, an instrumental one. It is linear, based upon a concept of goal-attainment with measurable outcomes. An example: some years ago, a massive attempt was undertaken in "rural arts development." A repertory theatre company, as well as well- known people like Boris Goldovsky and Lee Strasburg, and their students, spent an entire summer in a community of 1,100 people—an isolated community, forty miles from the nearest movie theatre. The notion was that the "arts people" and the "rural people" would come to understand one another. As the rural people watched the artists at work, and had opportunities in their home town to attend these very high quality arts events, they would reach a new appreciation of the arts; and as a result of living in the community, the "arts people" would have a new understanding of rural America and its values. In fact, the opposite happened, and anger and frustration ran high on both sides. The project outcomes had been carefully planned; the human side had not (Ewell & Ewell, 1975).

This pattern recurs time and again. Barbara Polk observes that partly as a result of the cultural analysis, which argues that the institutions of society are corrupted by their weddedness to masculine values, and partly for reasons of sheer survival, many women are engaged in building alternative institutions that incorporate feminist values and can thereby serve as models for institutions in a new society (Polk, p. 411).

Let us allow a feminine value of affiliation to guide us: and if we do, our language shifts to the language of transformation and the counterculture.

Work and non-work life are no longer dichotomies. Community arts now emphasizes the creation of settings grounded in love and dignity, which nurture the mutual growth of the people involved. A woman, a community arts council board president, once told me that she felt that her greatest strengths as president were that "I am a little bit in love with every member of my board, and I know that my town is the finest community in the world." I believe that she is approaching the activities of that group in the truest possible sense of community arts.

4.   "COMMUNITY ARTS IS A WAY OF HUMANIZING
     OUR NOTION OF THE FUTURE."

a. One common composite scenario of the future suggests
that Western society as we know it is growing and
disintegrating. The quality of education is declining.
Reading and writing skills become less important as we
become a visual/oral society. Here, community arts often
focuses upon integrating the arts into the technology
available to us—cable television, for instance.
     Consistent with this scenario is a vision of the future
as a time when runaway growth catches up with us. Cities
have grown uncontrollably; Manhattan will be abandoned
before long. Zoning and environmental issues count for
little as more urgent problems of survival—water supply,
public safety, the crumbling physical
infrastructure—dominate collective existence. Here, the
role of community arts is to promote almost any creative
activity which provides an urgently needed vestige of
humanity in a world becoming ever bleaker, ever less able
to attend to people's social or spiritual needs.
     Or the future is a time of anomie, where growth and a
dominant Protestant/White culture plus the presence of a
powerful media industry encourages homogeneity. Huge
growth in the white collar, service sector means miles of
unbroken suburbia replacing cities; "pop" culture, now
accessible to all, sets universal standards for music, dance,
theatre, and local or regional traditions in the arts are
threatened. Here, the role of community arts is to remind
people of their roots, and to assist them in retaining a sense
of place, a sense of uniqueness, in the face of growing
anomie.

b. A second contrasting scenario imagines people both
discovering appropriate technology and high technology.
People become more concerned with mental and physical
health; health care becomes more holistic. People become
more concerned with self-sufficiency, with responsible
utilization of the world's resources. At the same time, they
communicate by computer mail; acquire information

through computerized services such as CompuServe; meet via holography; vote and shop via their television screens; and work at their home workstations and communicate with colleagues via modem. The "electronic cottage" vision outlined in such publications as The Futurist intrigues me, for it suggests a new type of self-sufficiency. People will be freed from traditional roles; and the place that the family used to occupy may be replaced by that of the community.

Certainly the first notion of the future is the one I hear the most. And its language also is masculine: we project declining scores and skills, shrinking amounts of open space, growth of major population areas. We describe, in short, an abstract future, apparently devoid of people and of human relationships.

But allow the future vision to become that of a world rediscovering that small is beautiful; of a world returning to a proper, human scale. As technology frees us from many traditional tasks, we are freed to replace the family with the community. If we need no longer emphasize the communities which form, for instance, around our children's school or the workplace (I currently spend more informal time with my colleagues in Denver than with my neighbors in Boulder), then an emphasis may naturally return to the physical neighborhood.

If I spend most of my time in my house, then the people I will naturally socialize with—and there will be a new urgency to socialize— will be my neighbors. We will care about our shared space in new ways. Does it make a statement about us? Are there good recreational and social opportunities open to us and to our neighborhood's children? The electronic power available to us will enhance our creative selves—rote learning gives way to an educational process which is right-brain, which emphasizes play in thought and intellectual risk-taking.

Finally, the arts themselves will occupy a new-old role in our lives: as the arts-via-technology become commonplace and accessible to all, the unique arts will be the live arts, produced at the community level, by and for neighbors. The "elite" stigma of the arts can no longer exist. Participating in the arts will truly be democratic; people will participate because they live together, not because some are better educated than others.

Within each of the four paradigms, I suggest that confusion over the meaning of "community art" has resulted from forcing an essentially affiliation-based set of activities into dominant masculine traditions and language. I return to Gilligan:

> It has not been recognized that this psychic starting point, of recognizing affiliation as a legitimate organizing principle of adult life, contains the possibilities for an entirely different (and more advanced) approach to living and functioning....Thus Miller points to a psychology of adulthood which recognizes that development does not displace the value of ongoing attachment and the continuing importance of care in relationships (Gilligan, p. 171).

Community arts, to me, is at the heart of a transformative vision of society. But, ironically, we have allowed community arts to be managed and to be produced in a masculine tongue. We have never allowed ourselves to recognize community arts as ultimately feminine, in Gilligan's sense, with an essence of affiliation, caring, and self-respect. To speak in this voice allows self-expression and community to mesh. Recall the board president who said that she was a little bit in love with each member of her board. And then return to one of Gilligan's subjects: "By yourself, there is little sense to things. It is like the sound of one hand clapping, the sound of one man or one woman, there is something lacking. It is the collective that is important to me, and that collective is based on certain guiding principles, one of which is that everybody belongs to it, and that you all come from it. You have to love someone else, because while you may not like them, you are inseparable from them. In a way, it is like loving your right hand. They are part of you; that other person is part of that giant collection of people that you are connected to" (Gilligan, p. 160).

Within such a voice, delivery, art, change process and vision become synonymous. Programs and services, participation and observation, are no longer dichotomies.

The roles of the cultural animation artist, the public sector folklorist, and the countercultural change agent are identical.

In this context, the debate over "quality" becomes moot for process and product are no longer artificially severed. Judy Chicago said that "women's work has been taken out of our historical context and put into some mainstream context it doesn't belong in; then it is ridiculed or incorrectly evaluated" (Dewhurst et al, p. xvii). We will now be able to provide a context for not only women's art, but that of any individual.

By taking such a perspective we endow the term "community arts," finally, with meaning. We have been guilty, I think, of artificially placing the arts at the perimeter of life in the name of "quality," "excellence," and "training"; we now allow the arts to return to their place at the center, not at the perimeter, of every human being's life, and of their lives together. We can allow the arts to once again be synonymous with what people do, love, and worship.

What, then, do we "do," now that we've arrived at a meaning of this term? As I have said, I'm a practitioner, and meaning, to me, is not only a mindset but also a way to translate thought into action.

Let me just begin to make a list:

We can view the 2,500 community arts councils as potential alternative institutions. It is a network, already in place, already in large part run by women, many of whom are uncomfortable because something is wrong, something doesn't quite "work." We can help them see themselves as alternative institutions—as agents of transformation.

We can look at the spaces we share—the lobby of our apartment building, the plantings around the recreation center's pool, the blank walls left as buildings are torn down, the spaces for placards in our buses, the mini-park created in the center of the traffic circle—and see whether these reflect the same attributes that we find important in our homes. If we do not see in them a statement of our common life, if we do not see in them personality, uniqueness, self-expression, then we can take it upon ourselves to change them. We can undertake the decorating of our community in the same way that, formerly, women undertook the decorating of their homes.

Decorating shared spaces—through public artworks, through gardens, through a new concern with color, signage, park and street furniture—may be the place where "community" and "folk" arts become one.

We can take time to listen and to understand what drives people to create what they do, instead of merely staring at their product: we can, therefore, finally allow the arts to be animate. We can change evaluation procedures from emphasizing product to the presence of the personal, the contextual, the process of creation.

We can stop, however tacitly, acknowledging single standards of "excellence" and "quality"; indeed, I would be happy if we never again used those words. We can subscribe to In Context, a journal dealing with people's transformative visions, and read it for the same reason we read Art in America. We can acknowledge that people are moved by different things, and celebrate this rather than condemn it.

We can encourage any community activity in which we participate to be endowed with a sense of caring, of beauty, of the creative process. We can undertake and support programs which celebrate our common life in the performing, the visual, and the literary arts.

We can undertake and support programs which emphasize the individual as active creator, not passive participant, "getting educated." We can drop the term "audience development" and "outreach" from our community arts vocabularies as terms relevant to institutions but not to human beings.

We can insist that for every activity which takes place in our arts centers an equally important activity must take place outside those centers in places where people live and work. Indeed, we can help our community re-think the role of the arts center, whether it already exists or is being planned, for arts centers potentially perpetrate the homage to the passive.

We can then sing and care, write and love, paint and converse, compose and listen, in the full recognition that they are the same thing, and that we are all human beings whose lives, separately and together, are distinct and for that reason alone, are of unutterable value.

Bibliography

Brownell, Baker, Art is Action, Harper & Brothers, New York, 1939.

Crowfoot, James E., and Mark A. Chesler, "Contemporary Perspectives on Planned Social Change: A Comparison," in Warren G. Bennis, Kenneth D. Benne, Robert Chin and Kenneth E. Corey, eds., The Planning of Change (3rd edition), Holt, Rinehart & Winston, New York, 1976.

Culbert, Samuel A., "Consciousness-Raising: A Five Stage Model for Social and Organizational Change," in Bennis et al, op. cit.

Dewhurst, C. Kurt, Betty MacDowell and Marsha MacDowell, Artists in Aprons: Folk Art by American Women, E.P. Dutton, New York, 1979.

Ewell, Maryo and Peter Ewell, "Planning for Grassroots Arts Development: A Research Study of Nine Communities in Transition," Arts in Society, v. 12, no. 1, 1975.

Franklin, Richard, "Toward the Style of the Community Change Educator," in Bennis et al, op. cit.

The Futurist, various issues, Bethesda, MD.

Gard, Robert, Grassroots Theater: A Search for Regional Arts in America, University of Wisconsin Press, Madison, 1955.

Gilligan, Carol, In A Different Voice: Psychological Theory and Women's Development, Harvard University Press, Cambridge, 1982.

In Context: A Quarterly of Human Sustainable Culture, various issues, Sequim, WA.

Kahn, Si, Organizing: A Guide for Grassroots Leaders, McGraw-Hill, New York, 1982.

LaFollette, Robert M., LaFollette's Autobiography: A Personal Narrative of Political Experience, University of Wisconsin Press, Madison, 1968.

McCluskey, John, "Beyond the Carrot and the Stick: Liberation and Power Without Control," in Bennis et al, op. cit.

Polk, Barbara Bovee, "Male Power and the Women's Movement," in Bennis et al, op. cit.

Posten, Richard W., Small Town Renaissance: A Story of the Montana Study, Greenwood Press, Westport, 1971.

Royce, Josiah, "The Good Community: What Would It Be?" in Roland L. Warren and Larry Lyon, New Perspectives on the American Community, Dorsey Press, Homewood, 1983.

Schlissel, Lillian, Women's Diaries of the Westward Journey, Schocken Books, New York, 1982.

Women's Culture
and Building the New Society

by Robin Morgan

Women's culture and the building of the new society
are inextricably interrelated: any concept, vision, let alone
reality, of a new society is linked not only to women's
culture, but feminist culture and I mean feminist in the
broadest possible sense of the term. I believe that
feminism, quite simply, is the politics of the 21st century
for the entire human species, the main hope of saving
sentient life on our planet, just that simply.

At the center of that politics is the capacity and indeed
the desire to make the connections. When the power
structure as it now exists changes and when the more than
half of humanity which is female becomes empowered,
enfranchised, voiced, nothing will ever be the same. At the
very center of that majority of humanity becoming
empowered and voiced is women's culture. The women's
movement is unique to political movements, certainly in
written history, recorded history (i.e., patriarchal history),
in that it has always seen women's culture as central to its
politics.

At times we have felt guilty about women's culture.
We have batted around the words, "She's a cultural
feminist," or we have marginalized culture in the way that
male political movements almost always have. The idea
that the Garcia Lorcas are stood up against the wall and
shot once the revolution is won is hardly a new one. The
revolution accomplished by the women's movement will be
different because at its core the women's movement is
different, and the very politicizing presence of culture and
art in the politics of the women's movement, not disparate
from them, is the hope of our own salvation, in not only
gaining but in redefining power; not power over, but power
to.

The connections between art and politics which I see
as central to this vision are not simply the obvious

connections. Patriarchal politics has always compartmentalized by race, sex, age, class, sexual preference, geography, national boundary—you name it. If there is a possible way to separate and divide and compartmentalize—the main genius of the Big Brothers of the world has resided in creating those divisions. I think what feminists seek is a holographic, holistic politics, what I like to call holopolitics, which is to see, to recognize, not even to have to make, but to <u>understand what has always been there</u> —the integral, inextricable connections between racism and sexism and agism and homophobia and classism, etc., and to deliberately reject all forms of compartmentalization. This does not mean overlooking differences, and it does not mean amalgamating everyone into some cookie-pattern replica. On the contrary, our diversity is part of our strength. It simply means that we look to the similarities and the incredibly challenging euphoria of <u>recognizing the similarities through the differences</u>. It's like seeing a similar theme show itself in lots of variations, and that's terribly exciting.

I am going to do a deliberate genre mix because I believe that the form should reflect the content. I am going to start with a poem and finish with a poem. I write quite a few poems, it seems, about women artists—visual artists, musical artists, performing artists of the dance. This was never particularly by intention but obviously because the work is in a spiral of cross inspiration back and forth, and just as some of my poems have been set to music or used as alternative rituals—spiritual rituals—so the work of other women artists in various forms inspires me.

This particular poem which was in the second volume, <u>Lady of the Beasts</u>, was written as a dedication to Pat Mainardi whom you doubtless know as the feminist promulgator, in a sense the bringer forth to our consciousness, of the centrality of quilts, at least in Western women's culture. Pat is also of course a fine painter, and she and I were in our very first consciousness raising group together back in the mid-1960's in the Pleistoscene era of this wave of the feminist movement. We had been saying for years that since one of us was a painter and the other a poet, that one day it would be really nice if I wrote a poem to Pat and if she painted a picture of me and if we somehow

wrote the poem about the painting of the picture and the
picture in some way reflected the writing of the poem.
Well, of course, twelve, fifteen years went by during which
we saw each other at meetings, doing fund-raisings, at
marches, in jail, and other basic chic meetings, the way
women meet nowadays, as opposed to having lunch in a
tearoom. And one day we realized that our collaboration
would never happen unless in fact we made it happen. So
we made it happen.

This was around the mid-1970's. Pat came and did
her sketches and then the portrait; the portrait is in full
color on the back of the hardcover edition of this particular
book of poems.[1]

> Portrait of the Artist as Two Young Women
> (for Pat Mainardi)
>
> Old hands,
> both of us,
> at consciousness-raising sessions,
> at organizing, and at our respective crafts,
> and old acquaintances—
> we've both returned,
> not having really left, to this:
>
> You paint my portrait
> while I sit for you,
> writing a poem in my head
> about your painting me writing.
>
> Old hands, both of us
> we cannot help but try
> to raise each other's consciousness,
> reorganize each other.
>
> You care for the pigments themselves.
> Your glance quickens the practiced brush,
> streaking my eyes and hair
> in umbers and siennas, both raw and burnt.
>
> You mix my face

with ochre, cadmium red and orange,
titanium white.
Daylight is clarified
by lemon yellow strontium,
the floorplanks scoured with ivory black.

I care for the words themselves:
alizarine, viridian, cobalt.
I turn "cerulean" over in my mouth,
curling my tongue around it;

I roll it along my teeth, surreptitiously,
like a sourball.
Our methods impede each other.
You ask me to sit still.

We rest—only to compare
our miseries
as artists, women, feminists.
The world misunderstands us.
We two misunderstand this much,
at least, about each other.

Raised consciousness requires of us
we use the using usefully,
but art demands of us
we use the using for the use itself.

A communication thin
as ink or linseed oil
has filtered, tentative, actual,
between our veins.
Translation would have been
in such a different shade or language
had both or either of us been
women but not feminists,
feminists but not artists,
artists but not women.

As it is, even our different sets of tools
recognize each other better than we do:

the rhythm of shape, the color of a vowel,
a verb's perspective,
the Manichean values of chiaroscuro,
the adjectivial danger in a composition.

The making understands itself
more than the makers do.
It has a higher consciousness,
is better organized,
and freer than you or I

shall ever be—
except in those brave moments
when we become it,
even at the price of being doomed
to blur away afterward
like the autumn light—
brightness draining from us
as from rinsed brushes;
our own selves blank, but for that visitation's jottings,
as pages in a notebook laid aside.

Meanwhile we wait for its restoration,
invoking it with all our skill—
because without it
all the organizing fails,
and I will not
quite
catch your not
quite
catching me.

One of the things I want very much to do is help bring
even more center- stage a global perspective to women's
thinking. In part, I have to do this because I have suffered
permanent brain undamage from the thirteen years of
compiling and editing Sisterhood Is Global: The
International Women's Movement Anthology, and I can't
help but see everything in a cross-cultural, international,
global context. Most assuredly that's true of women's
culture. I want to give just three tiny examples in

affirmation of what Elizabeth Janeway said about
remaking the language. These are examples of the kind of
consciousness raising that needs to be done about
language— patriarchal language—even for us who thought
we already had a pretty good international feminist
consciousness.

All international studies on population and on
contraceptives and abortion practice, including those of
International Planned Parenthood (IPP) or the World
Health Organization (WHO), use certain basic terminology.
In preparing Sisterhood is Global, we would always
cross-reference these studies and do our own computations
from data provided by women's rights activists in the
region involved, do comparative studies, before the
documentation went into the preface about that particular
country. One of the things that got by us for about three
months was the automatic picking up of the terminology
that IPP and WHO and all of the other agencies still use in
discussing abortion legislation. They will say, for example,
"only available for the first trimester," "only in the case of
rape, incest, etc.," whatever the legislation is, and "only to
save the life of the mother." It was three months into the
project that in the middle of the night I woke up and I
thought: we, of course, should say "only to save the life of
the woman."

Another example is the references in data on many
Third World countries— and on the Scandinavian
countries—about "cohabitation." Whether for
customary-marriage-law reasons in many Third World
countries or in the alternate approach of the Scandinavian
countries, when the data refers to couples in cohabitation, it
will be assumed that those are heterosexual couples in
cohabitation. So we always, when citing that data, referred
to it as heterosexual couples cohabiting, because, indeed, it
did not include same- sex lovers who were cohabiting on
however long-term or committed a basis.

A third example of ethnocentricity came as a bit of a
surprise. All the way until one year before we finished the
book we had been using the date identifiers A.D. and B.C.
Fortunately, we were working on word processors and
computers, and we simply fed into Ida (we nicknamed our

computer Ida) that she should please do a search for every
B.C. and change it to B.C.E. (Before Common Era) and
every A.D. to C.E. (Common Era). Ida gamely did it. At
times she would flash up "No memory, can't handle." We
thought it was because she was getting very upset because
of the enormity of atrocity statistics that were being fed
into her on rape, battery, dowry murders, genital
mutilation, etc., but, in any event, she did flip herself
through all the disks of the book and change all B.C.s and
A.D.s. Our oversight had gone that far past us. One could
go on and cite examples indefinitely, so that part of the
process of inventing the new language that I think
Elizabeth was talking about is again recognizing the
incredible sneaky pervasiveness of the old language, even
when one is already dedicated and focused on looking
precisely for that sneaky pervasiveness.

In talking about women's culture, international and
domestic, I like to think of the obvious divisions of past,
present and future. For each, there has been a negative
and a positive.

The patterns of the past are fairly simple to describe:
They have been negative and patriarchal; their objective
has been to bury our culture, our voice, our existence, to
make us and our labor invisible.

Present, the feminist vision involves the unearthing of
what Paule Marshall refers to as the "mother poets."
Artists in the women's movement have been bringing forth
as a refrain now for twenty years the rediscovering, not
only of our mothers and our foremothers, but of ourselves
and our own past individually as women and where and
how they've been buried, our own silences.

Present, the negative, the patriarchal, exists rather
clearly statistically in the staggering situation and pain of
the majority of the human species, a few samples of which
I will cite. The positive in the feminist involves
empowerment, and when I think of empowerment, it is
again multi-faceted. I think of the kind of work that the
Women's Art Registry of Minnesota has been doing. I have
been to the W.A.R.M. Gallery; it made me very warm. I
think of the kind of work that Florence Howe has been
doing in the women's movement for years, internationally

as well as nationally, basic pioneer work in recovering our own history and in making it. I think of the kind of cultural affirmation and vision that Margie Adam has given and will continue to give us. And I think of new friends like Dr. Margaret Walker Alexander, who has survived for fifty years as a black woman feminist, artist, and educator. All of those connections, and more, go even beyond the definition of empowerment.

The future, the patriarchal negative future, is very simple to describe. There won't be any. A future won't exist! Or rather, it will exist in the shape of a large mushroom cloud, and such a future is quite imminent as we all know. The feminist, the positive, involves vision, audacity and enormous risk, and it involves making the connections from the spiritual, as Gloria Orenstein has done and is doing and will do, to the political, from the aesthetic and the cultural to the legislative, from the streets to working "within the system." The feminist future mandates that there be no more either/or bifurcated thinking, but that we look instead to both/and.

I want to read a few critical facts about the lives of women from the Introduction to Sisterhood is Global.[2]

Two out of three of the world's illiterates are now women, and while the general illiteracy rate is falling, the female illiteracy rate is rising. One third of all families in the world are headed by women. In the developing countries, almost half of all single women over age fifteen are mothers. Only one third of the world's women have any access to contraceptive information or devices, and more than one half have no access to trained help during pregnancy and childbirth. Women in the developing world are responsible for more than 50 percent of all food production (on the African continent women do 60 to 80 percent of all agricultural work, 50 percent of all animal husbandry, and 100 percent of all food processing). In industrialized countries, women still are paid only one half to three quarters of what men earn at the same jobs, still are ghettoized into lower-paying "female-intensive" job categories, and still are the last hired and the first fired; in

Europe and North America, women constitute over 40
percent of the paid labor force, in addition to contributing
more than 40 percent of the Gross Domestic Product in
unpaid labor in the home. As of 1982, 30 million people
were unemployed in the industrialized countries and 800
million people in the Third World were living in absolute
poverty; most of those affected are migrant workers and
their families, youth, the disabled, and the aged—and the
majority of all those categories are women. Approximately
500 million people suffer from hunger and malnutrition; the
most seriously affected are children under age five and
women. Twenty million persons die annually of
hunger-related causes and one billion endure chronic
undernourishment and other poverty deprivations; the
majority are women and children. And this is only part of
the picture.

Not only are females most of the poor, the starving,
and the illiterate, but women and children constitute more
than 90 percent of all refugee populations. Women outlive
men in most cultures and therefore are the elderly of the
world, as well as being the primary caretakers of the
elderly. The abuse of children is a women's problem
because women must bear responsibility for children in
virtually all cultures, and also because it is mostly female
children who are abused—nutritionally, educationally,
sexually, psychologically, etc. Since women face such
physical changes as menarche, menstruation, pregnancy,
childbearing, lactation, and menopause—in addition to the
general health problems we share with men—the crisis in
world health is a crisis of women. Toxic pesticides and
herbicides, chemical warfare, leakage from nuclear wastes,
acid rain, and other such deadly pollutants usually take
their first toll as a rise in cancers of the female reproductive
system, and in miscarriages, stillbirths, and congenital
deformities. Furthermore, it is women's work which must
compensate for the destruction of ecological balance, the
cash benefits of which accrue to various Big Brothers:
deforestation (for lumber sales as export or for construction
materials) results in a lowering of the water table, which in
turn causes parched grasslands and erosion of topsoil;
women, as the world's principal water haulers and fuel

gatherers, must walk farther to find water, to find fodder for animals, to find cooking-fire fuel. This land loss, combined with the careless application of advanced technology (whether appropriate to a region or not), has created a major worldwide trend: rural migration to the cities. That, in turn, has a doubly devastating effect on women. Either they remain behind trying to support their children on unworkable land while men go to urban centers in search of jobs, or they also migrate—only to find that they are considered less educable and less employable than men, their survival options being mainly domestic servitude (the job category of two out of five women in Latin America), factory work (mostly for multinational corporations at less than $2 US per day), or prostitution (which is growing rapidly in the urban centers of developing countries).

As women, the majority of the world's population, are beginning to mobilize, the goal is not only to change drastically our own powerless status world wide, but to redefine all existing societal structures and modes of existence. The pernicious patriarchal tactic to keep women divided and a permanent subhuman world caste, the lie that feminists are outside agitators, loses its persuasiveness as we unearth our true history. We continually document new evidence that an indigenous feminism has been present in every culture in the world and in every period of history since the suppression of women began. That indeed is the predominant theme of Sisterhood is Global.

The last section from Sisterhood is Global that I want to share is very much making the connections, particularly for those of us who work in the international movement. I hope more and more that means all of us. There is not only bringing-it-all-back-home phenomenon but a connecting-it-with-your-own-backyard-very-deeply phenomenon. It can totally transform the way one relates outward. A good illustration is the issue of genital mutilation.

As you may or may not know, some seventy million women on this planet are genitally mutilated, primarily, although not exclusively, on the Arabian peninsula and on the African continent. When Western women "discovered" this especially dramatic atrocity against women they responded with the best possible intentions and with missionary zeal. Calling it a savage practice, they said, "You people must do something about this." Not surprisingly, this was met with some irritation by women's rights activists on the African continent and the Arabian peninsula, who had indeed been working and campaigning on the issue, taking stands, and fighting this practice for decades. The minute that this Western insensitivity became apparent, the men in those countries turned to the women and said "Aha, you are pawns in their game." The result was a boomerang effect against the indigenous feminist organizers.

This "discovered" practice might not have been attacked with such missionary zeal and lady bountiful patronization by Western women had they known that it was done in England and in the British Isles in general through the 1900's. Clitoridectomy was in fact considered an elitist operation and was made available only to the wealthy (Harley Street physicians performed it). Before they had their debutante balls, daughters of rich families would be clitoridectomized. It was widely assumed that orgasm in women created catalepsy and epilepsy, and those wealthy enough didn't want their wealthy upper-class daughters to become epileptics by having an orgasm. The operation was also performed in the United States up to as late as 1947, and we are now hearing of rare cases even into the fifties in all parts of America as a cure for masturbation and "sexual deviance." It was also performed up to the 1950's in Australia and New Zealand for the same purposes. Now, that information changes the perception! It is recognition that we are all in the very same boat. Would it not change the way that a white Western woman discusses this issue with a woman from the Arab world, or a woman from the African world? She would not dare go in with any missionary zeal when she knew that genital mutilation was a part of her own history as well. Where it has been one place, it has been everyplace, but it takes looking, recognition, and acknowledgment.

These are just a few more quick aspects of the

connections. This is from the last section of the
Introduction:[3]
    Are we then really so very different? (This, Liljestrom
of Sweden implies, is the question men hate most for
women to ask.)
    Women are murdered for the sake of men's "honor" in
both Latin America and the Middle East. Genital
mutilation, psychological Freudian female castration, and
gratuitous mastectomies and hysterectomies all are
performed on women for the same purpose: male
convenience masquerading as custom or even "science."
Black veils shroud us in Ireland, Greece, and southern
Italy, in Iran as the chador and in Chile as the rebozo. The
patriarchy worships particular girl children as goddesses
incarnate in Nepal and sentimentally cherishes child film
stars in the West—but still evinces indifference or contempt
for female children the world over in terms of mere
survival.
    Our perception of reality is everywhere valued at less
than men's: the Halacha (religious code of Judaism) does
not recognize a woman as a witness or document signatory;
the Islamic Law of Evidence defines one man's testimony
as being worth that of two women (see Israel and
Pakistan). But is that so different from the West? The
Law and Language Project of Duke University explored the
difference between male ("powerful") and female
("powerless") presentation of testimony, using over 150
hours of actual courtroom tapes, and researched the effect
of sexism on the perceived credibility of women
witnesses—with depressing findings that women's
testimony carries half the weight of men's. Courts
everywhere are, in effect, functioning under the Law of
Evidence as far as women are concerned.
    The underlying similarities emerge once we begin to
ask sincere questions about differences. The real harem
tradition included intense female friendship, solidarity, and
high culture (as well as humor, bawdiness, and anti-male
ridicule). The real "belly dance" is a childbirth ritual
celebrating life; the Raqs al Sharqi (Eastern Dance, its
correct name) is meant as an exercise in preparation for
labor and childbirth, and still is danced only by, for, and

among women in many parts of the Middle East. The
examples could go on and on.

What this does to one's perception of culture and of
sheer facts is extraordinary. For one thing, one cannot
read anything without reading between the lines. The
major story all over the world of the Sahalian famine is a
perfect example. We read of the deaths, of the agony.
What we never read about are two of the reasons why it
happened in the first place, which have to do with sexism.

If a country uses coal as its primary fuel, the miners
are considered workers; coal is a product; the work is
factored into the gross national product or the gross
domestic product and the social services that recur back
upon those workers are valid.

If, however, a country happens to have wood as its
major fuel, and women are the primary wood gatherers, the
work is invisible. It doesn't appear in the GNP or GDP.
The social services that would be provided the workers
aren't available. The Sahel is such a wood fuel region,
women are the fuel gatherers, and since the work is
invisible, no planning went into that, and mass
deforestation accrued over a very long time.

The other example of sexism is even more dramatic.
After the last Sahalian famine, international agencies
poured a great deal of aid into the region including a head
of cattle to each family. AID and other Western aid
agencies gave that head of cattle to what they defined as
the "head of household," the man. Nobody bothered to
research the fact that in that particular part of the world,
cattle tending is considered women's work; it is taboo for
men. Women are the experts. Women own the cattle,
which are passed from mother to daughter. But the men
were given the cattle, and because the women had pride,
they would not tend the cattle and they would not teach the
men. The men on the other hand were too proud and
scared in their taboo to try to learn. And the cattle all
died. Next time you look at a news story, look between the
lines.

I want to share a few of the proverbs in Sisterhood is
Global.[4] If you doubt that there is a world's women's
culture, lend an ear:

Men are mountains and women are the levers which
move them.
—Afghanistan (Pushtu)

Now you have offended women; now you have touched
rock; now you will be crushed.
—Africa (Zulu women warrior song)

Where women are honored the gods are pleased.
—Arab

When a woman loves a woman, it is the blood of the
mothers speaking.
—The Caribbean

A man thinks he knows but a woman knows better.
—China

A rich widow's tears soon dry.
—Denmark

A poor woman has many troubles: weeping children,
wet firewood, a leaking kettle, and a cross man.
—Finland

Men are the reason for women disliking each other.
—France

Wherever you go, have a woman friend.
—Ireland

Men should leave women alone and go study
mathematics.
—Italy

A man who betrays a woman had best sleep with one
eye open.
—Japan

A brilliant daughter makes a cranky wife.

— The Netherlands

Quick-loving a woman means quick not-loving a
woman.
      — Nigeria (Yoruba)

Trusting a man is like trusting a sieve to hold water.
      — Saudi Arabia

When a woman loves another woman, it brings no
shame to her father's head and no swelling to her own
belly.
      — Saudi Arabia

The women will get there but the men won't.
      — Samoa

A woman's heart sees more than ten men's eyes.
      — Sweden

You need double strength if you quarrel with an
independent woman.
      — Zimbabwe (Shona)

These surely demonstrate one culture — one theme and
myriad multi-faceted variations.

Women writers from around the globe further confirm
the existence of one culture. The African novelist, Bessie
Head, is simply one of the greatest novelists alive on the
planet today — and yet there are women, intelligent,
educated, well-meaning, dedicated and strong feminist
women, who have never heard of her. Our ignorance is
profound in the West. We should be introduced to such
women writers as Buchi Emechetta, Bessie Head, Omalara
Ogundipe-Leslie (all three are African women writers),
Nawal El Saadawi, an Egyptian woman writer who has
now two of her 17 books available in English (one is The
Hidden Face of Eve, which is nonfiction and the other is
Woman at Point Zero, a novel). Keiko Higuchi has written
at least 22 books in Japanese, none of which is in
translation. Berit As is a Norwegian major feminist

theorist. Margery Agosin, the Chilean poet, now has a volume out with facing pages in Spanish and English in the United States.

The silenced, the utterly silenced ones, contributors to Sisterhood is Global, had to write pseudonymously, either because they were in a dictatorship of the Right or the Left, or because family was still there, or because it was not possible to speak the truth and stay alive; but they wrote nonetheless. That's one kind of silencing. Then there's another kind I call feminist imperialism, where our work gets translated and goes out there, but it doesn't come back. One of the future projects of the Sisterhood is Global Institute is a massive translation project to get some of these major feminist writers from parts of the world where it is said that feminism doesn't exist into English and German and French and the more general languages in the Western world. Keri Hulme, a Maori feminist novelist has written a brilliant book published in New Zealand called The Bone People. In addition there are Hinewirangi Kohu, a Maori feminist poet, Leonora Calvera from Argentina, Isel Rivero, the Cuban feminist poet. Feminists are creating all over the world. It only takes the looking.

So the last then would be for them, this poem which comes out of a little bonus gift, a reward for that kind of looking. As a poet in the West and as a woman in the Western English poetic tradition, I of course, would have died rather than write a poem about a flower. Why? Because in the nineteenth century, we were all thought to be "poetesses" lying neurasthenically on our chaise lounges with a lavender scented handkerchief nearby in case we should faint. We were all lady poets with three names. Actually many of the poets with three names were extremely strong poets: Elizabeth Barret Browning, for example, was intensely political and radical, but is mostly known for her sonnets to Robert when actually "Aurora Lee" is her great work, a book-length novel in verse.

Nonetheless, the chilling effect of the idea of a twentieth century woman poet daring to write a poem about a flower was pretty considerable; the tradition had to be given back to me from somewhere else because in my own tradition it had been taken so thoroughly from me. I

had come across a particular metaphor which happened to
be a valid horticultural fact, but I was paralyzed about
putting it in a poem. It was not until I learned of the great
medieval tradition of "the peony poem" of the bardic poets
of Japan and China (most of whom, I might add, were
women), that I was free to do this. At a certain point, after
Asian poets had passed many of the lower examinations
and gone through a great many of their own
self-and-other-set tests in their bardic progress, they could
then demonstrate their skill by writing "the peony poem."
This is a very different kind of tradition, so this poem is
something that my Asian foremother poets permitted me to
write:

PEONY[5]

What appears to be
this frozen explosion of petals
abristle with extremist beauty
like an entire bouquet on a single stem
or a full chorus creamy-robed rippling
to its feet for the sanctus —
is after all a flower,
perishable, with a peculiar
history. Each peony
blossoms only after
the waxy casing thick around
its tight green bud is eaten literally
away by certain small herbivorous ants
who swarm around the stubborn rind
and nibble gently for weeks to release
the implosion called a flower. If
the tiny coral-colored ants have been
destroyed, the bloom cannot unfist itself
no matter how carefully forced to umbrage
by the finest hothouse gardeners.

Unrecognized, how recognizable:

Each of us nibbling discreetly
to release the flower,

usually not even knowing
the purpose—only the hunger;

each mostly unaware of any others,
sometimes surprised by a neighbor,
sometimes (so rarely) astonished
by a glimpse into one corner
at how many of us there are;
enough to cling at least, swarm back,
remain, whenever we're shaken
off or drenched away
by the well-meaning gardener, ignorant
as we are of our mission, of our being
equal in and to the task.

Unequal to the task: a word
like "revolution," to describe
what our drudge-cheerful midwifery
will bring to bear—with us not here
to see it, satiated, long since
rinsed away, the job complete.

Why then do I feel this tremble,
more like a contraction's aftermath
release, relax, relief
than like an earthquake; more
like a rustling in the belly,
or the resonance a song might make
en route from brain to larynx—
as if now, here, unleaving itself of all
old and unnecessary outer layers
butterfly from chrysalis
snake from cast skin
crustacean from shell
baby from placenta
something alive before
only in Anywoman's dreamings
begins to stretch, arch, unfold
each vein on each transparency opening proud,
unique, unduplicate,

each petal stiff with tenderness,
each gauzy wing a different shading flecked
ivory silver tangerine moon cinnamon amber flame

hosannas of lucidity and love in a wild riot,
a confusion of boisterous order
all fragrance, laughter, tousled celebration—
only a fading streak like blood
at the center, to remind us we were there once

but are still here, who dare, tenacious,
to nibble toward such blossoming
of this green stubborn bud
some call a world.

Notes

[1]Robin Morgan, Lady of the Beasts, New York: Random House, 1976. pp 31-33.

[2]Robin Morgan, ed., Sisterhood is Global: The International Women's Movement Anthology. Garden City, NY: Anchor Press/Doubleday, 1984. pp 1-3.

[3]Ibid. p 36.

[4]Ibid. pp 756-7.

[5]Robin Morgan, Depth Perception: New Poems and a Masque. Garden City, NY: Anchor Press/Doubleday, 1982. pp 13-15.

The National Museum of Women in the Arts

by Anne-Imelda Radice

Wilhelmina Holladay is the person who deserves credit for the founding of the National Museum of Women in the Arts. I would like to sketch a bit of the history.

About twenty years ago Mrs. Holladay and her husband, Wallace, were touring Europe and decided to buy some art works. They came upon a still life painting by a women artist named Clara Peeters, who worked in the 16th century. They looked at it, thought it was beautiful and then went to another museum where they saw another work by her. It turned out that they finally saw three or four of her works.

They came back to the United States and Wilhelmina pulled out her Janson's <u>History</u> of <u>Art</u>, the art book that we all grew up on. She flipped through the index and not only was there no Clara Peeters, but there was not any woman artist listed. They then decided, "That's our focus." Twenty years later, the collection had grown—it goes back to the Renaissance—and incorporates a variety of art works. Well, what do you do with a first-rate collection and an extensive library? A number of museums approached the Holladays, but the late Nancy Hanks, who was then Chair of the National Endowment for the Arts, told Wilhelmina: "If you give this to a major museum, they'll have one exhibition. They will put the books on shelves. The exhibition will close, the paintings will go into the collection chronologically, and that will be the end of that. And the educational impact you would like to see—the reason for the collecting—will never occur.

A feasibility study was completed and it indicated that the idea of a women's museum was indeed practical. There was a great outpouring of interest. And in 1981 the Museum was incorporated. A generous woman, who wished to remain anonymous, donated a million and a half dollars as a kick-off. She and two other women then proceeded to say that if the sponsors could raise a million dollars each year for four years, they would match these sums. The Museum has easily met that challenge for the past two years and is presently into the third year. Now, there is a collection, there's a library. What about a home? In 1982, the search really began.

The museum's setting of Washington, D.C., the nation's capital, gives it an international role as well as a national one. For that reason it was extremely important to pick the right sort of building. Also there was concern about asserting a sense of presence within the community of Washington (as its residents are aware, the city itself tends to get overlooked because all the federal institutions that happen to physically occupy that area). The then head of the National Trust, Michael Ainslie, finally found a building which seemed to meet the Museum's needs. It was a former Masonic Temple and then designated as a national landmark. With almost 80,000 square feet, it is a very large building. It has an auditorium. It has an area for a great hall which is 20,000 square feet. There are two stories high of open space as you go into the building.

You've found the home. Now what do you do? Well, of course, you go out to raise money and you do it twenty-four hours a day. We've received donations from a variety of sources. Both the Endowment for the Humanities and the Endowment for the Arts have shown their confidence in what we're doing, and we've received all four of the grants for which we applied. We have received support from numerous foundations and corporations. The exhibition which will open our building in April of 1987—it will highlight American women artists, 1830 to 1930—was totally underwritten by United Technologies.

We have also embarked on a membership campaign throughout the United States. We did so, first, for informational purposes, because, you know, people who live on the East coast come to believe that the whole world is the East coast, and we didn't want to fall into that fallacy. Anne Sutherland Harris, the distinguished art historian, very graciously wrote a letter that we were able to use in our direct mail solicitation. We are now receiving 3,000 new members a month.

One important thing about the museum is that it's

called the National Museum of Women in the <u>Arts</u>. That means it's not limited strictly to the visual arts. I mentioned an auditorium. In Washington, you can appear at Constitution Hall, you can appear at Kennedy Center, or you can appear in somebody's living room. But there are very few other places where an emerging talent can perform or a poetry reading can occur. So we are fortunate to have an auditorium that seats 200 people. I can tell you that if we wanted to we could book that auditorium right now for every night for the next ten years. But we are not taking any bookings until we are actually in the building. We are going to be able to sponsor a variety of events heralding the achievements of women—women composers, women architects—anything that demonstrates creative achievement associated with women.

One question that we are often asked is: "Why a museum for women? Why not devote all of your efforts trying to push women into the mainstream?" The question confounds me, because if there were numerous women represented in major art collections you wouldn't need our efforts. What this museum is trying to do is not to pull away from the mainstream, but rather to make women's artwork more widely available so that people can come and see it. Our objective is to stimulate other museums to start buying works of art by women, to provide women composers with the opportunity for that first step. We don't expect to be everything to everybody, but we do expect to be the place where careers can start.

I recently had lunch with a very important woman who is connected with a well known New York museum. She said to me, "We have famous women artists in our museum." I said, "Yes. How many?" And she said, "Quite a few." Then she added, "So I don't see what the purpose of your Museum is—why you are doing all this?" I responded, "Those particular women artists, which you could count on the fingers of two hands, are just the tip of the iceberg. There are so many other people out there who need to be recognized."

I'm also asked the question, "What about contemporary artists?" Because of course, the collection as it exists now is primarily oriented to the past—it looks backwards as opposed to forwards. That is done for one reason. It is now very important to acquire the recognized works of the past because in recent years the prices have been sky-rocketing—going up and up and up. So for the present we are concentrating on putting our core group together. But acquisition of contemporary art is extremely important, and we will soon be doing that.

We have what is called a State Exhibition Hall in the Museum. Its purpose? To serve our state committees. These committees will sponsor exhibitions of local artists, and then after the state committee has made its decision as to what will be sent to Washington, that show will be in Washington, and we can integrate it perhaps with a presentation of the performing arts of that state. The possibilities are enormous. Now the state committees will be able to highlight exciting artists that the people sitting in Washington won't even know about. I am talking about the artists who deserve recognition, but are often ignored by institutions. And I think it is also very important to provide opportunities to come and show at the Museum to those emerging artists, or whatever, from states that might not have the chance to come to Washington. In addition, since we have Museum members in about 10 foreign countries, we are aware that we have a responsibility to show the artistic output of other cultures.

We are hoping, too, that we'll be able to acquire works of art that might not always be on display in the museum, but will be available for loan to various organizations, institutions and businesses at least within the Washington area, and perhaps on a more national level.

One thing that may be of interest to artists is our Art Registry. We are establishing vertical files on women artists who have had at least a one-person exhibition. We are working on computer link-ups with other museums and universities, so that our data base about these artists can be disseminated. If you are interested in being represented in the Art Registry, send information about yourself and perhaps some slides to Krystyna Wasserman, Librarian of the National Museum of Women in the Arts. She is internationally recognized in her field, speaks five languages, and is very much in tune with everything that's happening.

It is our intention to make the Museum financially self-sufficient, so that we won't constantly be going to the membership and asking for donations. We want to create a responsible and stable institution, one that women artists will be proud to be associated with. For that reason we have maintained a neutral position in the political scene in Washington. It is our role to serve everybody, not just one or two political groups.

Recently we established a committee of Afro-American art experts to gather the kind of information we need to be of fullest service to the Black community, and also to make recommendations for acquisitions. For the same purposes, we've established committees of Arab women, of Jewish women, and of Indian women. It is Wilhelmina Holladay's dream that the Museum will help all little boys and girls realize that a woman can be a painter, a dancer, a composer or a civil engineer—all of these things!—and that this might make a dent in some of the misunderstandings that have gone on for so many centuries.

The National Museum of Women in the Arts will be a place where you can come to learn about the past, see the present, and anticipate the future, where you can meet other women and men interested in common artistic endeavors. Situated as it is in Washington, with a role of national leadership, the Museum will shake up those other institutions. Someday women artists will be represented, as they should be, everywhere.

* * * * * * * * * *

Question: I applaud you. Everything that you are speaking of is so wonderfully ambitious. The state committees—that's such a fine idea and so is the whole idea of state artists and emerging performing artists being presented at the Museum. But on the other hand, you are a museum, and where do standards come in there? Standards have been used by other museums as a means of discriminating against women.

Radice: As far as who exhibits and who doesn't exhibit, the

answer is pretty easy if you are talking about artists of the past. In that instance you're dealing with people who are recognized, people who weren't recognized but everybody agrees should have been, and people who made important sociological statements—we're pretty safe if we are looking behind us. But as for the art of today and of the future that's more difficult. That's why we are setting up the state committees. We hope to get juried shows and we hope that knowledgeable people around the country will give us advice.

I believe we are going to be able to be a lot more avant garde in our contemporary shows than most other places. I mean, I'm sure we will have things on display that other museums will believe we should not be showing and yet will have an important message for women and women artists. We will be able to afford to be open-minded in ways that other institutions can not. You will not likely see the same kind of contemporary show at the National Museum of Women in the Arts that you would see at the National Museum of American Art. We hope that we keep the highest standards in regard to the acquisition of works of arts and also the highest standards in regard to the honest presentation of disparate views. So I'm sure we'll have some controversial shows. I'm sure that we'll even have shows that will make some people say, "Boy, is that dull! Why do they do things like that?"

Question: These are friendly questions. But I have spent ten years of my life dealing with disappointment, with advocacy on behalf of women who have been barred from institutions because of so-called standards, so I hope that you and Mrs. Holladay understand that you are going to be under a microscope until we fully trust you. Since you offer such hope for women—as you pointed out, you can open the door to other museums—you will face a very important challenge on this matter of standards: You will have to take large risks in order to open more doors.

Radice: I can't argue with that! You're right. If someone had said to me five years ago, "Anne, you're going to be the director of the Women's Museum," I would have laughed. I

wouldn't have believed it. Every bit of art history training
I received was in the most traditional way. In my day I
was the only woman in the class. When I was in school in
Italy, again I was usually the only woman. Having to play
the game according to men's rules—I'm very familiar with
that. And I think one of the reasons why I'm really
committed to this project, why I am sure that we are going
to be able to come through for you all is because the people
who are associated with it not only know what you're
saying but they have also experienced that other world.
And they are disillusioned with it, they know what's wrong
with it. They have now learned to play the game, if you
will, in a way that will help the people that we really want
to help. So, yes, we do feel like we are under a microscope
all the time, but we're not afraid of that.

Question: How can we contact our state committee?

Radice: If you give me your name, I will give it to our state
committee person, who will write you and give you
information.

Comment: I would like to get hold of the whole list, if I
might, for each state. Is that possible?

Radice: Sure, we can supply that.

Question: Is there any possibility of not only using the
state committees but also to have, in tandem with them,
some grassroots people on the final jury selection?

Radice: The first exhibition that's going to be in our state
gallery is going to be from the state of Kansas. Our feeling
is that the people in Kansas know better than we do what
they should show from Kansas. Now, we are really not
trying to impose what people might consider to be a
Washington standard or an Eastern approach or whatever.
We are treading very lightly. We'd rather have whoever is
doing the show in Kansas take leadership for aesthetic
decisions. We will encourage, and we will make
suggestions, but we don't plan to get involved in making the

final selections. I think that would be very wrong of us.

Question: Is the librarian, Ms Wasserman, already at work? Can individuals now submit slides or whatever?

Radice: Oh yes, absolutely. In fact, not only was the Holladay book collection donated to the Museum, but Chris Petys, has donated hundreds, really thousands of prints of the works of women artists; other individuals have donated books. So the library is quite well established and, yes, Krystyna is accepting material. Sometimes it takes her a little while to write you back because she's so careful about everything. Every piece of information that comes in she treats with the greatest of respect. She sets up the entire file and then she writes the letter to let you know that everything is in order.

Question: There are at least 350 organizations in this country who have already been serving the emerging needs of women artists, and I'm curious what your institutional relationship will be with us, in terms of helping us change the perception of women artists? It's also unclear to me whether these organizations, which have really been in the forefront of struggle and made it possible for the Museum to exist, will have an opportunity for input into policy-making.

Radice: Well, believe it or not, the process for this is already structured. The Board of Directors of the Museum will have members from the state committees. So that it will not be as though there are faceless people out there who are doing all the support work and not getting recognition. Grassroots people will be involved in policy-setting. Now you are absolutely right that the work of all those organizations and of the women who actually got into the trenches helped to make the Museum possible. Mrs. Holladay would agree wholeheartedly.

It is apparent to the Holladays and those people associated with getting the Museum underway that it isn't enough just to show artwork, that there are greater responsibilities. Because of all of your work, you have

changed the attitudes of people who can now help in ways
that they were never asked to before. If it weren't for the
women's movement, the Museum wouldn't be a
reality—and if there are barriers of communication,
obviously we want to get rid of them. I'm very open to
that, and I think you will find that the people associated
with the Museum are also very open. Now, because we are
in Washington we may seem a little remote to some
people. That's one stereotype we would like to break down.

Comment: I think what is being suggested is that there
might be a way of moving us forward from our collective
strength, of bringing together at the Museum
representatives from all the women's arts organizations
throughout the country for a planning session—a
conference. This might be a way for us to merge our
energies and forge some sort of strategy for the
future—because the future is at risk, desperately at risk,
more at risk really than it was in 1970.

Radice: I think you're right. We are in total agreement on
that. You would be amused by this. When I was doing my
public relations class I had to write a paper about
promoting an institution. I was at that time on the Board
of the Museum, so I said, "Oh, I'm going to do my paper
about what I think the Museum ought to do six months
before the building opens." And it was practically what you
suggested, to have a conference. I am hoping we can do
that.

THE MESSAGES AND CONCERNS
OF WOMEN OF COLOR

Panel Discussion

Statement by Tisa Chang

I started out as a performer working for other people
as a dancer and an actress. You audition; you wait for
other people to call you and to hire you. But it gave me a
very good experience in all aspects of American theater.

Although I was a music major in school, I ended up in
theater because it really incorporates all the elements that I
love—music, painting, poetry, movement.

I was born in China. My work now as a theater
person reflects a great deal of my bicultural, bilingual
experience. Ultimately in 1973 after twelve years of very
professional work, a lot of union work as a performer, I
went into directing, writing and promoting my own work,
because I wanted to be able to have greater impact on the
system. It's important that what we do is also heard and
understood. I felt that it was also important to dispel
stereotypes, preconceived notions. The roles I was offered,
clearly they were very limited. I think some very terrible
stereotypes exist. I don't believe the system intentionally
perpetuates them, but ignorance is no longer an excuse. So
I went into directing and in 1977 founded the Pan Asian
Repertory Theater. I like being in charge; I like being in
control; I like making things happen.

As a producer, you get to find money and put nuts and
bolts together. That's something I like to do and it gives
me a platform to promote certain ideas.

The Asian American theater movement can be said to
have begun about 1969 or 1970 with Frank Chin's play,
Year of the Dragon. However, the playwrights, Wakako
Yamauchi, Momoko Iko, Jenny Lim also were influential.
Wakoko's play And The Soul Shall Dance dealt with an
immigrant artistic soul lost in the dustbowl of California in

the thirties. Momoko Iko is another California Japanese American writer and playwright. Her Flowers and Household Gods dealt with choices, a woman coming into her own and is very autobiographical. A second play, Second City Flat, dealt with interracial relationships. Jenny Lim's Paper Angels deals with immigration, detention at Angel Island. Maxine Hong Kingston—of course, you all know her book, Woman Warrior — is not a playwright and she will not write plays. She's a novelist, a very superb novelist, and, of course, her novel deals with the bicultural dreams of childhood.

There are also the younger voices, the newer women playwrights. They include Lionelle Hamanaka, whose play that we did in 1982 dealt with the internment camp experience; Karen Huie; Fay Chiang who heads the Basement Workshop in New York City, a community group, a multi-arts community organization. Fay's first play, Laundryman deals with an autobiographical experience. Her father was a laundryman.

So you can see that the Asian American women writers and playwrights wrote about things very close to them—things that we considered to be the landmarks in the Asian American experience. As a jumping-off point they dealt with the immediate questions of self-identity, of evaluation of our lives, and of the choices available to us. In the late 1980's I think our writers will start to broaden their outlooks.

I feel that the Pan Asian Repertory Theatre is a vital force, a very important influence in the American Theater scene. It's a small non-profit theater, but nevertheless we're the only professional Asian American theater company east of the Rockies. I am in a position to promote a lot of ideas and good work, and that's very important to me.

In the early years, things were very, very difficult, and to say that we started on a shoestring would be really an understatement. Our very first budget was $8500. That was for producing two full-length plays, with fourteen to sixteen people in each cast—and in New York City!

I'm lucky that Pan Asian Rep has good coverage by the press. That's very important. And it is supported by interest to Asian Americans. Clearly, theater that's valid must be for all people, with universal themes.

I would urge those of you who are starting something, or sustaining something, not to give up hope—just keep at it. You've got to have that compelling drive to make it work. Those first years were difficult, but this is our eighth season. So now I'm trying to tackle the wonders of institutionalization, the secrets of marketing and some of those other things that make for financial stability in theatre.

QUESTION: I'm wondering how you feel about being invited to participate on a panel of minority women artists?

TISA CHANG: I am a Chinese American. I guess I'm used to the minority label. For instance, Pan Asian Rep is a minority theater company. That simply means that we are fewer in this society—in the American society. I don't feel that this intentionally separates us from the mainstream. I think perhaps there was a reason for setting up this panel. In my case, the Midwest does not know too many of the Asian American theater artists. I felt that's why I was asked.

Statement by Sophie Rivera

Latino women's problems are really not very different from typical American women's problems. They are raised literally from birth in the most traditional manner, primarily to be housewives and mothers. They are definitely not encouraged to become professionals or artists. Artistic talent and intellectual vigor are commodities not appreciated in Latino women as they are growing up in the Latino culture which is, of course, predominantly patriarchal. A woman is really raised to be subservient to the man in the Latino culture; she is not encouraged to attend college, and if she does, the message from the culture is that she should not be an artist. This is traditional in Latino communities. If a woman wants to be an artist she must be very very tough, and chances are that she will not get support from her family. She will be that she will not get support from her family. She will be encouraged to have a family and children.

For example, a friend of mine who is an artist married a progressive Puerto Rican man, who happens to be a writer, and they were both in the same place in their careers. But he wanted and expected her to go out and work and support them so that he could continue his career. When they had children, he expected her to take care of the children and support them. She had no time to continue her art.

Last year while curating a photography exhibition for a Latino museum in New York City, I helped a woman artist finish her work of art so that the quality of the exhibit would be uniform. She was perplexed at my help as she had been unable to envision the completed piece. She didn't quite trust my intentions, being a victim of a patriarchal society where women distrusted each other. She had previously left it incomplete so she appreciated the help when the work was completed. Normally, the gallery owner would do this. Visiting artists in their studios and seeing works in progress, they would make suggestions to help finalize it. Showing works in progress to other artists and vigorous criticism and discussion is often the most helpful system for artists. The point I am making, in other words, is that Latino women have no support systems.

The woman I have mentioned has made excellent progress in her work. However, she feels constrained for both personal and societal reasons to find a husband and have children. In her case, as in many others, the time of biological and artistic creativity coincide. The powerful forces of the male-oriented Latino culture demand conformity for a woman while a man is permitted to attain artistic success and then raise a family if he so desires.

QUESTION: One of the things I'd like to ask Sophie is how has she broken out of the barriers that she has interestingly portrayed for us as the life in the Hispanic community. How did you get out?

RIVERA: Well, I guess I'm just naturally a rebel. Every woman has the potential to be a rebel because of the way rebel, and that's really about all I can say. That's what motivated me. I felt it was important to be an individual, to do and say as I felt I should, and not to wait for permission from anybody else to do or say what I wanted.

QUESTION: Do you feel that you have experienced any particular hardships as a result of having made that decision and having been rebellious?

RIVERA: Yes, in the first exhibition, a museum exhibition of Latino photographers, there were no women represented. I was told at the very last moment about this exhibition and thought a woman should be represented, though I already had another exhibition going on. It was my first one-person show, so I had all my original prints on that wall. I had only "seconds" to take for this museum exhibition. At the last moment, the curator who was male, said to me, "I'm sorry, but it's too late." He hadn't seen the work yet, but he said, "I'm sorry. It's too late. You can't show your work to the panel," (which was comprised of eminent people in the photography world, none of whom were Latino, of course).

I found out the date the panel would meet together and I went up with my work, and insisted that my work be seen and judged for the exhibition. While I was doing this, this man, the curator was whispering in my ear that he was going to destroy my career—I'd never photograph again—and he was really carrying on in the most ridiculous manner. The panel said they would see my work.

When I had trouble getting my work back from the museum after I had submitted it to the panel, I was told by one person I was in the show. I was told a gallery owner "flipped" over one of my photographs. I was also sent an invitation to the opening. It wasn't until the very last moment that I found out that I was not in the exhibition, and finally was able to retrieve my work. I was going to picket the museum but I couldn't find any other Puerto Rican women photographers to picket with me, and felt it would be unfair, more or less, to have white women picketing against Latino male artists, so I just let it go.

It was the last time that an exhibition like this

It was the last time that an exhibition like this occurred, because from this group of men who exhibited together a Latino photography group was formed and the very first exhibition they had was of ten women and ten men. They had learned their lesson well.

It took the Latino photography group, who has helped me very much in the last few years, almost seven years to get in touch with me to invite me to exhibit my work, not because the quality was wanting, but because I was a feminist and too outspoken. I was even told I should not be a panelist here. It's a hard road.

COMMENT from audience: I was interested in your saying, "I am a woman. How could I not rebel?" The mind-boggling thing to me is how few women have rebelled through the centuries. It's not the norm.

RIVERA: I come from a family of five girls and we were all together and we supported one another. Perhaps that had something to do with being a rebel. I was the youngest of five and we always watched each other's back and fought for each other.

Statement by Jean LaMarr

I'm presently working as artist-in-residence on the Susanville Indian Rancheria. I moved back there after working in the Bay Area for twenty-one years. I left the reservation many years ago, and I didn't think I would ever want to come back because of the poverty and the welfare system and all the things which go wrong when the government is involved in a community organization.

But after having been influenced by the arts in the Bay Area, I now feel that I am a very community-oriented artist and a political artist. A lot of my work states, "Stay off of Indian land with your jets and your pollution." These are some of my main concerns and a lot of my works have been based on the women's role in the Indian community.

There have been so many stereotypes about Indian women that I feel that there's an information gap in what is conveyed from the Indian world to the non-Indian world.

squaw; I have been working against this kind of attitude for a long time. In our community hundreds of years ago the women were the artists. The men were not the artists; the women were. They were the basket weavers. I always tell people that if I had been born a hundred years ago I would have been a great basket weaver. But I didn't learn my basket weaving technique from my grandmothers. They died before I was interested. Now I wish I had them with me. They did beautiful work to please themselves, and then the tourists came in and bought their baskets up, and now they are all sitting in Berkeley. It was interesting that when I went to school there the Art Department was above the museum which held all the baskets, and I would go down there and look at them and just dream about how it used to be.

What I'm doing now is working in the Indian community with the youth. We have a 95% dropout rate in high school; very few graduate. We have a welfare system. No one wants to get a job; no one wants to leave the reservation. But we have very talented youth on the reservation. They are very good draftsmen and they are very creative; and what I want to develop within the next three years is a group of young people who will become printmakers. I want to create a printmaking shop on the reservation, because the big push by the government right now is economic development. I want to employ these youths and I want to print for women artists. There's a big problem when you go to a fine art press because they charge you about $10,000 for one print—an edition of one hundred. It's pretty expensive.

And I want to set up a non-profit learning institute so these young people can be employed, plus we can do a service for minorities and women by printing editions of their art work. I have a friend who's working with me and she's a lithographer and a woodcut artist. I do etchings and silkscreens. So we have this great combination going.

Our goal is to eventually become self-sufficient—for example, use wind power for energy generation and have very little overhead. We will be on trust land so we won't have to pay taxes; we will use natural water; do everything possible to achieve self-sufficiency and a low-overhead. We possible to achieve self-sufficiency and a low-overhead. We also are very interested in making our own paper, and we want to incorporate natural things that are indigenous to our area—for example, sage and willow. And then eventually this will be a real service to a lot of women also. We want to work out a situation where women artists can come and serve a residency and work on printing their own art.

Going back to work in the Indian community has been really difficult. I didn't think I'd ever want to go back, but I now enjoy being there. We have a problem with American Indian art in that it's a big tourist attraction right now. If I was concerned about making money I could go down in the Southwest and do artwork of Indians in regalia and that would just "sell like hotcakes," but I think there's more to art than just making money. I think community artwork means involving the entire community.

We have wonderful artists in the community that have been totally ignored. They do such beautiful beadwork you wouldn't believe that their talent has never been recognized. They never get to show their artwork, and these are museum pieces that they have in their homes. I visit with a lot of these Indian elders, because we do oral histories with them. And in each home they have their own little museums—just amazing. If dealers came up there they could really make a clean sweep. I'm trying to document these things and take slides for these elders, because I think it is important that other people see their work.

We're going to have an Indian art show at the Crocker Museum in July and August, and it's going to be the first one of northern California Indian artists and it's dealing with how our work is related to dance. I think it is so important that our art not be just a visual form but that it also involve dance. This weekend we have the Bear Dance and it's a part of a Spring ceremony that welcomes the Spring. Every year it has included all kinds of artforms. For example, besides the dance we do singing, and we do posters. To support this activity the youth have been helping to make T-shirts to raise money, because we need to keep this dance and tradition going. I involved the youth too. I think it's been a long tradition that art is a total thing.

The project right now as it stands: one organization is now renovating a building; they are putting $20,000 into it. I told them that because there is no commercial silkscreening business in town, people have to go to Reno. So I convinced them that we can make money. However what we are really going to be doing is focusing on the fine arts. We are just going to do a little bit of the commercial on the side.

QUESTION: I am wondering how you feel in 1985, about being invited to participate on a panel as women of color?

LAMARR: I guess we have been categorized and color-coded for so long we get used to it. Hopefully in ten or twenty years we won't have to have a color-coded panel. We'll all be in one group, not in what I call "art menstream"(because it is run by men) but in the art mainstream—it will be "womenstream" too. We are all working towards this. In the meantime you've invited us to come voice what is happening to us now, and this is a women's conference because women are suppressed and Indians are suppressed and we have double problems.

QUESTION: Getting people's thinking sorted out at an early stage is very important, and that means awakening the minds of the young. For two years I have been supporting an American Indian girl from Colorado and I would like to know what you could tell me that I could write to her about (that's through the Save the Children program) to put her more in tune with an awakening dignity of herself as a woman and as an Indian woman in the world and maybe as a preserver of her own culture. Would there be an operation like yours in Colorado that I could tell her about? Is there any sort of networking or capitalizing on your own particular venture? What would you offer to me to offer to her?

LAMARR: What is her age?

QUESTIONER RESPONSE: She's twelve now.

LAMARR: Twelve. This is the perfect time. I work with ages twelve to twenty-one. The younger they are, the easier it is to reach them. I don't know what the situation is with her, but I feel that you must encourage her and offer her things she has never seen before. Send her brochures on the Women's Museum. Send her information constantly that she's never seen before, because they live in a very rural isolated community and television is all they get. Keep encouraging her to get an education. The reason why a lot of the young people do not get a good education is because their parents were sent to boarding schools and they were told to forget their culture and their language and suppress the idea of being proud of being Indian. You should really encourage her to go on in school. Send her stories cut out of the newspaper about Indian people. There are a lot of national Indian organizations that encourage young people. There are all kinds of Indian youth organizations that have conferences. I think Save the Children is going to have a conference in southern California and they are bringing in youth from different areas. They are really trying to focus more on youth because no one cares about the youth any more. There's preschool, and there are programs for after-school elementary children, but once they reach twelve, poof!—they're forgotten. They are totally ignored, and this is the crucial time that we need to contribute to their lives, because their parents have a difficult time dealing with the institutions of education. They went to boarding schools, and that was a horrible experience for them, so they can't relate to higher education.

Statement by Nellie McKay

I teach here at the University of Wisconsin in Madison. I hasten to say that I am not an artist. But then maybe I am an artist, and I may be an artist because in the training, in helping to train young minds (I hope I have some impact on young minds) there is a degree of artistry people see and understand what they can do and how they can do it. That in itself may well be a great art. We sometimes fail at it. We hope that we sometimes win.

My main focus at the University these days and in my life that goes on outside of the University seems to have moved from what was a very large area far away from who I happen to be, into what I now see sometimes as a rather small area. But that may not in fact be true, and I may well be in the largest area that I could decide to look at.

As an undergraduate at Queens College in New York in the 1960's I decided that I wanted to be a Shakespeare scholar. There was nothing wrong with that choice at Queen's College in the 1960's. There were no black professors in the English Department; there were no courses in black literature in the English Department at Queen's College; and everyone studied Shakespeare or Milton or Chaucer or maybe Hemingway or Faulkner. I love Shakespeare best, and I actually had visions of being one of the first of the black professors at Queen's College. Actually, there was one black professor in the English Department at Queen's College when I was there, but I never thought of him as being black, and I'm not just trying to be funny. But I was going to be the first black woman Shakespeare scholar in the country. That was one of my big ambitions in 1966, which was when I decided to be an English major.

By the time I graduated from college my intentions had changed. The Civil Rights movement actually caught up with me, not only in an intellectual way but in a rather physical way. I went to Queen's College in 1965 and graduated in 1969. The graduating class had 1700 students. There were four black graduates.

So that physically, the Civil Rights movement caught up with me, although intellectually, I had been aware and participating in it from very early in the 1960's. It caught up with me because when I left, although there were only four black students in the graduating class—and my way of protesting was not to go to graduation—by then, there were more than 400 black students on the campus. Once the black students got on the campus I could no longer be black students got on the campus I could no longer be separated from what it meant to be black in a white institution.

By then I had also decided that in spite of my love of Shakespeare, it was much more important for me to understand the American experience in literature. When I graduated, I went on to graduate school to study American literature. Because this area is still very secondary in many places, those of us in the field were often treated to a snide question: "Is there any American literature?" But I studied American literature in graduate school, and part way though my graduate education, because of the influence of other black peers in graduate school, I ended up doing a dissertation on a black writer.

There were no courses in black literature in my graduate school either. I recall doing term papers in classes and seminars in American literature and in which there were no black writers or other minority writers included. I recall that quite often I did my paper on a black writer out of protest. I once took a course on the modern American novel, in which we read 18 novels in a semester—graduate seminar—18 20th-century American novels with not a single black writer included. I did my paper on writer Ralph Ellison. I got an A on my paper. It would be difficult for one of my students to get by me with that paper today. I think it's safe to say that my professor never read the book; I think it's safe to say that my professor felt that the best thing he could do was get me out of that class. And so from the wide field of Shakespearean England to the smaller field of American literature, in 1985, I find myself, narrowed and broadened by the study of black women's lives.

I'm currently working on a project that I hope will eventually be a book on the autobiographies of 20th-century black women writers. I say without hesitation that it is the most exciting intellectual experience that I have ever had, or that the single most exciting intellectual experience has been the reading of the lives of black women who have lived in this century and who have chosen not to write fiction, not to write poetry, not to write plays, but to write about their own lives.

many people now ask me: "Are there any black women who wrote autobiography?" I can now reply that I have read a total of approximately 65 autobiographies by black women written between 1920 and 1970. Most of the names are unknown to most of us, which led me to another question when I started this project—the question of why did they write. I think we have some of the answers for why they wrote in what Paule Marshall says. I think I found a part of the answer in a conference that I went to at Wingspread in the fall of 1984 on women's autobiographies. I was in a session at the conference listening to white women talk about white women's autobiographies and the thing that came most poignantly to me during that session was the way in which white women were talking about white women's silences. I sat and listened, and for a long time I was perplexed, at first not quite knowing why I was as perplexed as I was, and then I realized, it was like a light bulb going off in my head, which is also something that Marshall said: black women have never been silent, nor have black women ever waited to be permitted to speak. And the reason that these, to us, faceless, nameless, 60 perhaps 65 women whom I've read, wrote about their own lives is because they took control and decided that they did not need to be permitted to talk about their own lives. They decided that it didn't matter how many people read what they had written. Like the poets in Paule Marshall's mother's kitchen they had something to say to themselves, for themselves and among themselves, and they said it.

And taking a step beyond the poets in the kitchen, these women not only said it among themselves and to themselves and for themselves, but they wrote it down; so that the daughter whom they never even imaged that they had—the daughter by the name of Nellie McKay—now goes and reclaims those narratives, those lives, and hopefully, will bring them into the public view which they deserve.

The women are poets and dramatists and storytellers and painters and they indulge in all the variety of the arts that we've been talking about without, as Toni Morrison says in one of her novels, "without paints, without easels," but because nobody ever told them that they couldn't speak, but because nobody ever told them that they couldn't speak, they spoke for themselves. Because no one could have told them that they couldn't speak.

It's been a wonderful experience for me. I wish that the book was going to be due in two years or three years or four years. I don't know when it is going to be ready. But again the process of working on this material is also a part of what has been very wonderful. And it is what I mean when I say, on the one hand, I feel that I have narrowed in from the vast world of Shakespeare's England in my thinking in 1966 to the small world of unknown black women in America. But it is not a narrowing; it is a broadening, because in the study of these women's lives I am also finding my own life.

QUESTION: I was just wondering how the you feel, in 1985, being invited to participate in a panel as minority women artists?

McKAY: I have no problems with it at all. I am a black woman, not just a woman who happens to be black, and I think in the study of black women's lives, by identifying as strongly as I am now doing, perhaps, stronger than I ever did consciously before, with the lives of black women, and the word "minority" is problematic only because clearly we are not a minority, so it's a bad use of words.

But to be in a group of women who are not a part of the mainstream is not at all problematic to me. I would have probably liked to have seen women of color integrated throughout the conference as a part of a variety of things that happened. On the other hand, I would also, in spite of wanting to see the integration, I would probably also have welcomed in addition a panel in which women of color spoke about themselves as women of color rather than spoke within the context of the larger culture. What I'm saying is that it is both ways.

I am not at all insulted by being on a panel with only other women of color. I think there are enormous differences between white women and women of color, at the same time that there are enormous similarities between women of color and white women. But I am also convinced women of color. All people of color have to deal with the fact that they are people of color in order to gain their own strength, because even if the larger culture is the minority culture, it is a powerful culture. And in order to gain power of our own to cope with the larger culture it is wrong to think that all we need to do is to be integrated into the larger culture. I think that first I have to deal with me as a black woman, and as a woman who is not white. That's my answer.

DISCUSSIONS—GOALS AND STRATEGIES FOR THE FUTURE

Each of the five discussion groups was composed of representatives of all the arts categories and all groups had the same assignment: to identify and examine the critical issues of the future and to project new possible goals and leadership roles for women in the arts.

The following compilation has been distilled from the rapporteurs' notes and the tape recordings of all the sessions, without specific attribution to individual groups. Major ideas advanced are presented under the following subject headings:

Advocacy and Allies: The Promise
Marketing and Outreach
Educational Challenges
Personal Survival
Preserving our Heritage

Goals and Strategies for the Future

Discussion Leaders:

Anne-Imelda Radice
Estella Lauter
Barbara Colton
Margot Kernan
Judith Tick

Rapporteurs:

Pat Quinn
Margot Peters
Nancy Deutsch
Mary Barrett
Fannie Hicklin

Advocacy and Allies: The Promise

Another reason to continue a special attention to
women in the arts: It's an important way of
promoting the feminist, humanist qualities which we
hope will change the world.
    —Ted Shannon

Art is not a leisure class activity, artists are workers.
Women artists (workers) are exploited in many ways.
As long as this is true we need to organize and act.
We need to be political, to make our voices really
heard and to create the changes necessary in this
society.
    —Betsy Damon

No one questioned whether women artists and art
groups should advocate. The question was how to be more
effective in mobilizing and directing the energies of the
growing constituency. More intense advocacy is essential in
shaping the future status and influence of women in the
arts.

As the connections between and among women's art groups multiply, these networks have the potential of highlighting additional ways in which they can be beneficial. The new roles of networks might include: timely notification of events, sharing strategies for a range of objectives, hiring other women, mentoring younger women, providing a ready pool of experts, exchanging techniques, and learning to expect help from one another. Expanding the multi-disciplinary aspect of art networks has underscored both the uniqueness of our histories and the commonality of our challenges; that expansion must continue.

The networks must also involve women's organizations outside the arts and utilize their experience in successful advocacy. Within the women's political movement there are many organizations with whom closer ties can mean an augmented impact. Women artists can thus strengthen their cause, while the women's rights groups become more knowledgeable about the political roles of the arts in society and more supportive of women artists.

In the process of broadening coalitions, it is urgent that women cross class and racial lines in an ever widening inclusive circle. Our culture is becoming increasingly diverse, with different voices and different ways of living. We must welcome and value this diversity, become aware of our own multiple identifications, and shed any reluctance to acknowledge them.

The basic goal of advocacy is to influence policy-making. While women may be justifiably suspicious of many existing institutions, feeling they can only trust the ones they themselves have created, it is nevertheless important that they attempt to transform the suspect institutions rather than simply rejecting them. It would be folly to ignore the traditional institutions, for they not only have amassed very rich resources but they exercise a signal influence within the culture. In the long run it is a necessary commitment to press for institutional and social change. The alternative feminist institutions can and do serve as role models, highlighting a growing heritage in women's creativity, and they furnish women the opportunity to experiment and grow without the risk of "creeping accommodation" to the patriarchal values of the traditional institutions. They provide the environment in which women can cling to and develop their philosophy and promulgate the humane qualities essential to new social structures. However, because they remain outside the mainstream, it is doubtful whether alternative institutions can by themselves have a significant role in the restructuring of our society—the aim implicit in the very existence of the women's movement.

Women artists are urged in their advocacy to become more politically sophisticated and to take action even when results are not immediately apparent. Unless artists seek to have an impact on elections they surrender to others who do. Public policy at all levels touches the lives of women and reflects the value system of the predominant electorate—those who vote. Women artists for the most part are successful in making their ideas visible; manifesting those ideas politically is more difficult. The gamut of their concerns reaches from the funding and monitoring of public art, pay equity, licensing regulations for TV and radio, copyright laws, tax codes, environmental protection, regulation of hazardous materials, to such global issues as peace, disarmament and world hunger. Acknowledging that decisions in the political arena are vital to women artists is the first step; learning how to be a significant force in making those decisions is the next.

Marketing and Outreach

We tried community outreach of women's theatre in Bowling Green, a conservative northwest Ohio town. We had what was called a Pink Collar Workers project—the title, of course, adapted from Louise Kapp Howe's book. There were four plays in the project, which we performed on-site—in a restaurant, in a beauty parlor, in a women's clothing store. The plays were about people who work in those kinds of situations. The fourth was about homemakers.

What was amazing was that we packed 200 people on a week night. By the 3rd or 4th performance there was some real tension in the room, as people began to

look at the issues. There is a great hunger out there for theatre and for ideas.
— Vickie Patraka

It was acknowledged that all the arts need to do a far better job of marketing the products of women's art. A number of art organizations and coalitions include the subject of marketing along with bookkeeping and business practice in their educational workshops for members.

Take art to where people gather and learn, to beauty parlors, farmers markets, shopping malls, flea markets. Fine art can be displayed and sold in supermarkets. Making art widely available will help it become a part of the flow of people's days.

Electronic media of film, television, and rock video have displaced the print media as influential shapers of our culture, often with mindless fare. Women artists must infiltrate these popular media and make every effort to change the content.

Pressure all the media to give time and space to the arts. One minute of each TV news half-hour would be a good beginning. Public radio and TV are helpful outlets and collaboration is urged to retain their funding which is in jeopardy.

Cable TV evoked controversy with respect to its limited geographic availability, high cost, the quality of its public access programs, and the future of the medium itself. It was pointed out that at the community level cable continues to provide women artists the opportunity to communicate in diverse ways with their audience. Home video viewing via VCR's is believed by many to be the market of the future. Women's video collectives are an emerging resource to serve this new home market, and they could well become as influential in shaping women's culture as feminist book stores and publishing houses.

Whether to encourage and invest in the development of community arts poses hard choices. Do community arts lower standards? Do they displace or compete with professionalism? Is self-expression confused with artistic creation? On the other hand, does the involvement of local artists and art groups educate and enrich the community while also providing creative outlets, building audiences and giving employment to artists?

As cultural resources, especially in isolated areas, community-based theatres, orchestras, choruses, dance companies and galleries have the potential of bringing people together in special ways. Such activities can create a sense of belonging, make for a better understanding and appreciation of the unique character of a place and its people, and they often produce new pride and self-esteem. Community arts groups are, in fact, agents of transformation.

Educational Challenges

We must continue to teach our students the history of women in the arts. There is so much to be known. Good will is not sufficient. Within the University of Wisconsin system we have an arrangement whereby we can exchange faculty around the state. This year I went to three campuses of the system and talked about women playwrights. It was very gratifying to be able to do missionary work outside my own campus.
　　—Rhoda-Gale Pollack

American society does not value the arts as many other nations do. To elevate the appreciation and respect for the importance of art in keeping vision and creativity alive, education—formal and informal—must undertake renewed responsibility. Teacher education programs should incorporate curricula that provide guidance for teachers from Kindergarten through 12th grade in the training of appreciative, knowledgeable audiences as well as performers. Field trips to theatres, concert halls, galleries and museums should be encouraged. By also relating art to other school subjects, the questioning and social criticism inherent in much of art will enhance the overall learning experience. Women artists can volunteer to serve in schools as Artists-in-Residence. By inviting teachers and school board members into women artists' networks this entire thrust can be enriched.

There is a fear among many women artists that
school children today are being taught an ethnocentric,
macho view of the world. The world view that is
imperative if there is to be a future must be inculcated from
the earliest years.

All of the college and university women's studies
programs should offer courses, as many of them do, in
Women and the Arts. Many young women are ignorant of
women's history and need to understand the struggles that
have opened doors for them. There is a great need to
publicize the availability of the new resources produced by
women's research efforts and to create mechanisms for
exchange. For example, art historians are eagerly seeking
tapes of women painters talking about their work. The
New York Public Library has a pamphlet listing the items
in their archives of music and composers. Many more such
resources are needed.

One successful model of interchange is the office of
Women's Studies Librarian-at-Large in the University of
Wisconsin System. This office for a decade has served all
26 campuses of the UW system by compiling, coordinating,
researching and publicizing new materials of interest to
Women's Studies. The computerized data base and periodic
bibliographies are available system wide. In addition, their
periodic inventory of Who's Who of Wisconsin Women, both
in and beyond the University, greatly expedites networking.

One particular caveat: art history appears to be
becoming a "women's field." Should it actually be perceived
as such, there is real danger of it suffering the denigration
that continues to infect women-dominated work.

Personal Survival

> As the pie diminishes, we are put in competition with
> one another. It is a miracle we are all still talking.
> —Margot Lewitin

Economic survival continues as the primary problem
for most American women artists in spite of a decade-plus
of the mushrooming and recognition of women artists and
their work. Because our society does not place a high value

on culture, and because artists like what they do, there is little financial reward for all but a handful of stars. Rather, their creative work is too often perceived as recreation or hobby for which they shouldn't expect to be paid. At the same time, income and prestige are measures in our society for whether or not one is taken seriously; hence, Catch 22.

Even the most devoted artist has other obligations and responsibilities in her life. As an individual she must find ways to integrate all of the segments of today's complex living. When she must add income-producing activity, such as teaching, to an already full schedule, her problems and frustrations multiply.

Women who belong to artists' unions often enjoy income and benefits not otherwise available. Yet in some fields the very existence of these unions is not universally known by people who might profit from affiliation. Opportunities need to be better publicized and explained.

The dominant attitudes in the United States toward the arts and toward "women's work" need drastic revision. The notion that only tangible, useful products merit public funding must be challenged and replaced by widespread affirmation of the centrality of the arts in everyday life. Shifting national priorities from the lionizing of contemporary athletes and rock stars as heroes, to a reward system that gives public honor to those people whose values we respect is an Amazonian undertaking.

Preserving Our Heritage

> As we think about the future, we become aware of the necessity for visionary thought. As women, we are nourished by the visions of other women, from quilt makers, diary keepers, to the chronicles of our mothers and grandmothers, to the work of artists, dramatists and painters.
> —Margot Kernan

American women artists face the ironic fact that while the important arts institutions in this country were more often than not built primarily by women, these institutions have not provided women artists with the kind of exposure that male artists have received. Women artists have not been aided by the National Endowment of the Arts to the same extent as male artists—a situation that has worsened in the past five years during which the percentage of support from NEA's overall budget allotted to women artists has dropped by 35%. (And this when, between 1970 and 1980, the number of women artists in America increased by 162%.)

Strategies to publicize the heritage of women artists include educating feminists about the centrality of women's art to the Women's Movement, exploring funding sources from the private sector, encouraging women to become collectors of women's art and comptrollers of museums, lobbying within state and national art organizations, and maintaining an active response when institutions blatantly ignore women artists' contributions.

The power of art critics cannot be overestimated. Much of women's art in all fields has been ignored or deprecated precisely because it fails to meet the prevailing male-dominated guidelines of the critics. A major task for women artists is to develop a coherent feminist body of criticism.

The National Museum of Women in the Arts holds real promise. The task of publicizing the heritage of women artists requires both integrating women's art into the mainstream of the art world, and maintaining separate institutions and organizations for women's art and artists. The National Museum of Women in the Arts might aid in synthesizing these approaches. There is concern among women artists that the NMWA realize its importance as a symbol, that it provide the opportunity for veteran women artists to have an active role in its operation at both the national board level and the state level. There must also be wide opportunity for women artists to take part in the peer panels that help select works for the permanent collection and for the museum's exhibitions. The NMWA might well consider establishing a Council of National Organizations as an ongoing mechanism to tap the women's art groups for advice.

The Conference's Accomplishments

by Florence Howe

This is in one sense the easiest and the most difficult of all jobs—to summarize the kinds of riches we have all been partners to these last three days. As I said again and again to people who have tried to commiserate with me, "I can't fail, except at order, clarity, and inclusiveness."

A summarizer brings a framework to the task and I'm no exception. I came asking, "What is the purpose of this conference?" Because I have spent all my life as an educator in the arts, at least in the literary arts, and the past fifteen years as a member of a feminist arts organization, I also came asking another question: "How can this conference serve artists, arts organizations, the arts, and the communities out of which they spring and to which they speak?"

I see myself as a reconciler, a recognizer. Like Elizabeth Janeway, I am interested in naming. I see myself as one who seeks to recognize and reconcile differences, but not, however, in order to eliminate them. Not to blur differences, but to introduce them as independent entities, often to each other, because they may not yet be recognizable to each other. And finally and ultimately, I come to serve a political purpose: to note that only when these independent entities join hands, link arms, and even on occasion, embrace, can we have the collaborative, cooperative process through which the arts and creativity and, yes, even change, occur.

I have two themes and the first of these, and maybe the second as well, will name some of these independent entities. For artists, especially, and I'm talking now of individual artists, personal circumstances usually do circumscribe their lives as well as their art. Two of these personal circumstances are there for men as well as these women. That is, race and class. Where we are born, into which race and which class, affect us all, male and female, they affect all our opportunities. Unlike men, other factors affect women and there are four of them, only one of which has been mentioned openly at this conference. Most of us take for granted that we still live in a patriarchal world in which women are born permanently into a position of subordination. Men are born permanently, still, in fact, into a position of superiority.

We have talked about gender and most of us understand the patriarchy we live in. We have not talked about generation very much. We've mentioned the pink-clad generation—the young people who are either ignorant that there has ever been a women's movement or who think it has accomplished everything it set out to. One could as readily refer to them as those in high heels and jeans. Generation matters a great deal to us and not simply to the old and the young but to all those in between.

But there is another factor for women, beyond gender and generation—namely, who your husband or father is or was. We haven't talked very much about that. But many opportunities have come to women in the past and still do in the present because of the persons they marry, and I think that needs to be named. It doesn't usually work that way for men.

Finally—and we've mentioned this slightly, in terms of the need for day care—there is the factor of sexuality. It's not important for men, by and large, just as marriage isn't important for men. Well, if male artists marry, they've got somebody to keep house for them, but it's not a really important factor in their lives, finally. For women artists, whether or not you marry at all, whether or not you become a mother, is extremely important. Perhaps this is a good time to note that while for males wars and laws have long been the way in which one broke history into periods, bite-size enough to be taught in the classroom, for women one of the great historical events is the invention of birth control. That is, if we were to write women's history, that would have to be a watershed for all of us. I emphasize this because of the comments I've heard through the conference and because I would like to repeat what Margot Lewitin said early on in the conference, "It is a myth that excellence rises to the top. What matters is where you are positioned." I think that's worth remembering.

The second theme that will move through my remarks is the contrast between the individual artist's need for uniqueness, separateness, isolation, for creation, that "room of one's own" that Paule Marshall reminded us of, that Virginia Woolf wrote so movingly of; the contrast between that and the fact that on the other hand certain arts are, by their nature, communal and cooperative. In dance companies, for instance, in publishing houses, stars may come and go, but the theatrical company, the publishing house, is by its nature, a cooperative entity. Some of the arts don't flourish at all except as cooperative entities.

What I now have to say applies to the various arts organizations among us. And here my theme is: the first ten years are the easiest. After the newness, after the excitement, there is the question of staying power, and the new generations of cohorts who may or may not follow us. It is more difficult to sustain institutions than to start them.

The first problem is language, and that's why it is so marvelous that Elizabeth Janeway began this conference. We are at different points along a feminist continuum. Some of us are just beginning; others are burned out, maybe not even for the first time. And somewhere in the middle of this conference I remembered what a very patient woman taught me in my most impatient period over the last two decades. One day when I was complaining about the low level of consciousness of people at a conference we were attending, perhaps ten or more years ago, she said, "You have to remember, if you are in this for the long haul, that we've got to have a first grade every year." And I think that those of us who get tired and burned out and impatient must remember that—we've got to have a first grade every year, even if it seems very boring. There are those teachers who have to be there in the classroom with a new set of kids every year.

What are our accomplishments? We have had a very very rapid growth in ten, or at most fifteen years. We have built very tall structures with very shallow roots and you know the problems of tall structures and shallow roots. They can be toppled easily, and so what I see ahead of us and what I hear people talking about at this conference is the need to strengthen these roots.

The roots that sustain the life of institutions are money, community, and history. Here, I want to become specific, to talk about one of the roots—money—and our experience at The Feminist Press. Like many feminist arts institutions, The Feminist Press began without capital, and survived through inventiveness, voluntarism, and the fiscal generosity of a community of feminists. Beginning in 1971, the State University of New York provided housing. Beyond that provision, The Feminist Press paid its own way with human capital: our authors wrote for us without advances and sometimes with late royalty payments; our staff worked at first with token salaries, then sometimes with late payments; and volunteers continued to staff our boards and committees and to contribute funds to us as well. No one will ever know whether we might have continued on this path, for a devastating fire in 1982, combined with the political shift in funding patterns that has affected all arts organizations, turned our course.

Even a large and committed feminist community could not substitute for an adequate and regular funding base, once the pattern of institutional life was disrupted by catastrophe. Our story, unlike that of other feminist organizations, has a happy ending. In 1985, responding to an invitation from Chancellor Joseph S. Murphy, The Feminist Press took up residence within The City University of New York, with plans for a future that would see it institutionalized.

As an institution, The Feminist Press has contributed to building the other essential roots: community and history. Let me say a few words about them. Community and communication first: the networks are easier to begin than to maintain. Conferences like this one are important, and yet, of course, how to continue what has been begun? How to draw on each other's strengths? How to share resources when we are a national network and when phone and mailing costs are staggering? Also, and we must at least mention this fact here, we are international as well as national.

Finally, the third set of roots, and they are perhaps

more difficult to achieve even than the first two which are
difficult enough. The third set of roots this conference has
been fine about—we need a deepened sense and knowledge
of our shared and individual history. The papers the
conference offered to us all have given us that sense of
history. And if there is one division of knowledge essential
to all of us and to the permanence of the institutions and
the women's art we are building, it is the history of
women. All kinds of history, including, as I have said, the
history of medicine and birth control for women. The
papers we heard were histories as well as analyses of the
last decade and a half of women and the arts as a
movement.

Are we women or artists? Ruth Dean's interviews
offered us several sets of paradoxes in answer to this
question. Some artists don't want to be called women but
rather artists, a familiar theme to those of us in and out of
the art movement. And yet the same women complain
about sexism. It is surprising to me that after fifteen to
twenty years of the women's movement which has had
some measure of success, especially in certain visible
economic areas like work, participation in work, and even
some payment for work, that some women offer as the only
solution, that individual women artists must be "excellent"
in order to succeed. More excellent, that is, than they
currently are, or even more excellent than male artists.
There are other solutions. In fact, that one doesn't even
work much of the time. Often we are told we appear
unattractive, not chic, if we are still strident feminists. I
don't know that I've ever been particularly strident, and
that word irritates me, but I certainly have been feminist
and continue to be and I don't see myself as changing. So
that when I hear that the period of feminism or strident
feminism is gone or over, I wonder which world I am in.

On the other hand, mothers are not wanted either, at
least in dance, and certainly not in some of the other arts.
So once again we have that familiar paradox. You are
damned if you do and you're damned if you don't.

We now have in contrast to the individualist
perspective the possibility of a women's audience, even of
women's arts organizations. Yet I heard at this conference,

and Ruth Dean reported, that such groups are considered
even by women artists themselves as ghettos. And the
"ghetto" is, by the way, possibly a positive term, not simply
a negative term. And yet, I heard it only in a negative way
here.

When we are free to be women and artists, we are
unafraid to illuminate our learning process. I found that
pattern marvelously available in Gloria Orenstein's paper.
We are even intrigued by the pattern. Gloria's story, her
search for the Goddess, is part of the search for history and
identity without which there can be no art. It's the key
search of Joyce and Lawrence, as a matter of fact. The
way out of their roots for them is through their roots. The
specific and the alleged universal are always in
equilibrium. It is not one or the other, but both.

As women and artists we think back through our
mothers. Paule Marshall made that palpable, not only
through her own mothers, but she broadened the concept
for many of us. Though she couldn't deal with the whole
world, she certainly reminded us of Virginia Woolf. She
returns us to Elizabeth Janeway when she describes her
mothers in the kitchen, language their art form. They
invented it and shaped and bent it to suit themselves.
"They used language to gain control over their lives," as
Paule Marshall said, ."attesting to the fact that they were
there." They used language as a weapon to deconstruct a
white male world.

Elizabeth Janeway said we cannot plan a new world;
we can only create one. The tools we need for that include
a language in which we can speak to each other truly and
truthfully and we don't yet have such a language. But
inventing a language is also a stage in creating a world.
Whose world are we creating? I am reminded of the
moments during the past three days when the several
worlds of the conference participants, of all of us, clashed.
The individual artist and the feminist art organizations.
White women artists claiming excellence and white women
art organizers claiming community. White middle class
women artists who see women and who may not yet
understand questions of race and class and women artists
of color who see as women but also out of a racial or ethnic

heritage, both a blessing and a curse.

And then the most promising clash of all—between the conference participants almost as a body, despite their own differences, and the idea of the National Museum for Women in the Arts. The clash between those who have been struggling to become, then to survive, who have survived, created a body of art, or restored one to view; and those who have more recently arrived to claim the territory, not only with the money and resources denied to the pioneers, but with the potential power to exclude them altogether, at least from the making and creating and naming of this new institution. A museum after all, even more than a library but somewhat like that institution, codifies, claims significance and permanence for what may have been seen as fleeting, ephemeral or not seen at all, invisible. If the conference had accomplished only this joining of language and purpose, it would have been declared of use.

But of course its accomplishments are more various still. I have not yet mentioned the extraordinary summary paper by Elizabeth Durbin, recording the decade-long progress of the various arts we are part of, the growing visibility and variety, " the incredible diversity," Kathryn Clarenbach's words, and mine, "the heterogeneity" of the conference participants, that reflect at least in part that real world of women artists out there. We might have had more women of color. We are missing a person, at least one person, from an open lesbian community that has nourished some significant achievements in women's music and women's literature.

Elizabeth Durbin's work calls attention to the explosion of women artists and arts organization and to their presence and disappearance through history. It should be clear to us by now that we both owe and serve a women's movement.

I want to call attention to the political aspect of art, especially the appearance, disappearance, and current reappearance and explosion of women's art. None of this is accidental. It is no accident that in the 19th century, in the middle of the first movement for women's suffrage, writers like Elizabeth Stuart Phelps wrote novels about women who made work, not love or marriage or childbearing, the center of their lives. And her vision included both working class and middle class white women. Other 19th century women living in that first feminist period read her work eagerly and not only in English, for it was translated into dozens of languages and read in other parts of the world in that same period that nourished a women's movement all over the world. And so Elizabeth Stuart Phelps' work disappeared along with hundreds of other women writers here in the West and in the East. We are reading it all again and perhaps it is even more important this time for it connects us to a past and reminds us of all we must do so as not to disappear again. I'm not using "political" in a narrow sense. In fact as I use the term, it encompasses social, economic and cultural.

Art is political, at least in that it reflects or questions the assumptions of the milieu from which it arises. Yet some art is universal in some sense, though the most universal subject has been the most ignored or abused even now, even perhaps in this esteemed company. For we were all born of women and whether or not we have been biological or cultural mothers we have had mothers who have birthed us. The birthing experience has offended male editors from time immemorial. I speak of a period as recently as the twenties when the person who was editor of the first appearance of Edith Summers Kelly's novel called Weeds (which is part of The Feminist Press's list, so I know about it in particular) excised a chapter from that novel that portrayed graphically the birth of the heroine's first child. It was simply cut out. He said it was unpublishable. When we republished the novel in 1982, we included that birthing scene as a chapter at the back, to call attention to the fact that it had been excised in the first place. Birth may offend both women and men today who may deride the process—and I've heard derided vulvic or womb art. Such imagery is political even if only because we learn to appreciate what we are taught is beautiful. We have had ample illustration of that in reference to ethnic and racial communities in the last twenty years and yet we don't quite understand it in relation to women. Women are still rarely taught even today that their bodies are beautiful, except for the way in which men have drawn their bodies. Certainly their genitalia are not beautiful—at least, that's what women are taught.

Art is gender specific, it is cultural, class and race specific, it is of course nation specific, and within nations, language specific. In India for example, for some reason the great female writers of autobiographies wrote in Maharati, the language spoken in the area around Bombay. And we will have in a year or two an English translation in a single volume of selections from some of the 132 autobiographies published by Indian women in Maharati between 1880 and 1930—a large number of books from a country in which the vast majority of the women are illiterate.

We heard James Joyce mentioned yesterday. There is no other artist I could name more bound to maleness, to a rising Irish Catholic working class population, and to the escape from all but the maleness to become an artist whose alleged universality resides in his subject matter which remains Irish working class Catholic from the male perspective. And yes, it is very narrow, this art, and yet it carries the claim of universality as does a great deal of Western male art. Should we join that claim with female artists in our fists or finesse it, turning our attention elsewhere to reclamation, to making it possible not for a fistful of female Joyces to make it into the male Pantheon, but thousands of women artists to have their days and nights in the sun? The answer is obvious in the creativity of the women's art movement. We have our Joyces, in fact, and if museums or critics may still be ignoring them, we are not. The Virginia Woolf "industry" just to take one example, and it is called an industry rather derisively by those outside the feminist world in which it flourishes, has still not managed to place her into the firmament that includes Joyce and Lawrence. But she is certainly in ours, and firmly in international terms. The Women's Center in Rome, the most important feminist center in Rome, is called the Virginia Woolf Center.

What is our feminist future? Our future as women artists? This is a question being asked by those of us also in Women's Studies and not only here but all over the world. In the Hague recently at an UNESCO Conference, the key question was: "Should we organize autonomous women's studies programs or integrated ones?" Autonomy versus integration, or "mainstreaming," that I heard for the first time yesterday as "menstreaming." I thought that was wonderful, a real contribution. The Conference dialogue certainly insists that we need both. We have had access, one participant said, not success. Were we in museums we would not need a museum of our own, but of course, we need to continue to press for the entrance of women's art everywhere. That is one of the Conference's recommendations, and I want to read it for its energy. And I am going to read a few of the other recommendations:

"We must continue to spread out, infiltrate, lobby, scramble, push, pull, take charge, activate, politicize, draw attention to ourselves, our points, our beliefs." Whoever wrote that or said that, I want to thank her. As an English teacher, I love verbs. "We must continue alternative networks, institutions, and create more places for study, work, research. We must create alternative galleries."

"We must seize opportunities in the new technologies, in home video as in international video letters, [our tribal notebooks, they were called] and in computer art."

"We must have a hand in the role of the National Museum of Women in the Arts. We must help there to make women's art visible including the art of women of color. We must provide a space for joint planning with women's arts organizations. We must develop women collectors of art."

"We must educate other feminists and the public more generally about the centrality of women's art to the women's movement."

Finally, "we must have more conferences like this one."

WOMEN AND THE ARTS:
A SURVEY OF RECENT PROGRESS

The Conference Working Paper

by Elizabeth Durbin

Women and the Arts:
A Survey of Recent Progress

Table of Contents

Women and the Arts: A Survey of Recent Progress

by *Elizabeth Durbin*

Enlarging and Enriching Our Views of Art

Quilts: Metaphor for a Movement

As no other art form, quilts have come to symbolize the feminist art movement. In 1973, Pat Mainardi, writing in the Feminist Art Journal, stated that quilts were "The Great American Art."

To understand the process by which quilts have come to be accepted as art, not craft, embodying a creative urge quite apart from their utilitarian purpose, is to understand how women artists over the past 15 years have been able to redefine art.

Quilting may be the art in which the process of redefinition has been most visible and dramatic. The male art world, said Mainardi, had defined women's quilts as if they'd been made only for the specific and limited function of covering a bed. On the contrary, she pointed out, quilts were made for display. The bed, topped by the quilt, was the feature piece of the room. Women also made quilts for display at "county fairs, churches and grange halls."

Nevertheless, the art world continued to define quilts as utilitarian and then ruled that something made to be used could not be considered art. Overturning this idea—in its full-blown form the idea that women's traditional domestic efforts, personal concerns, skills and lives could not be considered in any way artistic—is the big story of the past 15 years.

Anonymous works

Male art historians and critics also downgraded

quilts—and all the domestic crafts—by calling them anonymous works. Obviously, if the artist is unknown, it is easier not to deal with the art. Many quilts were unsigned, their creators forgotten. But the catalog for the "American Pieced Quilts" exhibit at the Smithsonian Institution, according to Mainardi, "bears a cover reproduction of a quilt signed "E.S. Reitz" in large letters." Yet within the catalog, the artist's name is not given, and Jonathan Holstein dedicates the catalog to "those anonymous women whose skilled hands and eyes created the American pieced quilt." It is Mainardi's contention that "These women did not choose anonymity. Rather it has been forced on them."

"Anonymous Was a Woman" was the title and the theme of Mirra Bank's film, one of the "Originals: Women in Art" series produced by WNET/13 in New York.

"Women have always made art," wrote Mainardi in "Quilts: the Great American Art." "But for most women, the arts highest valued by male society have been closed to them for just that reason. They have put their creativity instead into the needlework arts, which exist in fantastic variety wherever there are women, and which in fact are a universal female art, transcending race, class and national borders."

During the process of redefining women's needlework as art, quilts, especially, came to be seen as analogies for women's artistic struggles. In an essay by Lucy R. Lippard included in Charlotte Robinson's 1983 book, The Artist and the Quilt, the well-known feminist art critic establishes the metaphor. "In properly prim grids or in rebelliously crazy fields, [the quilt] incorporates Spider Woman's web, political networking and the collage aesthetic."

Prim grids or crazy fields

Lippard went on to itemize the ways in which quilts also metaphorically illustrated women's lives. Their geometrical and grid patterns stood for diversity within monotony, the penchant for bringing order out of chaos. The overdetailed, overdecorated tendency, the "fussiness," is characteristic of those whose time, organized around the interruptions of others with superseding claims, comes in small squares. The salvaging of bits of material from a family's old clothes echoes not only the necessity of thrift that structured so many women's existences, but also the desire to hold onto the past.

Lippard stated that before the "recent surge of feminism, few ambitious women artists on the New York art scene would have been caught dead making a quilt."

One reason, as Cindy Nemser, editor of the Feminist Art Journal, noted, might have been that "When women used geometric or organic designs in art work such as quilts, they were dismissed as mere decorators, while men who later used similar patterns were viewed as fine artists and abstract thinkers."

Off the bed, on the wall

Thus, what was once considered a humble necessity beneath the notice of male-defined art, the quilt today, its value as art recognized, is often used as a wall hanging rather than a bed covering. And "In a similarly paradoxical development," said Robinson, "quilting (along with crocheting, rug-hooking, and needlepoint) came back into middle-class and upper-class fashion in the 1970s, in part on the apron strings of feminism."

It began to be recognized, thanks to women's efforts, that op art—trendy in the '60s—owed a lot to 200 years of quilting; that white on white work foreshadowed minimal art, while applique and trapunto were bas-relief in fabric rather than stone.

Bringing their "personal female vision" (the phrase is Robinson's) into their art, professional women artists in the '70s and '80s reclaimed quilting and all other needlework arts as their own. In collaborative quilting projects improvised on traditional grid and basically geometrical designs, they used pieces of fabric to reproduce actual paintings, or such mixed media as crushed cola cans, ceramic, plastic or metal. Photographer Amy Stronsten photo-silk-screened her quilt.

It was not only artists who took notice of what was happening. Grass roots America rediscovered quilts and quilting in a surge of interest and affection. Quilt exhibits became more and more common at church suppers and county fairs (where they'd always been), in community museums and historical societies all over the country. Quilting classes sprang up in every city and many towns, and shops featuring quilting supplies and how-to classes mushroomed. In 1983 one Sunday issue of the Los Angeles Times listed scores of such establishments at the end of an article on the practical aspects of quilting.

Many women, traditional women, not feminists, who had formerly used the heirloom patterns for their quilts, began boldly to design their own patterns, and moved from there into producing and marketing original patterns to others.

The prices of old and new quilts escalated, as did those of other fancy work. Indeed one of the problems artists had in recruiting needleworkers for collaborative projects was the inability to offer as much money as the women could earn by selling their quilts for finally fair prices to clamoring private customers.

Two collaborations

Two noteworthy alternative collaborations had important creative impact after 1970: "Artists in Aprons," mounted in 1977, and the "Quilt Project," first conceived in the early '70s by Charlotte Robinson, Dorothy Gillespie and Alice Baber.

"Artists in Aprons," designed by Marsha MacDowell, Betty MacDowell and C. Kurt Dewhurst, focused on "those women who, without formal training and professional stature, nevertheless exceeded the traditional expectations of society in producing their art." The criteria for selecting works to be included in the exhibit and book were that each piece must be known to be by a woman, her name must be known and every piece shown must be of superior esthetic quality. The MacDowells and Dewhurst selected 125 items from hundreds of examples of folk art. Earlier state quilt exhibits in Michigan and Georgia inspired the project. Ohio, Pennsylvania and New York also mounted state shows in 1974, 1975 and 1976.

"The Quilt Project," though originally planned to

commemorate the United Nations-designated 1975
International Year of the Woman, was finally exhibited in
1986. In 1983, the collection was acquired by Philip Morris
and, after the exhibit circuit, will become part of the fine
arts collection at their corporate headquarters in New York
City.

Quilt artists

The 1984 book, The Artist and the Quilt, edited by
Robinson, described and pictured the quilts in the project
and the process involved. Robinson explained why the quilt
was chosen as the vehicle of expression. "By focusing on
the quilt as an art form," she said, "we would be making a
statement about our identities...as female artists governed
by both masculine and feminine principles, and shaped by
our cultural conditioning."
The project features the designs of 18 graphic artists
from New York to Los Angeles. Sixteen needle artists
executed the designs, working closely with the
designers. Altogether, more than 50 expert needlewomen
completed 20 quilts. Additional women helped administer
the project, which owed a great deal, over the years, to
Robinson's persistence.
The final artists who produced the quilt designs were
Alice Baber, Lynda Benglis, Isabel Bishop, Elaine Lustig
Cohen, Mary Beth Edelson, Dorothy Gillespie, Harmony
Hammond, Marcia Gygli King, Joyce Kozloff, Marilyn
Lanfear, Ellen Lanyon, Alice Neel, Betty Parsons, Faith
Ringgold, Charlotte Robinson, Betye Saar, Miriam Schapiro
and Rosemary Wright.
Quilters were Amy Chamberlin, Bob Douglas (a
woman), Chris Wolf Edmonds, Theresa Lanfear Helms,
Marie Griffin Ingalls, Angela Jacobi, Judy Mathieson,
Sharon McKain, Edith C. Mitchell, the Mitchell Family, Pat
Newkirk, Bonnie Persinger, Willi Posey, Marilyn Price,
Nancy Vogel and Wenda F. von Weise.
The schedule called for "The Quilt Project" to be
exhibited at the Moore College of Art in Philadelphia, the
Art Center Association in Louisville, Kentucky, the Herron
Art Galleries at Indiana University, Indianapolis, and the

206 / *The Green Stubborn Bud*

Huntington Galleries in Huntington, West Virginia.

Traditional routes in quilting

In spite of changing perceptions, "The prejudice against cooperative or collaborative art continues," Lippard wrote, "unless high technology is involved." She makes the distinction between designing the quilt and executing it. Recently made quilts, like their predecessors, are "individually conceived and collaboratively executed." They are still individual works of art, she stated.

Not many traditional institutions have seen it that way. As Robinson noted, "only occasionally in the past decade have quilts been shown in art museums as examples of fine art." In 1971, Jonathan Holstein organized the "Abstract Designs in American Quilts" at the Whitney Museum in New York City. Recently the "Baltimore Album Quilts" opened at the Metropolitan Museum in New York City and closed at the Baltimore Museum. According to Robinson, both these exhibits "broke attendance records and ensured a place in art history for antique quilts."

The American Quilter's Society commissioned two Wisconsin quilt artists to put together the "Quilt Art 1985" engagement calendar. For this first edition, Klaudeen Hansen of Sun Prairie and Annette Riddle of Marshall, both just outside Madison, sought out superb quilts that represented "a cross-section of the United States." The book contains 54 color photos of quilts, paragraphs about individual quilters (representing 38 states), and a description of the awards won. Five of the quilts selected were made by Wisconsin women. Hansen, a Madison Area Technical College quilting teacher and a national quilt judge, said many of these "masterpiece" quilts are appraised at $5,000. Hansen and Riddle also worked on the 1986 edition of the engagement calendar.

An article by Sarah Bodine, "At Long Last Art: A New Home for the Crafts," in a 1984 issue of *Vantage Point*, chronicles the growing acceptance by major museums of all the craft arts. "In recent years, over two hundred museums—from the Museum of Fine Arts in Boston to the Nelson-Atkins Museum of Art in Kansas City, Missouri—

have held major exhibitions of artists' work in craft media, heralding a new critical and popular acceptance of works formerly relegated to folk art, craft, and historical society museums."

And Jean Perrault wrote in an Artforum review of a 1982 show at the Whitney Museum in New York, "The distinctions made between art and craft, like those made between genders associated with each (men with art, women with craft), are often false."

Visual Arts: A Feminine Perspective

Over the last decade, women artists have been remarkably effective in articulating a new perception of what art is. Before 1970, a common attitude among male art historians, critics and educators was that women's artistic endeavors did not fit the patriarchal establishment's definition of art. Some men did not consider women great, or even serious, artists. Women browsed in vain through art history textbooks such as H.W. Janson's 500-page History of Art to locate even a single woman artist. When art activist Eleanor Dickinson interviewed him in February of 1979 at the College Art Association Convention in Washington, D.C., Janson explained his omission.

"I may very well in the next edition include women artists, but at least until the most recent edition (1978) I have not been able to find a woman artist who clearly belongs in a one-volume history of art."

Questioned further about the standard for inclusion in his book, Janson said the artist "must have changed the history of art." In 1984, however, Janson apparently found what he was looking for. Together with Robert Rosenblum he published 19th Century Art. It included eight women—seven painters and a sculptor. In another update, Frederick Hartt revised his two-volume A History of Painting, Sculpture, and Architecture to include 26 women.

As Elsa Honig Fine, author of Women and Art and editor of Woman's Art Journal, commented in the Spring/Summer 1985 issue: "We have indeed begun to broaden the art history establishment."

Since the first National Conference on Women and the

Arts sponsored by UW-Extension in 1973, women have
clearly changed and still are changing the history of
art. And uncountable numbers of them have, without
question, redefined it.

Female imagery

Whether or not there is a biologically determined and
socially conditioned difference in the art of men and women,
critics have noted and recognized what has come to be
called female imagery. Feminist art critic Lucy Lippard
suggested that some of these sex-linked images are "a
central focus (often empty, often circular or oval), parabolic
bag-like forms, obsessive line and detail, veiled strata,
tactile or sensuous surfaces and forms ... and
autobiographical emphasis."

Designer Sheila de Bretteville said that multiple peaks
are a feature of women's art, rather than a single center of
interest. Other observers point to often-used images that
have become metaphors for women's lives: the collage, the
grid, the patchwork quilt. These objects, formed piece by
piece of bits and scraps, are well suited to epitomizing
women's fragmented, multifaceted lives.

Sandra Roos, in her essay, "Women's Imagery/
Women's Art," noted during the last decade the consistent
appearance of central images or synthetic juxtapositions
uniting two or more opposing qualities in one form. These
echo the appearance in prehistoric art of circle and spiral
patterns, plants, animals, the moon and, preeminently, the
female figure, suggesting, according to Roos, the themes of
unity/duality, cyclic change, regeneration and the seasons,
all goddess-related. Roos identifies in women's art a "centric
and synthetic imagery grounded in life experiences."

The names of some women artists are by now
inseparably connected with the idea of a specifically female
imagery. Judy Chicago is one of these women. In her
autobiography, Through the Flower: My Struggles as a
Woman Artist, published in 1975, Chicago details the
evolution of her art. While progress has been made, the
struggle isn't over.

Avis Berman quoted Chicago in an article called "A

Decade of Progress" in the October 1980 issue of Artnews.
Referring to the last decade, the tireless lecturer and
fund-raiser told Berman: "There is no question that things
have changed enormously. Ten years ago there was no
space for me as an artist. There was huge resistance to my
femaleness....Now more women are showing, but female art
is still resisted. That's because the prevailing white male
symbolism has still been retained. There hasn't been
enough pressure to redefine the basic categories of the
nature of art, which are inherently prejudicial. For
example, we still have the difference between art and craft,
between art and decoration. If a man does it, it's art, if a
women does it, it's craft."

Chicago gives a dinner party

Now, six years later, it's clear that Chicago's
contributions to the art world, both political and esthetic,
have changed art history. In 1979 "The Dinner Party," a
reinterpretation of the Last Supper from the point of view
of women who have always prepared the meal and set the
table, was a national event.
The project took five years and the efforts of more
than 200 women to complete. The collective nature of the
endeavor, if nothing else, was historically significant. Have
men ever worked jointly as equals on such a scale to
produce a work of art?
But of course that wasn't the only revolutionary thing
about "The Dinner Party." Using the techniques of ceramic
sculpture, Chicago revived the art of china painting,
formerly dismissed as an inferior woman's pastime. She
also used painting, sewing, embroidery and weaving to pay
honor to real and mythical females throughout history. Her
supper table had places for 39 women and listed 999
others. It drew thousands of viewers.
In many of her works, Chicago uses vaginal
iconography, active, not passive, that "flies, bends, twists,
pushes and thrusts." She includes images of butterflies and
flower shapes, of flying and mother goddesses. She uses
materials such as lace, fabric, glitter, beads, quilts and

ornamentation of all kinds. Her goal, she has said, is to "make the feminine holy."

The Birth Project

The same goal clearly powered her latest achievement, "The Birth Project," which encompasses nearly 100 needlework creations celebrating the miracle of birth. It is a miracle largely overlooked by male artists. "I started looking for images of birth," Chicago explained in an interview in The New York Times, "and I didn't find any. There were almost no birth images in the history of Western art, although I did find some from pre-industrial societies." Chicago believes the oversight resulted because men do not themselves give birth. "If men had babies, there would be thousands of images of the crowning."

More than 150 volunteer needleworkers, most of them mothers, produced the wall hangings from Chicago's drawings and paintings. They worked in embroidery, quilting, needlepoint, petit point, smocking, weaving, macrame, crochet, filet crochet, applique and pulled threadwork, among other techniques. The hundred pieces of "The Birth Project" are designed to be broken up and shown simultaneously around the country. The first exhibits opened in the spring of 1985 in New York City, Los Angeles, Anchorage, Great Falls, Montana, and Columbus, Ohio.

In explaining the genesis of her five-year project, Chicago said the "idea that a male god created man is such a reversal of the reality of how life comes forth." She researched creation myths and was "struck" by "the changeover from matriarchy to patriarchy in creation stories."

The project doesn't celebrate only the joy connected with bringing a child into the world. Wrote Leslie Bennetts in The New York Times, "Although the project was intended as a celebration of birth, the images are by no means unambiguous. The pain of giving birth is integral to many of the works: women's mouths are rent by screams, and the rippling designs seem to pulse with the agony of labor. Others communicate the ambivalence many women feel about becoming mothers."

Chicago financed "The Birth Project" from individual contributions and revenues from "The Dinner Party." Many of the women who asked Chicago if they could help with the project found their lives changed by it. Bennetts quotes Dolly Kaminski, a Pennsylvania grandmother who devoted three years to a 20- by 8-foot filet crochet wall hanging. "My particular piece has made me realize that I personally have a lot of power in communicating with other individuals that I didn't realize before and that I don't have to take a back seat to anybody. I feel strong in myself because of it."

Artist Miriam Schapiro has worked closely with Chicago both on the frontlines of political activity and in changing the esthetics of art. Together they've championed "a female form language, the predisposition in women's work towards centered forms," according to a winter '80-81 article in Woman's Art Journal.

Schapiro's "femmages"

In Berman's words, Miriam Schapiro "convinced the art world establishment that domestic handiwork and iconography possess significant social and human content and deserve to be admitted to the realm of high art. Her activism helped to make pattern and decorative painting and sculpture a trend that no one had to be embarrassed about. Her contributions to the movement are shaped canvasses emblazoned with paint, paper and fabrics: velvet, calico, chintz, lace, gilded trimmings and brocade. These pictures, called "femmages," are vibrant and resonant, for Schapiro has painted and appliqued in bold allusions to Persian miniatures, Matisse and formal abstraction, as well as patchwork quilts and Sunday-best dresses."

So influential were Chicago, Schapiro and other artists working similar lodes that the pattern and decoration movement of the '70s caught the energies and imaginations of both men and women. As art critic Kay Larson declared in the October 1980 issue of Artnews, "For the first time in the history of Western art, women were leading, not following a major movement."

Double bind

Faith Ringgold, emerging to prominence in the last 15 years, has, in the words of Avis Berman, "expressed the double bind of being black and female in America." Ringgold recently turned to soft sculpture, dolls and wall hangings that "satisfied a tactile and spiritual need to work in textiles and create tapestries, masks and puppets similar to objects women in primitive societies traditionally made."

Wrote Berman, "These three-dimensional portraits of black women, humorous and frank, are both individual stories and distillations of larger ethnic narrative." A poster has been made from Ringgold's quilt, "Who's Afraid of Aunt Jemima," and she is the subject of a book, Faith Ringgold, Twenty Years of Painting, Sculpture and Performance, edited by Michele Wallace, her daughter.

In assessing the past few years, Ringgold says, "The biggest improvement for women artists is that they now feel free to do their work, to experiment, to create kinds of imagery that may be peculiar to women."

Chewed gum, chewed lives

Sculptor Hannah Wilke's images are "folded, layered forms that remind one not only of female genitalia but of flowering buds and fruit, honeycombs, seashells and fortune cookies," according to Berman. She works in clay and bronze, in pulled and snapped latex, rubber kneaded erasers and chewing gum.

The latter material, in Wilke's perspective, is particularly appropriate: "In this society we use up people the way we use up chewing gum. I chose gum because it's the perfect metaphor for the American woman—chew her up, get what you want out of her, throw her out and pop in a new piece."

Following the lead of artists like Chicago, Schapiro, Ringgold, Wilke and others, women began, in the '70s, to freely express erotic feelings: heterosexual, lesbian or masturbatory, that were previously repressed and suppressed in art, said Charlotte Streifer Rubinstein in American Women Artists, published in 1982. "Vaginal forms shown as clean, well-made and beautiful became a

kind of flag or banner, the women's equivalent of Black is
Beautiful."
    Elsa Honig Fine, editor of the Woman's Art Journal,
pointed out that women "removed the female sexual organ
from its hidden recesses and displayed it openly like a
powerful male organ, thereby inviting vagina envy."

Forebodings about space

    Not all women artists who have come to prominence
over the last decade and a half use specific female imagery,
materials or techniques. Mary Miss is one who does not. A
teacher of art at Sarah Lawrence College, her large
environmental sculptures include major installations on
Long Island, in Connecticut, Ohio and Colorado, in the
Museum of Modern Art in New York City and at the
Olympic Games site at Lake Placid.
    Berman said Miss's works create "an atmosphere of
foreboding and uncertainty that pushes viewers into
questioning the space in which they find themselves."
Another critic, John Russell, noted that a Miss construction,
"consistently eats away at our sense of inner security."
Contradictions and redefinitions of perspective are found in
her work. "Her schemes of traps, trenches, lattices,
passages, towers, slopes, enclosures, doors, partitions and
crossbars draw on archeology, engineering and an abiding
love of old castles, forts, ruins, burial sites and other
emanations of lost worlds only deceptively available to
rational understanding."
    Dare one suggest that these constructions may
symbolize the frustrations, obstacles and turnbacks women
typically experience? About her own work Miss says only,
"I can't pinpoint what sort of content or imagery in my
work comes from being a woman....There was a sense ten
years ago of being criticized for not doing something with
specific female content, being requested to make feminist
statements in our art. I feel that phase has passed."

The Neel legacy

A woman who surely changed the history of art, despite the fact that she never made it into Janson's textbook, died in 1984 at the age of 84. During the early part of her career she was discredited and ignored by the art establishment because she painted in a realistic style while males in positions of power were decreeing that realism was out and abstract art, the art men were doing, was in.

Alice Neel's superb portraits in the expressionist-realist style showed the vulnerabilities, the inadequacies, the mortality, the humanity of her subjects, especially her bursting, nude pregnant women. She worked completely outside the mainstream until 1974, when the Whitney Museum of Art in New York City held a major retrospective exhibition of her works. In 1976 she won the National Endowment of the Arts Award, and was elected a member of the National Institute of Arts and Letters. Suddenly, realism was in vogue and even men began abandoning abstractionism and painting in a realistic style.

Besides Neel, notable artists Audrey Flack and Janet Fish portrayed the real world as women saw it. Flack's vanity tables laden with lipstick, jewelry and other female accoutrements necessary to preserve youth and beauty strengthened the notion that women's own experiences were the proper subject for art.

Painting men like women

During the mid-seventies many women artists painted men as men artists had, over the centuries, painted women. Sylvia Sleigh painted a nude male posed in the traditional reclining, passive female posture. She also produced "Double Image," a nude portrait of a man seen frontally. Men criticized it as being "dirty or pornographic."

In the 1975 exhibition "Sons and Others: Women Artists See Men," men were shown from an entirely different perspective.

May Stevens's "Big Daddy" (1967-1975 Series) is one of a number of feminist statements against male

dominance. It equated male symbols with a warlike
oppressive society.

Women's themes and issues such as racial equality
also predominated in street art—the painting of walls of
buildings—a big city phenomenon of the last few years. Eva
Cockcroft and Caryl Yasko are well-known wall painters
and wall-painting collectives included the People's Painters,
the City Arts Group, the Haight Ashbury Muralists and the
Mujeres Muralistas.

Sometimes the women have worked side by side with
men to produce street art, which has the virtue of
bypassing traditional male-controlled art spaces such as
galleries and museums and bringing art directly to the
people.

Other artists depicted women as heroines, figures of
power, images worthy of worship or inspiration. Mary Beth
Edelson created a photo-montage goddess series and staged
rituals to celebrate the new feminist consciousness.

In 1978, 11 women working together produced "The
Sister Chapel," a traveling environmental work, now
installed at the State University of New York at
Stonybrook. Each painted a larger-than-life female role
model: Joan of Arc, Frida Kahlo, Bella Abzug, Lillith, Betty
Friedan, Durga: Hindu Goddess, Artemisia Gentileschi, to
form an 11-sided pavilion. Ilise Greenstein, who conceived
and organized the project, constructed a mirrored roof over
the panels so the viewer could look up and see herself as a
member of this group of powerful females.

Other women artists embraced a primitive style,
literally returning to earth with earthworks, constructions
and paintings that echo those of primitive times, some
depicting agricultural goddess images.

Music: Different Voices, Different Drummers

As in the visual arts, men's definitions of music threw
up major obstacles to women composers and performers.
Donald Jay Grout's History of Western Music, published in
1973, is equally as sexist as Janson's History of Art.

Edith Borroff, in her "Conference on Women in Music:
A Progress Report," defined the obstacle: "A scaffolding of

great music which is hierarchical, narrow and almost
suicidally exclusive, excluding not only women but all
ethnic musicians, American popular music composers—
almost every one, come to think of it. A lot of effort has
been wasted in attempts to hoist women (and other
condemned types) into this exclusive group, but it seems
wiser to build a new scaffolding."

That, essentially, is what women have done over the
last decade and a half.

A good way to introduce the subject of Women's
Music, to talk about content, is to consider Ronnie
Gilbert. Involved in music and politics since she was a
young child, Gilbert performed with the Weavers, one of
America's most popular folk music groups, blacklisted in
the '50s by the House Un-American Activities Committee.

Certainly one of THE folk music events of the last 12
years was the 1980 Weavers' reunion featured in the film,
"Wasn't That a Time." Gilbert's collaboration with popular
singer and songwriter Holly Near, also in that film, led the
two of them to arrange a national tour. And in Madison,
Wisconsin, in the fall of 1984, Gilbert gave her first solo
concert in 20 years.

Gilbert's choice of songs for the Madison concert
revealed much about the content of Women's Music,
women's lyrics since the Weavers' breakup. It spotlighted
the gulf between these lyrics and the lyrics of some popular
and rock tunes that concern themselves with the
competition between women over a man, emphasize
women's dependency on men, make something whorish of
their sexuality, portray cruel and harsh ways of relating to
women and diminish women's place in society.

Women's love songs

A rock lyric about "love": "Just shut your mouth and
turn out the light."

A woman's lyric about love: "I loved you for using
your strengths to build mine."

In her Madison concert Gilbert said she had always
hated lovesongs, until she discovered Malvina Reynolds's
song, "If you think you'll love me for a long, long time,

plant an apple tree." It tells about a woman enjoying a
relationship with a man but who isn't going to fall apart
when he leaves. "Whether you stays or whether you goes,
I'll have an apple and I'll have a rose."

The Madison audience, both men and women, cheered
wildly for all Gilbert's songs, but they gave her a standing
ovation following the Betsy Rose lyric about how women
reached America on different ships, but "We're all in the
same boat now."

Other songs dealt with the effects of stripmining,
corporate greed and nuclear naivete. She sang her way
through the eras of McCarthy, Nixon and Reagan. She
included several songs by Tom Paxton, noting that she is
not a separatist and is encouraged to see songs coming from
men with feminist consciousness, "some of them wonderful
songs." She did a whole section of songs about mothers and
daughters.

Music for women's lives

The lyrics of the songs like those Gilbert sang in
Madison were delightfully liberating and Ruth Scovill, in
her essay "Women's Music," explained why: "The creation
of Women's Music reflects a consciousness of women-
identification. Written by and for women, it speaks to their
real lives, providing role models and choices that popular
music has rarely offered to them. In contrast to popular
music's prevalent degradation of women, Women's Music
holds the feminist and humanist ideals of self-affirmation
and mutual support." It speaks of "women working
together in new ways; of women caring for, sharing with,
and loving each other; and of women getting in touch with
their power by getting in touch with themselves."

According to Scovill, the entity called Women's Music
began to emerge about 1973. One of its first harbingers
was the album "Lavender Jane Loves Women." In 1974,
the First National Women's Music Festival, held in
Champaign-Urbana, Illinois, ushered in a period of
phenomenal growth as women began to understand the
"uniqueness and commonality" of their music.

Concurrently with the explosion in the numbers of women writing their own lyrics, and singing their own songs, women have been staging, producing and providing the technical backup for their performances. As Scovill pointed out, "There would be no point in presenting non-oppressive lyrics in an oppressive atmosphere."

So women, who up till the early '70s had rarely been involved in the production end, gained competency in the skills necessary to ensure artistic control of their concerts. "Women have consciously altered the concert environment to suit...their own needs," Scovill reported. "In a Women's Music production all the women—producers, technicians, performers and audience—are constantly interacting with each other."

Trusting rather than testing

There are no Women's Music "stars" who posture and punish like the male rock stars who keep fans waiting for hours, then dominate stage and performance. Instead women performers work to build a "trust that creates a balance of power." They consider the audience, not only by writing lyrics that speak to the real lives of women, but also by offering several ticket prices, holding after-concert workshops, meeting members of the audience, and doing away with any pretense to model womanhood. The woman performer's honesty in admitting her "own humanness has became part of the...strength of Women's Music," concluded Scovill.

Gilbert too commented in Madison on the revolution that brought women into the production end of the music business. In her Feminist Connection interview she cited the "network of women all over this country...who are incredibly competent production managers, concert promoters and record promoters....Nowadays there is a huge network of people who carry alternative music to the people. This is all because of the women of this generation who have taken it out of the theoretical and put it to work."

Art music: a women's form

In art music, as well, women may be creating their
own unique structures. Karen Grimsted, in liner notes to
"Mooncircles" by flutist Kay Gardner, reports, "Women's
Music...has also evolved steadily from its unpretentious
beginnings when feminist content was simply infused into
conventional popular music forms. While such lyrical
innovations continue to inspire, delight and raise
consciousness, feminist musicians have begun the profound
and far-reaching search for [the kind of] breakthroughs [in
this music] that are occurring daily in women's lives."

As a musicologist Kay Gardner has detected and
defined a women's form, a circular form in women's
compositions, perhaps related to the primitive round or
rondo. As distinguished from much music composed by
men, the "climax or moment of most tension is in the
middle" and the musical structure "following the climax is
the same as that leading up to the climax, only backwards."

Many women musicians contend that there is no such
thing as a woman's form in music. Composer Elizabeth
Vercoe, chair of the Massachusetts Chapter of American
Women Composers, said, "Women's music can be identified
as different from men's only in the texts revealing a
feminist orientation."

A middle-of-the-road view was expressed by composer
Judith Lang Zaimont, whose music has been widely
recorded. She said that "Women seem to excel in the fine
art of balancing and synthesizing: that is, they are quick to
make use of techniques perhaps innovated by others in very
apposite ways...to achieve something quite fresh and
impressive."

Women are acknowledged as paying scrupulous
attention to detail. "This translates," said Zaimont, "into
art music that is consistently well-made, with particular
attention to articulated surfaces that have a strong
coloristic focus or emotional impact."

From gowns to jeans

Not everyone, of course, perceives structural characteristics common to Women's Music, and distinguishing it from compositions by men. A "Meet the Women Composer" course of 11 concerts, devoted to the music of 18 contemporary women composers, was offered at the New School for Social Research in the fall of 1976. Describing the event in the Feminist Art Journal, Ruth Julius wrote, "Despite the common bond of creativity and gender, there was an enormous diversity of compositional style and personal politics. From velvet evening gowns to blue jeans, from richly-textured Brahmsian sound to unfamiliar quarter tones, the composers and their music reflected a wide range of feelings and ideas."

Perhaps when we have all had a chance to listen to more women's music, we can decide whether there is or is not a woman's structure as such, or whether, as Kay Gardner suggests, women tend to choose different instrumentation, the use of treble instruments, because that is their hearing range.

In closing her essay on Women's Music, Roth Scovill recalled that Sophie Drinker, author of Music and Women, predicted in 1948 that women would have to "sing first for themselves," to create and present their music. Women are doing that today and, in Scovill's words, the "result is an art that validates women's lives and helps strengthen their identity as women."

Gender-linked instruments

Another aspect of women's music began to change over the last several years: audiences' and performers' perceptions of what instruments women should properly be playing. Not too long ago, the only women in symphony orchestras were likely to be harpists. Speaking of that era, Karen Dobbs, a trumpeter and now general manager of the Louisville Orchestra, recalled in the December 1982 issue of Symphony Magazine, "The woman who chose a nontraditional instrument faced isolation and discouragement."

Today the picture is much brighter, though old stereotypes die hard. In 1978, a study by Abeles and Porter measured instrumental sex stereotyping among adults and children. They discovered that, starting as early as third grade, all age groups had stereotyped ideas of which instruments were appropriate to men or women.

The reasons for the strength of these gender associations can be traced back to the Renaissance when instrumental music became popular. Women were expected to take up "feminine" instruments that required no "alteration of facial expression or physical demeanor." Many male musicians have long maintained that women "don't have enough breath" to play brass and woodwind instruments.

Expanding choices

Kay Gardner wondered if women's treble hearing range affected their choice of instrument. At any rate, according to Symphony Magazine, the facts in 1982 were that 80 percent of all women in major orchestras played stringed instruments, compared with 11 percent playing woodwinds and 4 percent playing brass. But opportunities were expanding. In that year, women were playing principal trumpet in the St. Louis Symphony and principal bass trombone in the Cincinnati Symphony. A few major orchestras by then had female percussionists. The New York Philharmonic, in 1982, hired a woman as principal bassoonist. The National Symphony Orchestra had a woman horn player and women were playing the cumbersome double bass and the big, wrap-around tuba. It was an illustration of the same trend away from stereotyping that a man in 1982 played the harp with the San Francisco Symphony.

Theatre: Staging the Personal and Political

In one sense, trying to describe the content of feminist plays is like talking about all the things your mother told you never to mention in public. Over the past decade and a

half, formerly taboo female subject matter, now spotlighted
on center stage, has caused mostly women audiences to
applaud, cheer and weep. It was such a relief to see their
most personal everyday concerns made valid and valuable
and woven into the stuff of plays that dealt with women's
real lives.

Women's concerns had never before been considered
significant or artworthy by the male-dominated art
establishment. As Linda Walsh Jenkins said in <u>Women in
American Theatre</u>, co-edited with Helen Krich Chinoy,
"menstruation, mothers and daughters, pots and pans,
dolls, rape, childbirth"—it was all there in feminist theatre.
There is shock value as well as humor and a "female is
fine" bravado in a play titled, for example, "The Saga of
How I Lost My Hairy Legs."

The range of subject matter is astonishing. Myrna
Lamb's play, "But What Have You Done for Me Lately?",
features a pregnant man in search of abortion. Short
"guerrilla events" put on in elevators of office buildings and
department stores shock "by their verbal assaults on
familiar persons and institutions."

A 1984 festival of 12 plays staged by the Women's
Project at the American Place Theatre dealt with a
woman's health spa; foot binding in China; a family of
disfigured children; and the only woman military general in
America. But whatever the specific themes, all 12 plays
showed "women who, whatever their circumstances,
attempt to live their lives with strength, vitality and a
sense of humor."

Materials of our lives

Patti P. Gillespie, chairwoman of the theatre and
speech department, University of South Carolina, reported
that Womanspace Theatre attributed its success to
"working in a very organic way with the materials of our
lives." Burning City performed a series of episodes, "each
drawn directly from the life experience of a different
woman. Scripts are often built from interviews held with
performers' mothers, or from dreams related by members
of the audience. The fusion of the personal with the political

in these theatres is very strong indeed," said Gillespie. The fact that audiences like what they are seeing means the theatres have successfully transformed the personal into the political.

Women's dreams, feelings and fantasies have become fitting subjects for many plays. In an essay in the 1978 Quarterly Journal of Speech, Gillespie quotes from the It's All Right to Be Woman Theatre: "Making theatre out of these private parts of ourselves is one way we are trying every day to take our own experiences seriously, to accept our feelings as valid and real....To believe that what happens to us or what we feel or dream is important enough to share with each other and other women, that it is, in fact, the most important thing we have to share."

Feminist playwright Megan Terry's early interest in revealing the lives of strong women first motivated her to write "Approaching Simone," on the life of Simone Weil. The play won Obies for both Terry and the director, Maxine Klein. Terry's "American King's English for Queens" is about how language is used to control people. Her "Hothouse" reveals the positive side of a matriarchal love, and how women hold things together while men are off fighting wars. "Attempted Rescue on Avenue B" shows a woman coming to terms with her power.

Provoking action

The goal of feminist theatres is usually to provoke action rather than create "art," to increase awareness of the issues of feminism or to advocate change. This goal clearly influences the content of plays they produce. According to Jenkins, The Onyx Women's Theatre "strives to reinforce a positive self-image" for black women; the Circle of the Witch attacks old ideas and seeks to learn "new ways of thinking and seeing the world"; Bread and Roses uses theatre to educate audiences about feminism; and the Caravan Theatre wants "to produce plays that reflect ways of changing the social system."

Very few plays before 1970, for example, dealt with the "issue" of lesbianism. "In the '70s, said Jenkins, "lesbian theatres and other feminist theatres could explore

lesbian life choices and challenges with a new
consciousness, confidence and humor." An example is the
Lavender Cellar Theatre that "provides a positive
perspective on lesbian lifestyles."

Not only is the content of feminist theater new but the
form is also. According to Susan Suntree, "Today's
women's writing is characterized by experimentation with
form that yields new attitudes about the content of plays."
In many plays, like Megan Terry's "Viet Rock" and "Calm
Down, Mother," Terry concentrates "on how circumstance
and images stimulate personal responses and discoveries by
actors and audiences."

Good parts for women

Obviously, feminist playwrights like Terry write good
parts for women into their plays, even if the plays also
contain parts for men. In an interview with Dinah
L. Leavitt in 1977, Terry talked about how traditional
plays allowed the typical male lead to show many aspects
of his character, but the other characters were allowed to
show only one aspect of themselves, usually in support of or
opposition to the main character.

During the '70s, in fact, women playwrights became
increasingly suspicious of male-created woman
characters. They felt that even "sensitive" male
playwrights could only create women characters during
times of culturally accepted, stereotyped views of
women. And these are the times, of course, that they hope
to change.

With their women characters, women playwrights are
creating stylized, surreal, metaphorical or totally
autobiographical women characters—one of the today's
most important theatrical innovations.

Good parts for men

And what kinds of plays have men been writing?
Evidence that the war between the sexes is far from
over appears in some of the newest plays written by men,
according to Frank Rich, in The New York Times. Such

works, he says, as David Rabe's "Hurlyburly," David
Mamet's "Glengarry Glen Ross," and Sam Shepard's "Fool
for Love" portray women and men as chasms apart.

"Hurlyburly," says Rich, though set in present day
Hollywood, "dramatizes a set of [male-female] attitudes
that might be considered retrogressive in a Marine barracks
of 40 years ago." The women in the play are either
"bubble-brained" and promiscuous or "out-and-out bimbos."

The all-male cast of "Glengarry Glen Ross," which
Rich characterizes as containing "some of the most
interesting writing available in the theatre right now," is
about a group of cutthroat Chicago real estate salesmen
who regard women as beside the point. Rich comments that
it is laced with scatological insults from beginning to end,
but it's the four-letter word for the female sexual organ
that its characters deliver as the worst epithet of all.

In "Fool for Love," Shepard has put a major female
character on the stage but she and her lover "circle each
other like wrestlers for most of the 90 minutes that they
spend trying to erase one another in a seedy motel room."
They both believe that the only real men are those who
"half kill themselves falling off horses or jumping on
steers."

Rich concludes his analysis by noting that all three
plays boast enthusiastic audiences, "and it may not only be
the skill of the writing and acting that is winning theatre
goers over. There remains the heretical, not to mention
distressing, possibility that these gifted writers reflect the
real world of men and women in 1984 more accurately than
most of us would care to think." Not a comforting thought.

Performance Art: Powerful Women

In performance art, the themes of personal
introspection, goddesses, strong women, biography and
autobiography, and political commentary are paramount.

In her 1980 Artnews article, Kay Larson, art critic for
the Village Voice, wrote: "The female self is a fountain of
mysteries. It has provoked women into recreating rituals
rooted centuries ago in matrilineal, matriarchal,
agricultural ways of thinking. Goddess fascination attracts

spiritualists such as Mary Beth Edelson, a New York artist, whose performances and installations, documented in ghostly photographs...are focused on the artist as primogenitor."

Women artists, gazing into this fountain of mysteries, behold their own reflections, like a female Narcissis, and the image is translated into the now-familiar goddess image, with arms bent at the elbows and upraised.

Rites and rituals

Because of the search for women's roots and expanding definitions of what theatre is, ritual is increasingly being used by women's groups. Sherry Mester, editor of Earth Rites Press: "Many of us as feminists have felt that we needed to develop an integration of our political analysis and our spiritual and psychic awareness...at the present time women are trying to recreate or reestablish rites and rituals to remember our old power, our collective unconscious which has been buried throughout recent history.

"Thus a growing interest in Wicce and Native American women's rituals and point of view has inspired the creation of dramatic forms expressing women's welling experience of inner strength and connection with nature, symbolized for many by the various images of the Goddess," wrote Mester.

Edelson was creating solo rituals that she documented as performance pieces as well as group rituals. "What I am hoping for," she wrote in an introduction to her 1977 proposal for "Memorials to the 9,000,000 Women Burned as Witches in the Christian Era," is that "the performers and the audience will participate in connection with each other as a single body during the brief life of the ritual..."

According to Moira Roth, editor of The Amazing Decade, published in 1983, other performance artists in the '70s depicted women's lives. Lynn Hershman's character, Rebecca, had a complete identity, a job as a secretary and a bleak past, and "conveyed the terrible loneliness of a shy woman in an aggressive, marriage-oriented culture."

Betsy Damon's archetypal, blind "Thousand Year-Old

Woman" squatted on the steps of St. Patrick's Cathedral,
inviting passersby to tell her their stories. Laurie
Anderson's blond-haired androgynous punk told shaggy dog
stories in almost vaudevillian style.

Rage against violence

Performance art in the '70s often expressed rage at
the violence perpetrated against women. In 1977, Suzanne
Lacy and Leslie Labowitz staged a costumed, week-long
media event, "In Mourning and in Rage," on the steps of
the Los Angeles City Hall, protesting the wave of
rape-murders in that city. They also performed works with
abortion and incest themes.

A more recent theme of Labowitz was her 1980
"Sproutime" that drew the viewer into a world of
germinating seeds and plants with luxurious foliage and
brilliant artificial flowers and birds. Shown in both Los
Angeles and New York City, the performance, with its
accompanying readings from "The Secret Garden," echoed
the garden theme of women's literature.

Lacy's works in the '80s celebrated history rather
than violence. "In her citywide network pieces in Los
Angeles, New Orleans, and Ithaca, New York, she
developed new ways people (men and women) could
symbolize and strengthen their sense of community." A
particularly notable aspect of Lacy's work was following up
her event-making visit in the community with the
development of a women's network.

In May of 1984, Lacy's "Whisper, the Waves, the
Wind," over a year in the making, featured older women
sitting at a white-clothed table on the beach near San
Diego, talking about "aging, freedom, death and the
future."

On the 31st of the same month on the East Coast,
mostly black women from the Hodson Senior Center in the
Bronx performed in "Ready for Love," also a year-long
project. According to Lucy Lippard in the Village Voice,
"The play was one of three from Bronx senior centers
presented under the aegis of Elders Share the Arts, a
citywide program directed by Susan Perlstein." Comparing

both these events, Lippard wrote, "Lacy and Perlstein, et al. are concerned with destroying stereotypes, altering the way elderly people perceive themselves, reducing the fear of aging, recognizing the beauty of each stage of life, while reinforcing the "resources this society shuts off in its flight from death"....By giving people access to the creation of their own self-images, both Lacy and Perlstein integrate the functions of artist and organizer—a combination that comprises activist art."

A strong political theme of performance art in the '80s has been the threat of nuclear war. Nancy Buchanan turned away from her earlier focus on the experiences and attitudes of women and women's relationship with men toward the "subject of war and the abuses of political power in America," according to Roth.

Family fallout

Buchanan's 1981 "Fallout From the Nuclear Family" was about her nuclear physicist father. In this event, Buchanan read accounts from diaries of, letters by and articles about her father and his role as a key advisor to the American government on defense and nuclear weapons.

"In her current work, Nancy Buchanan is setting up models for highly effective political criticism as art directed at awakening people's consciences and fears about issues of nuclear war and political abuses of power in America," wrote Roth, who believed that much of the "most effective feminist performance is moving in these global and historical directions.

"Feminist performance art offers a highly imaginative form, to men as well as women, for using art and learning how to live in such a difficult and frightening world," Roth concluded.

New York's WOW festivals in 1980 and 1981 capped the-day-and-night, for-love-not-money-efforts of four women calling themselves the Allied Farces. Their second annual WOW festival featured 40 pieces and attracted women performance artists from several other countries. Writing in the Village Voice in October 1981, Barbara Baracks characterized the event as "a festival of contradictions:

funky and feminist, sexually eclectic, international in tone, racially various."

The women's movement has drastically altered the way we look at erotic art, wrote art critic Lippard in the Village Voice in February of 1984. Her case in point was Carnival Knowledge, another young feminist artists collective on the New York scene, that concentrated on reproductive rights. In "The Second Coming," a month-long performance series, they "included real live porn stars, mud wrestling, artworks, and other attractions." They intended "to confront the distortions of pornography and revitalize our erotic perspectives by creating a feminist porn."

Comedy: Out of the Closet

Before 1975, there hardly was such a thing as a female stand-up comedian, except for Phyllis Diller, Joan Rivers, Totie Fields and Lily Tomlin. Now, a New York agent who books comedy clubs across the country has added the names of 54 female comics to his files, most since 1979.

A funny thing about them is not only their recent proliferation but the way they get laughs from things we never even talked about before.

Faithlessness and foolishness

An example is the lesbian humorist Kate Clinton who goes into a lengthy examination of sanitary napkins and the subliminal messages that advertising about them bombards us with. Her advice, if you want to make waves: "Take a sanitary napkin, unpeel the back and stick it on your face." The thought is not only outrageous but voicing it aloud is both shocking and embarrassing. And how about the names of deodorants? Men's deodorants are called Arid, Mennen Speed Stick, Old Spice. Women's deodorants are called Mum, Ban, Secret. Clinton's humor makes us think as well as laugh.

Some of the grist for the female millers is, of course, more traditional, or the flipped coin of men's humor: the faithlessness of men and the foolishness of the women who fall for them. The relationship between the sexes has always been a source of comedy. But today, with women humorists, it might be double-edged. Carol Siskind, talking about her latest boyfriend: "We had a typical love-hate relationship. We both loved him and hated me." At one and the same time she puts down men's narcissism and women's lack of self-esteem.

Putting themselves down?

Siskind, an emcee with the Improvisation, a comedy showcase in New York City, said, "I think men and women are very much alike. That's really the gist of what I try to say."

In the old days, pre-1975, women comedians had to put themselves down, denigrate their own looks or sexuality, talk about the importance of landing a man or looking pretty, or make fun of their husbands to get a laugh. New funny women can talk about an expanded range of female issues: birth control, the life of the single urban woman, pre-menstrual syndrome, herpes. Food and dieting, depression, therapy are mined for their humor. So are current events and everybody's everyday problems.

As Adrienne Tolsch, comic and emcee at Catch a Rising Star, another New York comedy showcase club, explained in an article in the October 1984 Ms., women today "don't feel they're the only victims. Now they have a little perspective."

Often this women's humor comes from the identities the comedians have fashioned for themselves outside of the comedy club scene, in their jobs as cook, cosmetologist, bicycle messenger, teacher, manicurist, waitress or cleaning lady. But whether or not they call themselves feminists, their comedy represents a female point of view.

Beverly Mickins: "I love the lines men use: "Please—I'll only put it in for a minute." What am I, a microwave?"

Most of the new female comics adopt one of two main styles of delivery: a "sweet, ditsy approach," or a "strong, brassy manner," said Larry Amoros, a comic who, for several years, wrote jokes for women comedians.

The reason audiences didn't accept women comics until recently is the long-standing proscription against a woman's coming across with the aggressiveness and power necessary to control audiences. Today a few women comedians, like Rita Rudner, continue to project the more stereotypical persona: a sweet niceness. "My humor is more offbeat hysterical than it is raucous," she said.

Many other women, however, revel in the chance to express anger, exert power and be in control in front of an audience. And with few exceptions, even males in the audience not only accept it, they crack up over it.

Politics with a feminist spin

But women's personal concerns and the updated battle of the sexes aren't the only themes. Mickins digs at the crassness of men but she also does political humor, taking swipes at the Ku Klux Klan and President Reagan.

Maureen Murphy gets laughs by putting a feminist spin on her political jokes: "Maybe we should have a woman president. She'd save the country money because she'd only make half what a man makes."

Some women comedians work in pairs. Susan Fuller and Rita Paskowitz, based in the Twin Cities, are among the few women working the Midwest. Publicizing their arrival in Madison, Wisconsin, in September of 1985, Walt Trott wrote in the Capital Times: "As the kooky pair noted in a press release, they weigh in—collectively—at about 210 pounds, measure 109 and one-half inches tall (in flats) and boast 15 million strands of hair (or 30 million if you count split ends)."

They've performed both on network TV and on Public Television. Their humor is not particularly issue-oriented or political but their repertoire includes a sketch on capital punishment.

A trio of women—The Sleazebuckets—specialize in irony and trendy terms: "post-modern, multi-media new mime and cross-dress lip syncing fashion shows in the classic avantgardeey tradish, natch."

Hurray for Whoopi

Carving a special comedic niche is Whoopi Goldberg, who calls herself a comic actor. She has been compared with Richard Pryor, Elaine May, Laurence Olivier, Groucho Marx and Ruth Draper. Her cast of off-the-wall characters reminds you of the collection of crazies impersonated by Lily Tomlin.

Harry Haun, writing in the New York Daily News, dubbed them "a menagerie of misfits and malcontents." Her brood is a weird mix: a street-smart pothead named Fontaine; a Valley Girl bubblehead; an old wino who once danced with the Nicolas Brothers; a disabled woman who is marrying a man who charmed her by asking her to dance ("This is not a disco body," she demurs); a Jamaican lady who marries into money and the United States; and a little black girl who wears on her head a yellow skirt (her long, luxurious blond hair) because you have to have blond hair to be on "Love Boat."

Haun concludes that "Whoopi's art and compassion conspire to make them eminently believable and, on occasion, heartbreakingly human."

Goldberg's most recent success is her moving portrayal of the heroine in the film version of Alice Walker's The Color Purple.

Whoopi makes a point of preferring to be called an actor, rather than an actress. Maybe women will know they have really made it as stand-up comics when The New York Times calls them comedians—instead of comediennes.

Film: New Roles, New Lives

Ever since the beginnings of the Hollywood film industry, women in film have been portrayed in stereotypical ways. By 1934, the vamp and the "straight girl" were easily recognized by appearance, behavior and characteristics.

Fifty years later, the straight girl (representing virtue) has at last evolved, in Hollywood movies such as "Country," "The River" and "Places in the Heart," into a strong woman. All three movies concerned a family's fight to save their farm against both natural and bureaucratic catastrophes. Each featured a strong-willed woman who gave courage to the others.

Strong career women, equal-partner types, appeared throughout the '30s and '40s in Hollywood-made movies, before numerous versions of the apron-clad, "Yes, dear," housewife swarmed back to movie (and television) screens. It was not until the early '70s that strong women began to reappear occasionally, notably in such films as "Three Women," with Shelley Duvall and Sissy Spacek, written by freelance film writer Jane Wilson; "Julia," starring Jane Fonda and Vanessa Redgrave; "The Turning Point," with Anne Bancroft and Shirley MacLaine; "An Unmarried Woman," with Jill Clayburgh; and "Alice Doesn't Live Here Anymore," with Ellen Burstyn.

Television scenarios

Television programs echoed the same trend. 1984's lineup of primetime TV shows could have been and was interpreted as evidence that women were finally getting a break. Of 22 new primetime series, eight featured females in strong leading roles. In addition, the networks renewed two previous-season shows whose scripts called for strong, capable working women, realistically portrayed.

"Cagney and Lacey" and "Kate and Allie" continue, as does "Hill Street Blues" with its competent female police officers and its awesome attorney, Joyce Davenport. Unfortunately, few of the new women's shows first aired in the fall of 1984 survived the ratings shakeout. Yet even the few that do remain are an improvement over the time when women on television were either victims and/or prostitutes.

Men outnumber women

As recently as 1978, a University of Pennsylvania study found that men outnumbered women three to one in primetime. "Charlie's Angels," airing in 1976, was the first show to feature women in leading roles. Even though their appeal was based on their jiggle-prone attributes, the show probably did help pave the way for more realistic leading women.

Part of the credit for the improved situation belongs to the women who have moved into decision-making roles within the industry, said Lillian Gallo, a producer and former network executive. "More women are becoming network executives and they tend to do more stories with women."

However, Susan Baerwald of NBC noted that even the strong female characters, such as Joyce Davenport, are still idolized as women who have brains, guts and are still incredibly beautiful, feminine and sexy.

A study by the National Commission on Working Women found that women on television are more likely to be younger, white, professional and either upper middle class or wealthy.

Two exceptions to this stand out. "Murder, She Wrote," is a successful new show starring the vintage Angela Lansbury. And on "The Bill Cosby Show," Dr. Huxtable's wife, Claire, played by Phylicia Ayers-Allen, is black. But she is definitely upper class, and while she is ostensibly an attorney, the scripts so far have shown her almost exclusively in home settings, acting the wife and mother. It's a delight, however, to see Cosby's character cooking, taking care of the children and catering to her.

Documentary and news stories featuring women have, quite properly, garnered awards. Among these are "A Matter of Sex," about eight women employees of a Willmar, Minnesota, bank; "Working Women"; "Educating Rita"; and "Poverty Has a Woman's Face."

Strong women pitch products

Strong women are more often seen in TV and magazine advertising in recent years, after marketing studies won them the right to be portrayed in commercials as financially successful. In some ads for both the print and electronic media, they appear as professionals who buy their own cars, talk knowledgeably about financial instruments and use credit cards. But again, the change over the last decade has not been as drastic as some had hoped it would be. During the same time span, there has been a resurgence of women as romantic and feminine, not to say blatantly sexual. Images of women touting products in the kitchen and bedroom still abound.

In fact, recent University of Michigan research shows that sexual stereotyping of product use in advertising did not change at all from 1960 to 1979. "During those two decades of social change, advertisers consistently portrayed women modeling clothes or performing domestic work, while men were shown on the job and rarely in the home," wrote Hilary DeVries in the Christian Science Monitor.

Even since 1979, says Dr. Jean Kilbourne, a long-time media observer and author of the illustrated lecture, "The Naked Truth: Advertising's Image of Women," "Content analysis shows that women are still very much portrayed in the home while men are still considered the figures of authority."

It has been the independently produced, alternative, feminist films since 1970 that have explored the strong woman theme in depth and quantity. A recent example is listed in the 1984 catalog of Women Make Movies, a film collective founded in 1972 to teach, produce and distribute media related to the history and experiences of women.

"Annapurna: A Woman's Place" is, quoting from the catalog, "The powerful story of ten women who in 1978 set out to do what no American had done before, climb Annapurna, one of the world's tallest and most dangerous peaks."

Ishtar offers a number of films on outstanding women: May Sarton, Kate Chopin, Madeleine L'Engle, and "One Fine Day," celebrating American women from the 18th century to the present.

It's only natural that strong women as role models should form a significant theme in the movies of independent women filmmakers, whose numbers grew from 30 or 35 in 1972 to over 200—with 250 films to their credit—by mid-1976.

Film festivals

In 1973, the First International Festival of Women's Films spotlighted the explosion of independent films made by women and the occurrence of the strong woman theme. Perry Miller Adato, by 1973 a veteran filmmaker for television, entered her feature-length documentary, "Gertrude Stein: When This You See, Remember Me." Later she and others would make films about famous women artists Mary Cassatt, Louise Nevelson and Georgia O'Keeffe.

In 1974, this "second wave" of feminist films— biographical and autobiographical portraits— crested. The first wave of women's films (1970-1974) had concerned social and political issues. The biographic content took over as the emphasis on the personal as political became the dominant feminist theme. It was part of the thrust throughout the arts to discover women's personal stories, to search for roots and predecessors and to gain strength from them.

These film portraits also reflected feminists' mounting concern with private life. They zoomed in tight on the identity of a specific woman facing typical problems: divorce, job discrimination, motherhood. In contrast to political, social issue films that are concerned with the present and future, and feature representational women, they used the particular to show women's strengths in coping with such situations.

Biography

In addition to women of significant achievement, well-known in their time if not well-remembered, women frequently cast their own relatives or themselves as the central characters. Joanne Woodward and her daughter in the film, "Rachel, Rachel," is a Hollywood example. These films showed ordinary women encountering typical problems and responding to them with strength and courage. Rothschild's "Joyce at 34" and "Nana, Mom and Me" revealed one woman's response to the problem of trying to establish and maintain an identity as wife and mother.

These autobiographical films often sprang from an event in the filmmaker's life, such as the death of a mother, that triggered a more introspective, personal examination of her life. The theme of the relationship of mothers and daughters is common to all types of artistic expression since the early '70s.

"Antonia," a film about the vastly talented conductor Antonia Brico, could be interpreted as a film portrait as well as a social issue film. The focus was on the sex discrimination that dogged every step of her career. "Antonia" pointed out Brico's unique, distinctive qualities, rather than her ordinary or representative ones. Ironically, the film did more to boost Brico's career than did rave reviews about her conducting.

Thus, film portraits, which reclaim and integrate the past, reveal connections between public and private aspects of women's lives. "Like the women's movement, they identify points at which the personal and political dimensions of women's lives intersect," according to Women's Reflections: The Feminist Film Movement, by Jan Rosenberg.

One of the more recent film portraits is "Master Smart Woman," by Jane Morrison. It unearths the life of the 19th century feminist writer Sarah Orne Jewett. It is not only a much-deserved reevaluation of Jewett's contribution to American literature, but, says filmmaker Morrison, "It gives me great satisfaction, as a woman film director in the 20th century from Maine, to find [in it] inspiration for my own work."

Women and social protest

"Testament," a recent film produced outside of Hollywood and starring Jane Alexander, combined the strong woman theme with social protest, although the latter assertion is denied by its director, Lynn Littman.

"What came first with me," Littman said in an interview with Neal Gabler on PBS, "was the story of a mother and her children—the family story." Also denying that "Testament" was a woman's picture, Littman goes on,

"In my experience, men and women do not respond the same way to the question of nuclear warfare....women tend to simply jump to the heart of the matter and say, this cannot happen, while frequently men get involved with questions of strategy or political issues...."Testament" is a woman's point of view of the big bomb, but...it's a guy's subject."

The film, written by John Young, was based on a story by Carol Lehman that first appeared in Ms. Public television's American Playhouse producer Lindsay Law helped raise the money to write and produce it outside of regular Hollywood channels.

Picking up the social issue documentary form that had been more recurrent in the early '70s, nuclear warfare continues to be a popular subject in women's independent films. Women Make Movies lists three in their 1984 catalog: "For Life's Sake, Let's Fight," by Margareta Wasterstam, a Swedish journalist; "Carry Greenham Home," by British filmmakers Beeban Kidron and Amanda Richardson; and "Stronger Than Before," a videotape by the Boston Women's Video Collective.

Another political film, "Louder Than Our Words: Women and Civil Disobedience," released in 1983, "would program well with the nuclear films for stimulating discussions on women's involvement in politics, the nuclear disarmament movement and women organizing for social change," according to the catalog.

Obviously, a number of women filmmakers feel that the threat of nuclear war has superseded in importance issues such as the plight of poor and working class women, women's emerging feminist consciousness and other political responses to the conditions of women's lives.

Avant-garde films

Another category of women's films can be called avant-garde. These films go beyond notions of time, reverberating with private expressions of an individual's values. Even when those films concern feminist themes (women's sexuality, identity, childhood) the approach is highly personal, not political. These films contain no narrative, factual or realistic material or action sequences but rather express the filmmaker's own subjective moods and feelings. Creative self-expression has been the subject of many women's avant-garde films since 1974. The numerous avant-garde films that predate the 1970 beginnings of the women's movement have been reinterpreted and reclaimed by it.

Literature: Telling Their Stories

The most revolutionary thing women can do is tell their stories, said Sonia Johnson. Although the ex-Mormon feminist who ran for president in 1984 is not a writer, her statement accurately characterized the recent revitalization of women's story telling.

As women writers have realized that the personal is political, they have searched their histories, their mythic pasts, their own feelings and lives, their mother's gardens for the roots of artistic literary expression. The books that have poured forth—the diaries, biographies, autobiographies, journals, letters, fiction, poetry and essays—have made up what Robin Morgan calls the "new woman's renaissance of the '70s." It is an unprecedented deluge and one qualitatively different from what went before.

In poetry before the '70s, for example, women often earned their way by conforming to male tradition, wrote Debora Ashworth in the essay, "Madonna or Witch, Women's Muse in Contemporary American Poetry." Female themes, when women's poetry was mentioned at all, were considered neither interesting nor suitable material for "serious" poetry.

Women creating themselves

Now, said successful book publisher Florence Howe, "Women write about themselves as artists, their (female) muse, their lust for fame....They create and re-create themselves, their feelings, in thought or in action." One of the ways in which the woman poet explores her art is through religious and myth images, according to

Ashworth. The poetic awareness comes, she suggested, as she wades "through the countless mythologies" of her own life. Poet Audre Lorde has effectively combined history, biography and mythology, calling the result, "biomythography."

The past decade and a half has been characterized, particularly, by an astonishing output from black women writers. Paule Marshall, the author of Brown Girl, Brown Stones, and Reena, credits her mother and sister, with their Barbadian way of putting things, for developing her ear for language and her writing style. One of their favorite sayings was, "In this man world you got to take yuh mouth and make it a gun!"

Nikki Giovanni, Ntozake Shange, Maya Angelou, Toni Cade Bambara, Gwendolyn Brooks, Alexis Deveaux, Kristin Hunter, Gayl Jones, Gloria Naylor, Toni Morrison, Sonia Sanchez, Margaret Walker, Alice Walker, Sherley Anne Williams, Ann Petry, Rosa Guy, Louise Meriwether, Andrea Lee, Eleanor Traylor and Mary E. Mebane have all reoriented the literary world and readers' perceptions during the last decade and a half.

Claudia Tate interviewed many of these writers for her book, Black Women Writers at Work, published in 1983. But she said that contrary to what many believe, "Black women writers did not suddenly begin to write in the 1970s." They had been writing continuously since the 18th century, but only recently have they finally begun to find publishing outlets. Even so, wrote Tate, "They seldom receive the same marketing attention or support of the academic community their male counterparts do."

Searching for identities

Bambara, Giovanni and Brooks took part in a symposium on "Black American Women Writers," at William Patterson College in Wayne, New Jersey, in 1982. Each read her own poetry, which differed in theme as well as style. Brooks focused on black pride, and what it means to be black; Bambara spoke about the treatment of blacks in society, and Giovanni "expressed her individual feelings as a black woman," according to Maureen Murray, writing in New Directions for Women.

Tate identified several themes, some of which, she said, seem to be "unique to the writings of black women." An example is the quest theme, "a character's personal search for a meaningful identity and for self-sustaining dignity in a world of growing isolation, meaninglessness, and moral decay." Like women in general, these black women writers usually project their vision from the point of view of female characters whose quest is constrained by the "close boundaries" of their lives.

"Complex personal relationships" either while the protagonist is "confused or troubled" or "after she has achieved some understanding of herself and of others..." occur during the search. Self-esteem, Tate elaborated, "is so primary an issue in writings by black women that it deserves special attention. Many heroines suffer from a loss of pride and personal worth." Often at the end of the story, the women realize that a sense of pride and self-worth must come from within rather than be linked to relationships with men. Only then can this pride be shared.

Ntozake Shange, author of the play, "For Colored Girls Who Have Considered Suicide When the Rainbow Is Enuf," emphasized this perception. In her interview with Tate she said, "When I die, I will not be guilty of having left a generation of girls behind thinking that anyone can tend to their emotional health other than themselves."

Another theme common to women's writing is strong women as role models. Alice Walker, whose The Color Purple won the 1982 Pulitzer Prize and the 1983 American Book Award, published her collection of critical essays and autobiographic writings, In Search of Our Mothers' Gardens, in 1983. Walker speaks of the need women have for role models. She earlier published an anthology of the writings of Zora Neale Hurston, a black American writer of the '20s and '30s, whose story was not only valuable, but in danger of being misrepresented, distorted or lost. In fact, Walker sees the effort to resuscitate the lives of women who would otherwise "remain silent and invisible" as a social mission.

Foremothers and role models

The title piece in Walker's collection, originally
published in the May 1974 Ms., "has become a touchstone
for women interested in unearthing the lives, deeds and
writings of their foremothers." She cited her own mother as
an example of an artist whose creativity was channeled into
her garden, the one source of expression available to her.

About that artist mother she wrote: "Whatever she
planted grew as if by magic, and her fame as a grower of
flowers spread over three counties. Because of her
creativity with her flowers, even my memories of poverty
are seen through a screen of blooms—sunflowers, petunias,
roses, dahlias, forsythia, spirea, delphinium, verbena..."

This legacy from her mother enables Walker, the
daughter, to grow her own flowers—her stories and poems.

Mothers and daughters—the relationship depicted in
song and story, researched by social scientists, tilled for
inspiration through the last decade and a half—is indeed a
recurrent theme in women's art. A recent publication from
The Feminist Press was Mother to Daughter, Daughter to
Mother, a collection of 120 writers past and present on that
theme.

Another compelling theme is the rediscovery of the
lives of unrelated women. Carolyn Heilbrun, feminist
scholar and literary critic, and a professor of English at
Columbia College, discussed in The New York Times Book
Review Section the growing number of biographies written
by women.

Explaining the anomalies

Before 1970, Heilbrun wrote, "biographies of women
were scarce and rigidly restricted to royal women or those
attached to powerful men." In contrast, contemporary
women biographers are writing about women whose lives
are "not scripted by the patriarchy, not lived by convention,
not in most cases properly acknowledged by their
contemporaries."

Women have been able to write about these
unconventional women, Heilbrun pointed out, because they
are now "freed from the anxiety of portraying, defending,

explaining an anomaly": an unconventional woman's
life. "New lives for women have become imaginable," she
wrote. "In contemplating new stories about women's lives,
biographers have begun to see new plots in old lives."

Zelda, about the wife of F. Scott Fitzgerald, published
in 1970, was significant, wrote Heilbrun, in its revelations
of her husband's "assumption of his right to the life of his
wife as his artistic property."

Since then the stories of other women—Edith
Wharton, Alice James, Margaret Fuller, Vita
Sackville-West, Vanessa Bell, Dorothy Richardson, Simone
Weil, Frida Kahlo, Kathe Kollwitz and Barbara
McClintock, the Nobel prize winning scientist—have hit the
bookstores.

Women's words and diaries have achieved prominence
in the literary world of the '70s and '80s. Kay Larson,
writing in the October 1980 Artnews, said, "When women
began to piece together an identity not based on male
models, they turned to ... words." Many women in
consciousness-raising sessions kept diaries. The students
involved in Womanhouse in Los Angeles plunged into their
diaries in search of new, quintessentially female images.

As Larson pointed out, women in the last two decades
explored the personal use of words, recorded dreams,
worked their way out of emotional crises or detailed daily
lives no longer deemed "unsuitable" to art.

The dark side of women's writing over the last decade
is the romance fiction phenomenon. Publishers who have
contributed to the flood—and it is a lucrative one—bring out
hundreds of titles every year. The main character in these
potboilers is always a woman, usually one who has a job
but not, per se, a career. She must be a virgin who believes
her life will not be complete until she finds the man of her
dreams. The romantic settings in these books complement
the fantasy-land situations, the happy-ever-after
endings. There are now religious romances and another
segment of the market is moving toward soft core
pornography.

Whether the right-wing backlash has created or
merely identified the market for this escapist fiction, its
message is clearly designed to get women back into the

home, dependent upon the men who choose to rescue them from a life of spinsterhood. Writers who earn their money writing romances invariably use pseudonyms.

Working Through Traditional Institutions

Visual Arts: High Visibility, High Hopes

Some compared it to a scene from a childhood nightmare, recalling almost forgotten pain. Sign-carrying women artists marched the picket line in front of New York's Museum of Modern Art, just reopened after a two-year, $55 million renovation in July of 1984.

Hadn't anything changed since that day in 1970 when Women in the Arts pickets first carried signs protesting the low numbers of women—the museum itself estimated 10 percent—in MOMA exhibits?

Apparently not much. Fourteen years later, MOMA's grand reopening exhibit, "An International Survey of Recent Painting and Sculpture," included only 14 women—8.5 percent—among its 165 artists.

The WIA estimated at least 400 women came to protest: short-notice turnout all the more remarkable considering that the retrogressive statistics were not known in advance. With banners proclaiming "Old Boy Museum: formerly MOMA" and "MOMA Dislikes Her Daughters," many of the marchers complained bitterly about the lack of progress in the last decade and a half.

Joyce Weinstein, writing in the WIA newsletter, said, "The sad thing is that, although things have gotten better for women artists since that day 14 years ago when we first picketed, there is still so much discrimination around."

Early statistics

Perhaps it's best to begin with numbers. How many women artists are there? Encouragingly, the numbers have gone up over the past 13 years. Both women and minorities increased their participation in the arts during the decade of the '70s, according to a report published by the Research Division of the National Endowment for the Arts. Between 1970 and 1980, the number of women artists increased by 162 percent while the number of men artists increased by only 53 percent.

In 1980 women comprised 38 percent of the total

artistic work force, up almost 12 percent from 1970. This increase in the proportion of women artists in the artist labor force was two and one-half times greater than the 4.5 percent increase in the proportion of women in all occupations during the same time period. And it occurred in spite of the fact that women artists still earn not only one-third less than what male artists earn, but also a full 26 cents less than the national average for all women's work.

According to the NEA report, "Minorities' participation in the artist work force has also increased, but not nearly as dramatically as that of women." The number of minority artists increased by 2.6 percent. At 10.7 percent of the total, minorities are not even as well represented in the arts as they are in other professional occupations (11.6 percent).

The short end of the brush

In the face of the discrimination against both women and minorities, the participation figures are reassuring. Much of the discrimination has been documented. Statistics from a 1972 issue of Time magazine revealed that "in Manhattan, the leading art marketplace, the 100 principal modern art galleries represent about 1,000 artists. Of these, 20 percent are women....The Metropolitan Museum collection of contemporary art includes 10 percent by women. At the Museum of Modern Art women provide 9 percent of the collection; at Washington's Corcoran Gallery, 6 percent....In its 43-year history, the Museum of Modern Art has mounted 1,000 one-artist exhibitions. Only 5 were by women."

In 1978, Ellouise Schoettler and Cynthia Navaretta testified before Congress in connection with funding for the National Endowment for the Arts. In documenting discrimination against women, they complained that, in the fall of 1977, the federally supported National Collection of Fine Arts show, "The Painting and Sculpture of California: the Modern Era," featured only 19 women out of 200 artists.

Because of this long-standing and dismal record, museums have been a frequent feminist target. In a letter to the Human Rights Commission as far back as 1971, Women Artists in Revolution wrote, "Women, who constituted 52.5 percent of the U.S. population and 50 percent of the artist population, made up 60 to 75 percent of art school students. Yet they received only 3 percent of the representation in museums." At the Brooklyn Museum, for example, all its special exhibitions from 1966 to 1970 featured men only. Only male teachers taught in the associated art school. Men had created 89 percent of the acquisitions of paintings and sculpture, and 83 percent of the prints and drawings.

A flat or even downward trend characterized the record of one-person exhibits at three major New York Museums. From 1969 to 1980, at the Guggenheim, MOMA and Whitney, female representation was virtually unchanged, at 0 percent. At MOMA the change went from 0 to 1, with two "high" years of 3 and 2 percent; at the Whitney the percentage actually decreased from 2 to 1 percent, with four intervening "high" years of 3 and 4 percent.

Figures from an article in the winter 1976 issue of Visual Dialog showed that in the decade before 1972, MOMA had 5 female exhibits out of 995; the Los Angeles County Museum had 1 female exhibit out of 52; the Whitney had 8 female exhibits out of 129; and the Corcoran Gallery of Art had 4 female exhibits out of 76 one-person shows. Schoettler's figures indicated less than 2 percent of all shows given for living artists by major museums were for women artists.

There were exceptions, of course. The Guggenheim Museum's 1985 retrospective exhibition of Helen Frankenthaler's 56 "Works on Paper: 1949-1984," is a tribute to a woman artist who held her own among her male contemporaries—Motherwell, DeKooning and Pollack. Critics now commend her as a role model for women, a female artist who was as good or better than the most acclaimed male artists of her time.

Lois Mailou Jones is an artist who, in the '40s, began to deal explicitly with her own background as a black

American. She received national and international recognition through traditional channels: 50 one-person shows of her work, a 1973 retrospective at the Boston Museum and another at the Phillips Collection in Washington, D.C. Work by Jones also hangs at the Corcoran, Hirshhorn, Brooklyn Museum and the Metropolitan. "But," wrote Marcia Newfield in a March/April 1985 New Directions for Women newsletter, "Jones's work, heavily influenced by three decades of intense contact with Haiti and extensive travels in Africa, was not included in the 1984 important show at the Museum of Modern Art on "Primitivism in 20th Century Art." Only two black Americans were represented, both male."

One obvious reason for the paucity of women's artwork previously on display was, in Schoettler's words, that "very few women are to be found working professionally at policy-making levels in the field of art." Even by 1978, no major museum in the United States had a woman as its director.

Demonstrating to gain access

For women artists, it was clear where the problems lay, and feminist groups organized to fight the injustices. Demonstrations in the early '70s did seem to bring results. Picketing the Whitney and MOMA led indirectly to the New York Cultural Center's offer to exhibit what became the "Women Choose Women" exhibit of 1973. The Brooklyn Museum, after many roadblocks, much haggling, and the threat of a demonstration, also made gallery space available in the last half of 1975 for the "Works on Paper—Women Artists" exhibit.

Alice Neel, Sari Dienes, Lil Picard, Irene Moss, Dina Baker, Laura Schecter, Constance Schwartz, June Blum, Buffie Johnson, Ilise Greenstein, Clare Romano, Eunice Golden and Joyce Weinstein were among the 141 artists showcased.

June Blum, who put three years of work into the show, also managed to raise funds to print a catalog. But the museum itself paid for a full color catalog for their concurrent exhibit, "Of Men Only."

For the woman's exhibit, Blum set up a new system of judging artwork to achieve a high standard of quality. She knew women were already too familiar with the traditional male-favoring jury selection process where the artists' names are known and men get chosen. Blum's idea was to ask each artist to choose as her own jurors two women known to her and well-qualified in assessing art. The system worked well for new as well as established artists.

Blind judging

Throughout the art world, women began to pressure traditional institutions to employ blind judging—where the name of the artist is unknown to the judge—in selecting art. This procedure began to bring more women artists into the picture. By 1983, the NEA was using blind judging to award fellowships for composers and jazz artists in the music program, for creative writers in literature and for playwrights in theatre.

Not everyone is in agreement about the usefulness of blind judging, but in many arts—music is a good example—blind auditions have been one of the main reasons why women have been able to move into symphony orchestras.

Gallery space

Difficult as it has been for women to find places for their work on the walls of museums, they haven't fared much better in galleries. A 1979 Women in the Arts survey of 18 leading commercial New York art galleries showed that of those artists represented, only about 10 percent were women. When Ellouise Schoettler and Cynthia Navaretta testified before Congress in 1978, they presented the following figures. Of the National Gallery of Art's 1,800 pieces of sculpture, 5 were by women. Of 2,800 paintings, 55 were by women; of 35,000 works on paper, 603 were by women, and of 17,000 listings in the Design Index, 4,500 were of women. In prestige galleries in major cities, according to Schoettler's testimony, only 15 percent of one-person shows featured women artists.

Another set of 1975 figures comes from several sources and was published in Art Documentation, the Bulletin of the Art Library Society of North America. The 11 galleries selected for study represented in 1975 a total of 215 male and 24 female artists (9.2 percent); in 1977, 205 male and 24 female artists (9.2 percent); and in 1979, 294 male and 42 female artists (also 9.2 percent).

Reviews

The showing of an artist's work is, obviously, crucial to that person's ability to sell works of art and survive as an artist. But economic survival requires not only that an artist's works be exhibited but also reviewed.

An unpublished 1980 study by the New York Chapter of the Women's Caucus for Art examined the number of artists, male and female, reviewed in four major art magazines: Artforum, Art in America, Artnews and Arts Magazine. Quoting again from Art Documentation, "Although each magazine has its own special character, the findings indicated that feature articles heavily favor the male artist. In the case of history shows, women were almost never included, except when the exhibit focused only on women artists. In studies of art movements, women's ideas and contributions were poorly represented. Even most women reviewers did not seek out women artists to discuss."

These 1976, '77, '78 and '79 figures for reviews of women were not much better than they were in 1971 when June Wayne, director of the Tamarind Lithography Workshop in Los Angeles, published a statistical 1970-71 survey of all art magazines and newspapers. That study also revealed that male artists received the overwhelming majority of reviews. A sample of Wayne's statistics: Artnews, 78.6 percent male, Arts Magazine, 82.5 percent male, Artforum, 87.8 percent male; Art in America, 92 percent male; Newsweek, 96.5 percent male.

Men received a similar proportion of line coverage and reproductions of their art work. Wayne's study concluded that "a woman artist who might have spent many years and huge sums of money in order to prepare for and mount her first solo show can only hope to receive, at most, a six-to-eight line review in some art journal."

In her 1975 review article in Signs, Gloria Orenstein said, "It is clear from such statistics that we are being programmed to believe that 85 to 90 percent of our best contemporary art is being produced by men."

Documenting progress

Stressing the need for women to seek answers to such fundamental questions as who decides which artists are exhibited and reviewed, she added, "It is from these reviews that art history is written."

Orenstein insisted, "Women artists in collaboration with feminist critics must pressure museums and galleries to change their policies. Feminist art historians must document women's art history...through bibliographies, articles, books, new textbooks, videotapes, film exhibitions, panel discussions, conferences and the creation of museums and galleries where women can exhibit their works..."

Seven years later, Paula Chiarmonte, art historian and art librarian, and editor of Art Documentation, seconded that view: "I am very concerned about the lack of critical documentation on contemporary women artists. Generations of scholars to come will have as much difficulty as we, in the past 20 years, have had in rewriting art history. Even if women succeed in being represented by a gallery and having exhibits, there is no guarantee that the media will publicize and review their work, especially since much of contemporary women's art has evolved outside of the mainstream....Women cannot afford to rest until there is better representation of women's art in galleries, museums and pages of art journals."

Trouble in academia

How many women study art? Eleanor Dickinson, a professor of art at California College of Arts and Crafts, testified in 1978 before the State of California Commission on the Status of Women. She quoted statistics gathered with great difficulty from a variety of sources: In 1976, equal numbers of men and women graduated with degrees in art and in 1977 men and women received master of fine arts degrees in equal numbers. Yet women were hired for only 12 percent of faculty jobs in studio art, which require evidence of exhibits and other visible signs of success—the art world's equivalent of "publish or perish."

In 1978, women, according to Schoettler, received 50 percent of Ph.D.s in art history but held only 22 percent of all positions in that field and only 14 percent of tenured positions. The top level faculty were still virtually all men.

In the early '70s, college art department chairmen were 100 percent male. Men held 86 percent of full professorships, 87 percent of associate professorships, 74 percent of assistant professorships and 67 percent of instructor posts.

During the same years in college art history departments, 95 percent were men, including 89 percent of the full professors.

In 1973, statistics published by Ann Sutherland Harris showed irrefutably that women were discriminated against at all levels in the academic world. Thirty percent of Ph.D.s in art history went to women. But the proportion of women subsequently at the rank of full professor was far from what would be expected: around 25 percent, as a modest estimate. Instead, the statistics of the Women's Caucus of the College Art Association, based on a survey of 1970 and 1971 catalogs of 164 art departments and accredited institutions in the U.S., showed that women held only 11.1 percent of the full professorships, 17.5 percent of associate professorships and 23 percent of instructorships. A still lower proportion of women taught art studio courses. By 1975, men held an even higher percentage of full professorships: over 90 percent.

As Gloria Orenstein stated in her Signs review article, "Since women are rare in the higher ranks of the academic community, women students are being denied the opportunity of encountering role models who might

encourage them to take themselves seriously as scholars
and artists."
Dance is the only exception to this general rule.

Low end of the wage scale

Even when women did make it to the higher academic
ranks, they earned less than their male colleagues. 1975
college faculty salaries in all fields showed male professors
making $27,650 while females made $24,740. That same
year the average difference in earnings between male and
female faculty in two-year colleges was $1,600; in four-year
colleges, $2,538; and in universities, $4,300.

A 1978 survey of American institutions granting the
M.F.A. degree, by Janice Koenig Ross and Linda
L. Trentham for the College Art Association, found that
men held 88 percent of full-time faculty jobs, while women
held 12 percent. For part-time faculty jobs, the figure was
76 percent for men, 24 percent for women.

A 1978 American Association of University Professors
study showed that the art faculty figures were no fluke. It
revealed that deans of U.S. colleges were 82 percent men;
33 percent of the colleges had no female deans; full
professors were 92 percent men; tenured positions were 84
percent men; and full-time college faculty were 75 percent
men.

In many cases the amount of progress women made
from the early to late '70s can be exemplified by a
comparison of the figures at the San Francisco Art
Institute. In 1972, 50 men and nine women were on the
faculty; in 1978, 55 men and 15 women.

One might feel justified in taking hope from a
comment by Rose Weil, executive secretary of the College
Art Association, that in 1980 "hiring patterns tend to be
fairly close to equitable." However, artist Joyce Kozloff,
who visits art departments around the country, said in a
1980 article by Grace Glueck in Artnews, "Women are
usually hired on a part-time basis. The slots for women
were formed in the early 1970s when the feminist ferment
began....But it was set up very cynically, so that women

would be in and out the door. They knew it would all blow over."

Muriel Magenta's article, "Feminist Art Criticism: a Political Definition," first published in 1981, deals with the situation in higher education: "The feminist art movement has been less successful in placing women in the academic establishment. The ratio of females to males on college and university art faculties remains low despite federal and state affirmative action guidelines."

But 1983-84 figures from the CAA Women's Caucus showed that, indeed, things had improved. While "a greater percentage of men than women are employed full time," more women are being hired. In studio positions, 36 percent of the job applicants were women, and 53 percent of those hired were women. In art history, 55 percent of the applicants were women, and 68 percent of those hired were women. Comparable figures for salaries are not available.

Women's income from art

The situation in art education is a large part of the overall economic picture for women. Women artists must have access to teaching jobs in order to support themselves and yet they are still clearly at a disadvantage in terms of earning power.

"Their economic status in the art world," commented Muriel Magenta, "reflects the lesser value society at large still places on goods and services produced by women."

NEA figures in 1970 showed women artists, both visual and performance, had median earnings of $3,400 per year; male artists earned $9,500 per year.

In 1976, while women artists were earning $4,000 per year, male artists were earning $10,000 per year.

Women are making inroads into art administration, but here again, their salaries are lower than those of men holding comparable positions. According to Bill Dawson, executive director of the Association of College, University and Community Arts Administrators, "the compensation gap has not narrowed." The 1983 ACUCAA study shows that while the average salary of all full-time arts administrators is 20 percent higher than two years ago, the mean salary for full-time administrators who are male is $31,940 and for females, $22,615.

There are differences in every age group. For the 20 to 29 group, women's salaries are 20 percent lower; in the 30 to 39 group, women's salaries are 16 percent lower; in the 40 to 49 group, women's salaries are 35 percent lower; in the 50 to 59 group, women's salaries are 43 percent lower; and in the 60 plus group, women's salaries are 31 percent lower.

Women earn less even when level of education, number of years in the field and level of the position are accounted for.

In other words, the salary gap remains constant when comparing salaries of both males and females of the same age, level of education, experience and administrative position. Women earn significantly less than men. Overall, the figure is 29 percent less.

These figures confirm that there has been little change from the situation revealed in the 1974 "Museums USA," published by the NEA. It showed that "museum directors are most often male, white, 40 years of age or older." Male directors of museums earn almost twice as much as women in this position, an average of $16,000, compared with $8,000. One reason for this, the report said, was "the high proportion of men among directors of large-budget institutions." But even at small museums, there was a consistent $2,000 to $3,000 difference.

Moving into administration

Women are moving into higher echelon jobs. By 1978, a growing number of small and medium-sized museums had women directors, though none of the major museums did. Anne D'Harnoncourt, director of the Philadelphia Museum of Art, Jan Muhlert, director of the Amon Carter Museum in Fort Worth, Suzanne Delehanty at the Philadelphia Institute of Contemporary Art, Lisa Taylor at the Cooper-Hewitt Museum in New York, Susan Stiff at the Museum at Stony Brook, Long Island, Joy Ungereleider at the Jewish Museum, and the late Katherine Mead at

Madison, Wisconsin's Elvehjem Museum of Art are examples.

By 1978 also, women held more top curatorial positions than ever before, up from the 325 calculated by a survey on museum personnel taken for the National Endowment for the Arts in 1973. For years, custom decreed that men would curate sculpture and major paintings, while women got drawings and prints. But now women are moving into all curator positions.

The proportion of women in top positions, however, drops sharply from 46 percent in museums with budgets under $50,000 to 2 percent in museums with budgets over $250,000. In 1973, the Association of Art Museum Directors, an invitational organization that extends membership to art museums it considers "major,"—those with budgets of $250,000 or more—had 125 members. Only five of them were women.

According to Kendall Taylor, arts professor and director of Arts Management Associates, "Most women who have broken into directorships have been hired to head small museums or museums that have had a troubled history. Or they have been on the spot when the directorship opened—perhaps in an acting director capacity or as an administrator or curator. A few were connected with a particular institution through family wealth, association or perceived professional influence."

In 1984, the American Association of Museum Directors had 182 members, 19 of them, or about 10 percent, women. Of 135 active members, 9, or 6 percent, were women. Of associate members 20 percent were women.

Museum boards, who do the hiring, are changing as old board members retire and women professionals take their place. One indication of women's determination to move into museum administration is the increased numbers enrolling in museum management training schools, workshops and seminars.

Problems at the top

Though women are unquestionably moving into middle and top management positions, there are still problems, as Kendall Taylor pointed out: among them, being patronized by men. More than 25 percent of women in a Gallup poll said that, "on the whole, their life and work experience was still largely undervalued and that men all too frequently did not take them seriously." Younger women in particular complained that men often exhibited resentment and had difficulty taking orders from them. They described compromises with personal life as tremendously taxing, to the point that many women executives frequently chose to stay single or become separated or divorced. "Less than half, 48 percent, of female executives Gallup polled had ever had children....The married woman museum director, returning home late from her institution, may still feel she has to put something together for dinner. And if she has children, the responsibilities are manifold. In contrast, male counterparts frequently have a spouse at home who can provide that support base. It makes a difference," wrote Taylor.

Taylor's prediction: "Within this century the male-dominated leadership of America's museums will become a phenomenon of the past." In her February 1985 article in Museum News, she profiled women museum executives such as Juliana Force at the Whitney Museum, Ellen Johnson at Oberlin College in Ohio, Dorothy Miller in the Museum of Modern Art, Hilla Rebay at the Guggenheim, Susan Bertram of Museums Collaborative, Inc., Bettye Collier-Thomas at the Mary McLeod Bethune Museum and National Archives for Black Women's History, Edith Tonelli at UCLA, and Mary Schmidt Campbell at the Studio Museum in Harlem.

The Tucker touch

Arts Management named Marcia Tucker, director of the New Museum of Contemporary Art in New York City, the 1982-83 Arts Administrator of the Year. Cited for outstanding achievement, she was also praised for her "radical, yet highly effective mode of operation." All senior staff members, including the director, are paid the same salary and each individual participates on an equal basis in the decision-making process. A co-worker said, "We've all benefited from her creative approach to administration. Her unique style of participatory administration serves the museum well and might very well serve as a model for other arts organizations."

In addition to making an impact on traditional institutions, Magenta said, "Local feminist art organizations and the national organizations are sponsoring art marketing workshops and business seminars specifically tailored for women art professionals.

"They are also contacting corporations about art purchasing programs and apprising them of the availability of the work of women artists on local and national levels. Women collectors, whom the feminists refer to as matrons of art, are being encouraged to purchase and commission the work of women artists."

Women and funding

The availability of funding for women artists often means the difference between surviving as an artist or taking another job. The NEA, established to provide the best of the art produced in this country with a forum before the public, thus plays a large role in artists' economic survival. In 1970, the NEA awarded 20 visual arts fellowships, all but two of which went to men. Schoettler's 1978 figures indicated that 23 percent of the NEA fellowships for artists went to women.

Among other awards, the NEA nominates artists for public commissions under the General Services Administration's Art in Architecture program. The 1978 figures showed only 10 percent of all those major commissions went to women. Although in 1977-78, the nominating panels selected 73 men and 25 women, "it is more revealing that 216 men were considered and only 60 women," Schoettler testified.

The NEA has been criticized by various women's groups for the low percentage of women on the panels that nominate artists for awards. In 1977, for example, women composed 23 percent of the music panel; 61 percent of the dance panel; 13 percent of the literature panel; 18 percent of the museum panel; 12 percent of the theater panel; and 30 percent of the visual arts panel.

However, in her 1981 testimony protesting proposed NEA budget cutbacks, Schoettler applauded the NEA for being "extremely responsive to the concerns and efforts of women in the arts," itemized the specific grants that had helped women artists, and urged Congress to approve full funding for the agency.

Other funding organizations also becoming more responsive to women were the Ford Foundation which, in 1982, more than doubled its grants to women's activities, from $4 million to $9 million a year.

In 1983, arts groups were encouraged by the formation of the major, independent National Arts Stablization Fund, established with an initial commitment of $9 million from the Ford, Andrew W. Mellon and Rockefeller foundations. It is expected to grow into a $25 million fund with additional grants from other national sources to help recipients either liquidate accumulated deficits or build a working capital reserve. Some 100 arts groups will receive grants ranging from $150,000 to $1 million over a five-year period.

In addition the U.S. Conference of Mayors, one of the first organizations of elected officials to develop a specific arts program, last year published a major new study on cities and the arts, providing city officials with examples of the arts-boosting strategies available to them. The conference supports the National Heritage Resource Act introduced in Congress by Congressional Arts Caucus Chairman Thomas J. Downey (D-N.Y.).

The 184-member caucus recently added House Speaker Tip O'Neill to its executive board, which has been in the forefront of the battle for increased federal funding for the NEA and new legislation benefiting the arts.

State officials and legislators are also becoming actively interested in arts funding and the National Conference of State Legislatures has shown its concern.

Corporate support

Business has too. Corporate donations to the arts in
1982 increased over the previous year. Several major
surveys on corporate giving show new marketing programs
aimed at the arts, and some major grants and gifts to
cultural groups.

On the other hand, recent upheavals in corporate
boardrooms around the nation, coupled with diminishing
government support for the arts, is leading arts groups to
fear that their share of corporate charity may
diminish. Exxon Corp., the largest corporate philanthropist,
for example, in 1983 shifted more than $3 million from arts
and public television to health and social welfare. And a
spokesman for the Philip Morris Company said, "With the
Reagan Administration asking companies to do more in
social services, it will be harder to justify cultural.
programs."

Meanwhile, in 1984, numerous arts groups undertook
campaigns to raise endowment funds, with some cultural
institutions in a single city joining forces.

Reagan's budget

Early in 1985, Reagan requested $144.5 million for
the NEA for fiscal 1986. That figure was $500,000 more
than he sought for the 1985 fiscal year, but almost 12
percent less than the $163.7 million appropriated by
Congress. Because of their concern about the federal deficit,
it is quite possible Congress may not fight the proposed
cut. Inevitably, theatre, opera, music, and dance groups,
which in the past relied heavily on government grants, say
they would suffer. While large dance companies and the
more experimental ones seem to get funded, "the companies
in the middle who have been working in the grass roots
area are being passed over," according to Joan Woodbury, a
dancer in Salt Lake City, Utah.

Dance: A Unique Position

There is absolutely no argument about the explosion of interest in dance since the 1960s. Many have called it a dance boom. The 1979 Dance Catalog, edited by Nancy Reynolds, reported the existence of more than 850 performing companies (amateur and professional) and "countless other groups giving occasional recitals."

As early as 1971, the Wall Street Journal recognized the dance phenomenon when it reported, "The nation boasts 250 civic or regional dance companies, 10 times the number 15 years before. As the government's leading cultural export," 16 companies visited 10 countries and presented 160 original works in 1970.

Foundation support

Leila Sussman, a sociologist at Tufts University, observed that the growth of ballet companies, funded by the Ford Foundation, grew far faster than modern dance companies during the '60s, but modern dance groups, funded by the National Endowment for the Arts, pulled even by 1980.

Foundations have been lavish in their support of dance. Even back in '78, federal funding amounted to $7 million annually, and corporations and private foundations, particularly Ford, have been equally generous.

Dance has never been a high-paying art, perhaps because of the traditionally high preponderance of women in it. In 1971, men and women dancers were the lowest paid of performing artists, earning on average less than $5,000 a year. In the 1971-1972 NEA publication, "New Dimensions for the Arts," it was conceded that dance "continues to suffer, in spite of growth and recognition, from a financial insecurity which in many instances threatens its very existence."

And it hasn't improved greatly since. Genevieve Oswald, curator of the dance collection at the New York Public Library, said women dancers are "vastly underpaid and greatly underrated." This is in marked contrast to other professional athletes such as tennis players. Men and women have to go on unemployment as dance companies struggle to survive. According to a recent survey by the Labor Institute for Human Enrichment, 76 percent of professional dancers of both sexes experienced some unemployment in 1980, compared with 18 percent for other members of the labor force. Few other arts demand so many years of training (at least 10) and offer such short-lived careers.

The televising of staged productions has obviously been one factor in popularizing dance. And the interest of young people may be explained by the vigorous nature of dance and renewed interest in physical fitness. Whatever the reasons, dance concerts on college and university campuses are more popular than rock concerts, Dance Catalog editor Reynolds claimed.

A growing audience

"In 10 years," she noted, "audience attendance has increased an incredible 1,500 percent; in 1978, the year in which the United States Post Office issued four dance stamps and the president declared a National Dance Week, it was expected to reach 25 million." In 1984, according to a survey by Louis Harris and Associates, it reached 58 million.

Today, movies about dancing and dancers make big money by appealing especially to young people. At the 1984 Olympic Arts Festival in Los Angeles, dance events contributed 46 percent of ticket revenues, and though dance events made up only 18 percent of the programs, they brought in 38 percent of the performing arts audiences, according to Anna Kisselgoff in The New York Times.

A report by Dance/USA, the national service organization for professional dance companies, showed that in 1983-84, total income for nine designated ballet companies had increased 352 percent since 1970-71.

Have women benefited?

But what has the boom meant for women, for feminists? Reynolds takes an optimistic view of new employment opportunities "in administration, therapy,

notation, filmmaking, clothing manufacture, entertainment
law, college teaching, photography, journalism, recording,
grant writing, consultation, television, book editing, studio
or company management, research, scholarship, archiving
and much more—all with a dance orientation for which
there was no demand just a few years ago."

But in the academic world, according to Gill Miller,
chairwoman of the Department of Dance at Denison
University in Granville, Ohio, not that much has
changed. "Dance is usually the last of the arts to be
recognized as legitimate on college campuses." In addition,
many campuses do not have dance departments, some
campuses "pay lip service to it, allowing classes to be held
but not assigning academic credit to them," and often
courses are part of physical education or theatre
departments, usually under a male chair.

"If a dance department does exist," said Miller, "the
chair is often the only female in the midst of an old boys
network. Theatre, music and art department chairpersons
and deans of fine arts are generally men. Provosts,
academic deans and presidents are usually men.

"Unlike all the other arts," Miller explained, "there is
no published, tangible, fixed means or product at the end of
months and months of laboratory work that can be
submitted for tenure decisions. While dance notation could
serve as proof that a piece was done, it is a second skill
altogether, very time consuming and very expensive."

Miller also questions other opportunities: "At the top,
in large companies, those well-paying jobs are all held by
men. In small companies (local, regional modern dance, for
example), those jobs are held by women, but are volunteer
or very very low-paying: $4,000 per year salary for
executive directorships and the like. And all in all, the
mark of success of a small company is (still) getting the
named [male] partner in the big law firm to head the board
of directors. If the women artists can get the men
professionals to give them their stamp of approval, then
and only then are they successful."

The situation for women dancers today is even
stranger when you consider that the history of dance has
been written by women—a contrast to the situation in the

visual arts, music, theatre and literature, in which most of
the visible and successful artists have been men. When
women in these latter fields organized their own alternative
institutions, it was, as Leslie Satin noted in the <u>Guide to
Women's Art Organizations</u>," a strategy against the male
establishment."

"The only art in which women did not have to fight for
a position," Satin went on, "was dance...." Women dancers
and choreographers, from Loie Fuller to Agnes De Mille,
were the figures of prominence and authority in the dance
world.

Oswald declared, "Women have been so commanding
a force in dance—as creators, company directors,
administrators, performers, even cultural symbols—that it
is hard to imagine how they might be more prominent than
they already are."

In 1977, 85 percent of all dancers were women, a
situation not paralleled in any other art. As Satin pointed
out, "There was no need to band together for strength in
numbers."

In modern dance, women choreographers pretty much
held the field, at least until recent years. The 1979 <u>Guide to
Women's Art Organizations</u> listed 91 women
choreographers. Not all of them were feminists exploring
the personal themes prevalent in the other arts, themes of
women's politics and sensibilities, but many were.

Men move in

In recent years, however, men have moved into dance
as women have moved into formerly male-dominated art
fields. The downside, according to Miller, is that men use
women. Often ballerinas have neither artistic control nor
comparable salaries.

The past decade has witnessed the growing
prominence and authority of superb male dancers.
Examples are Edward Villella and Jacques d'Amboise, who,
according to Reynolds, "laid the groundwork for American
men in ballet," and the "dynamic Russians, Rudolf Nureyev
and Mikhail Baryshnikov, who have made a tremendous

difference." Writing in The New York Times, Kisselgoff declared: "The age of the ballerina is over."

As choreographers, men such as Cunningham, Gordon, Robbins, Nikolais, Louis, Ailey, Joffrey and Taylor have hit the big time, reaping the rewards of 20 years of effort. Twyla Tharp is the only woman who stands out in this masculine company, not only for her sex but for her ability.

A hot commodity

In a 1984 article in Dance Magazine, David Vaughn described her as a "hot commodity." He explained why: "With two new American Ballet Theatre ballets and an upcoming collaboration with Jerome Robbins, this modern dance innovator is breeding a new American Classicism."

Over the previous year, in addition to the two dances for the ABT, Tharp had worked with her own company as a choreographer and dancer, and staged the opera sequences for the film "Amadeus." No one, wrote Vaughn, "has choreographed more brilliantly for Baryshnikov." An example is her choreography for Baryshnikov and Gregory Hines in the 1985 Hollywood film, "White Nights."

The number of women choreographers in ballet and modern dance is large. And they're not all in New York. But Tharp, because she works in ballet, has gotten more recognition. Martha Graham, now 91, is, of course, in a class by herself. Her company opened a three-week season in New York in March 1985. Another nonagenarian is Hanya Holm, a recent choreographic award winner, who still teaches dance.

Women have been recognized by Dance Magazine's annual awards to both men and women "who have made important contributions to the field of dance." Heather Watts, of the New York City Ballet, was the only woman to receive an award in 1985. Alexandra Danilova received an award in 1984, Martine van Hamel in 1983, Laura Dean in 1982, and Selma Jeanne Cohen and Twyla Tharp in 1981. Between 1980 and 1972, eight other women were honored. But with 46 men receiving Dance Magazine Awards between 1972 and 1984, the percentage of women winning was about one third, hardly comparable to their numbers in the field.

In April 1985, however, about 64 NEA fellowships went to women, compared to 43 to men. Figures on how many of each sex applied are not available.

Women have been prominent as dance critics, not only in New York but all over the country. Kisselgoff has been mentioned, but others are Arlene Croche and Deborah Jowett.

Despite obvious successes on the part of women, a more or less steady reading of The New York Times Sunday Arts and Leisure Section over the last year and a half brings one to the conclusion that men as choreographers and performers are either doing most of the interesting work these days, or are getting the lion's share of the publicity.

Music: Muted Progress

As writer Elizabeth Wood pointed out in her 1980 Signs essay, "Women have had greater difficulty than their male colleagues in gaining commissions, performances, recordings and publication of their work." Throughout the 1970s and early '80s, nevertheless, women have made a significant impact on traditional musical institutions.

In a 1979 article, "American Women Composers," in Music Educators Journal, Jeannie G. Pool wrote, "the history of women in music is beginning to appear in music history textbooks."

The 100-year-old Grove's Dictionary of Music and Musicians-- the major encyclopedia of music in English—had never included an article on women and music until Judith Tick, a pioneer in women's studies in music, completed the first such article for the 1985 volume.

Girls play well; boys have careers

In her 1983 article in Music Educators Journal, Donna Pucciani wrote: "Girls are encouraged during their education to excel in music as students while boys are discouraged from many musical endeavors at the risk of being labeled effeminate. Yet when it comes to careers in music, it is the young men who are encouraged to pursue ambitious career goals, while women are discouraged from high professional aspirations."

In addition, Pucciani points out, the lack of male role models in elementary and vocal music and the lack of female role models in secondary school music, particularly in instrumental music and supervisory positions, "also reinforces stereotypes that limit the potential of students."

Pucciani reviewed 14 studies of sexism in educational materials, curriculum, guidance counseling, teacher behavior and teacher training and role models. They showed that "within the past ten years there has been a renaissance of scholarship" on women's contributions as performers and composers, but "Very little has been done to analyze the crucial role of the music education in reinforcing and perpetuating the bias against women."

The obvious cause of the lack of female role models for aspiring female musicians is sexism in hiring practices. Yet, Pucianni charged, "music education apparently considers sexism a non-issue."

Few women on faculties

In higher education the problems are compounded. Statistical studies by the National Association of Schools of Music compared numbers of women on music faculties for 1973-74, 1980-81, and 1981-82. The results showed that there was slight improvement and then a downturn in percentages of women on music faculties.

In private institutions in 1973-74, women comprised 24 percent of the faculty; in 1980-81, 29 percent; and in 1981-82, 27 percent.

In public institutions in 1973-74, women comprised 20 percent of the faculty; in 1980-81, 27 percent; and in 1981-82, 21 percent.

The lowest percentage of women was found on faculties in institutions that granted the doctorate degree: 19 percent in 1973-74 compared to 23 percent in 1980-81 and 21 percent in 1981-82.

After detailing similar statistics in their own report, the College Music Society concluded: "It is apparent that the status of women in college music is not improving. Regardless of the increasing number of qualified women within the field...the opportunities for appointment appear to be increasing only at the lowest levels, especially within the ranks which do not lead to advancement." This despite increasing numbers of women earning advanced degrees. Statistics from Judith Tick's Grove Dictionary article on women in music show that in 1979-80 women earned 28.3 percent of Ph.D. degrees, compared to 14.7 percent in 1969-70, and half the master's degrees, compared to 47.4 percent in 1969-70.

Given the demographics of a decline in the college-age population, noted the College Music Society report, opportunities for women in education can only be expected to decrease. While a two-year study cannot be used as the basis for a trend, the authors pointed out, the figures provided evidence that "women in college music, although qualified, are under-appointed and under-promoted." The CMS elected its first woman president in 1981.

Breaking the symphony orchestra barrier

"Women are breaking the symphonic barriers," headlined a 1983 New York Times article by Donal Henahan (based on an article written by Phyllis Lehmann and published in Symphony Magazine in December 1982.) Noting that symphony orchestras were once the "musical equivalent of the all male club," he recounted the increasing acceptance of women. Still much of the progress has been very recent, and it was threatened by the recession of the early 1980s.

According to a survey by the Labor Institute for Human Enrichment, 61 percent of singers and 35 percent of musicians experienced some unemployment in 1980, compared to 181 percent for other members of the labor force.

In 1983, 13 years after hiring their first woman player, the New York Philharmonic numbered 18 women among its 105 regular members. Judith LeClair, a bassoonist, was the first woman to hold a principal chair in

that organization. Among other orchestras with women as
principal chairs are the St. Louis Symphony (trumpet) and
the Cincinnati Symphony (bass trombone).

A gloomier picture

The situation for black women in classical music was
much gloomier. Charlotte Davis, a violinist with the
National Symphony Orchestra in 1983, was one of only a
handful of black instrumentalists. However, a number of
black women singers frequently grace concert stages and
they have had success in opera, jazz and popular music.

The Minority Artists' Project offered its first concert
series in conjunction with the College of Charleston and the
Piccolo Spoleto Festival in 1979. In 1984, reported the
International League of Women Composers Newsletter,
Piccolo Spoleto featured works by contemporary women and
minority American composers. The Piccolo Spoleto concert
was dedicated to composer Vally Weigl and her son,
John. The Weigl Archive, housed at the Albert Simons Fine
Arts Center of the College of Charleston, is a collection of
works chiefly by women and minority composers.

According to Lehmann's article, quoting American
Symphony Orchestra League statistics, 40 percent of the
musicians regularly employed by major, regional and
metropolitan orchestras in 1980-81 were women. (Major
orchestras have an annual operating budget above 3.25
million; regionals from $900,000 to $3.5 million; and
metropolitans from $250,000 to $900,000.) Five years
previously the figure was 35 percent, and in 1965, only 28
percent.

Other statistics indicated that roughly half the
musicians in regional and metropolitan orchestras are
women. An example is the Oregon Symphony whose 83
members include 41 women.

The figure for the major orchestras is only 26 percent;
nine of the majors employed less than 25 percent; none of
the top five employed more than 15 percent. In the
remaining major orchestras, women comprised from 30 to
40 percent. In other words, the higher the prestige and

budget associated with the organization, the higher the ratio of men to women in all positions.

Lehmann explained that one reason for fewer women in the major orchestras was the fact that those orchestras have male European conductors, traditionally opposed to the hiring of women. (The Berlin Philharmonic admitted a woman musician for the first time in its 100-year history only in 1982.)

One music director of a major orchestra who objected to the influx of females was heard to remark that "all these women on stage make it look like a kitchen." Other conductors confided that they feared women musicians would be offended by male musicians' harsh language.

Playing musical chairs

Women's progress is real but patchy. 1980-81 figures showed no unusual progress by women in obtaining principal chair positions. Opportunities for women as concertmasters, brass and percussion players haven't greatly increased either. In 1982 no women held concertmaster (concertmistress?) positions in major symphony orchestras, although Jean Ingraham succeeded as a freelance concertmaster in New York. Eleanor Shapiro was the orchestra manager for the Syracuse Symphony, Joan Briccetti for the St. Louis Symphony Orchestra, and Deborah Borda for the San Francisco Symphony.

Many people credit new support systems by and for women for enabling them to develop skills and strategies for coping in such a competitive career field. But the system of blind or screened auditions, insisted upon by women, probably made the most difference. According to Lehmann, "most of the top orchestra jobs today are filled through open, national auditions that are designed, literally, to screen out prejudice on the basis of sex, race, age or physical appearance. In a majority of these orchestras, applicants perform hidden from view, at least through the preliminaries. Carpet muffles even the sound of telltale footsteps."

A few major orchestras, such as the Denver and Houston symphonies, use blind auditions through the finals as well. When the potential for bias is eliminated, women are frequently the winners—"to the chagrin of some men," said Lehmann.

On the other hand, "hiring is still concentrated in the hands of predominantly male audition committees, male conductors and male management," Lehmann wrote.

There should also be anonymity in competitions, something Nancy Van de Vate, founder of the International League of Women Composers, called "of crucial importance and something women should insist on."

Not surprisingly, opportunities for women remain much greater in regional and metropolitan orchestras where frequent turnovers occur as musicians work up to the majors. But the numbers gap is also a reflection of a society in which the woman's career is considered secondary. The dedication required to play in the major orchestras is so all-consuming that women have traditionally felt they could not sacrifice home and family life for it.

A climate for babies

In the new climate of acceptance, however, even maternity is no longer taboo. In 1981, at least seven pregnant women played in one Carnegie Hall concert by the Detroit Symphony, without apparent harm to the music, said Henahan. In fact, one sign of American women's orchestral progress is the increasing willingness to spell out maternity-leave policy in union contracts. Orchestras can no longer revoke the contract of a woman who becomes pregnant or force her at a certain point in her pregnancy to take a leave without pay.

The Women's Caucus of the International Conference of Symphony and Opera Musicians, through their publication, Senza Sordino, advocates the availability of child care as well as maternity leave and insurance coverage. "The fact that women bear babies and men don't does not mean that working is a privilege for women and a right for men. The problems of raising the next generation are the concern for all society and not just of females," the publication declared.

That is indeed a far cry from 34 years ago when a Boston Herald music critic could comment on Doriot Anthony Dwyer's debut as principal flutist of the Boston Symphony with: "...the breaking of a tradition considerably older than the mere 72 years of the Boston Symphony seems to me a serious matter and I am not a little dismayed by it."

As opera singers, women have long been prominent, but as decision makers in opera companies, Beverly Sills broke new ground when she became head of the New York City Opera in 1980.

Women's work: composing

Wrote Pool in her 1979 article, "America's Women Composers," in Music Educators Journal: "Attitudes are changing as a result of the strong women's movement of the last ten years and, although prejudice still exists, more works by women are being performed, published and recorded..."

Indeed, as composers, women have faced nearly insurmountable obstacles. Yet their progress in the '70s has been astonishing, in spite of the fact that they have not had equal access to commissions, grants, recordings, academic posts and major orchestra and opera performances. In 1970 the National Federation of Music Clubs, for the first time since 1936, published a Directory of American Women Composers.

As Laura Van Tuyl wrote in October 1985 in The Christian Science Monitor, "During the past 10 years, women have entered the ranks of composers seemingly from nowhere. Opportunities for getting published, performed and recorded have never been better. Two women composers now have residencies with major symphonies, and have a good chance of getting their music performed. And Broadcast Music Incorporated, the world's largest performance rights organization, says the number of royalty payments it has made to women composers of serious music has doubled since 1977."

Van de Vate told Carol Neuls-Bates, "Yes, absolutely, the climate is changing! Women composers are becoming more assertive about themselves all the time, and are

receiving more performances of their works. We still,
however, lag very much behind men in the important areas
of orchestral performances, commissions and grants,
competitions and recordings. We still need to fully integrate
ourselves into the musical mainstream."

Few women composers hold academic positions, for
example. In 1975, noted Van de Vate, the College Music
Society conference on the status of women reported "only
67 women were teaching composition in the entire United
States, and my impression is that the situation isn't any
better now." In fact, the College Music Society in 1975-76
found 10.6 percent women teaching composition compared
to 5.8 percent in 1972-74.

Quoting from Tick's article for the New Grove
Dictionary, "In 1973, Louise Talma became the first, and
in 1975 Miriam Gideon became the second woman
composer to be elected to the American Academy and
Institute of Arts and Letters. Barbara Kolb won the Rome
Prize Fellowship in 1969 and received major orchestral
performances in the 1970s."

Musical big time

In her 1980 review essay in Signs, Elizabeth Wood
stated: "Few works by women have been performed by
major orchestras; few are recorded; few women gain
positions which sustain creative freedom."

Indeed, until 1983, no woman had ever won the most
prestigious award in the field, a Pulitzer Prize for music
composition. The first woman winner, Ellen Taaffe Zwilich,
was honored for her "Symphony Number 1." This was a
second first for Zwilich, who had been the first woman to
receive a doctoral degree in composition from the Juilliard
School.

She credited the publicity she earned as the first
female recipient of the Pulitzer with encouraging more
people to look at her music. In fact, a number of American
orchestras since then have expressed interest in her works,
to the point where she has had to turn down
commissions. She has even appeared on national television.

In the fall of 1984, her winning composition was

performed by symphony orchestras in Oregon, Pittsburgh and Indianapolis and an album of her music was recorded on the New World Label.

Still Zwilich is an exception, according to Van Tuyl, writing in the Christian Science Monitor. "Women composers are still really a novelty," said Marjorie Merryman, a composer and assistant professor at Boston University."

Zwilich's agent told Van Tuyl that virtually no composers today are able to make a living from composing alone. Thus women are finding more opportunities just at a time when contemporary music is less in demand.

In 1972, Laurie Spiegel's electronic piece traveled to Jupiter on Pioneer 10. And in the '80s, a number of women besides Zwilich have gained a measure of recognition as composers. Marga Richter's chamber music and orchestral works have been heard throughout the nation; Joan Tower, a pianist with the Da Capo Chamber Players, received a Guggenheim Fellowship; Judith Zaimont recorded a song cycle, "Greyed Sonnets;" Barbara Kolb recorded several major works and had her music performed by the New York Philharmonic and the Chamber Music Society of Lincoln Center; Elaine Barkin, a serialist composer, received acclaim for her "String Quartet."

Opera composer Thea Musgrove premiered her work about Harriet Tubman in Norfolk, Virginia, March 1, 1985. The opera, "Harriet: The Woman Called Moses," recounted the struggles of the woman who set up the underground railroad for fleeing slaves. It was commissioned by the Royal Opera House of London and the Virginia Opera Association.

Avant-garde composers

According to Jeannie G. Pool, in a 1979 Music Educators Journal article, women have also made outstanding contributions to electronic and avant-garde music. Alice Shields, Pril Smiley, Daria Semegen, Pauline Oliveros, Jean Eichelberger Ivey, Netty Simons, Ann

McMillan and Ruth Anderson "are all respected electronic music composers."

Pool added women prominent in the recent surge of multimedia and intermedia experimentation: Joan La Barbara, Beth Anderson, Doris Hays and Annea Lockwood. And Laurie Anderson was recently described in a New York Times article as the "best-known American performance artist." A trained classical violinist, she had commissioned work performed by the American Composers Orchestra and has had recent success with the rock music audience.

In 1976, the 11-concert series, "Meet the Woman Composer," offered at the New School for Social Research, showcased woman composers for the first time ever. It was organized by composers Doris Hays and Beth Anderson, who also served as concert administrators and music programmers, positions seldom filled by women.

Eighteen composers, including Nancy Van De Vate, took part in the event, conceived, planned and executed by women only. It was calculated to bring women composers out of the closet. No longer would they have to use first initials when submitting their works as did Van de Vate. When she appeared in person before the conductor who had scheduled a performance of one of her early orchestral works bylined "N. Van de Vate," he asked, "Where's your husband?"

The fact that such subterfuges are no longer required benefits all women, especially younger ones. Pamela Marshall, a 1976 graduate of the Eastman School of Music, said that she never felt that the field of composition was closed to her because she was female. She was quoted by Ruth Julius in the Feminist Art Journal, summer 1977.

In 1978-81, Katherine Hoover's Festivals of Women's Music brought three or four concerts a year of chamber, choral and electronic works to Manhattan music lovers. In 1979 the American Women Composers produced an eight-event series at La Guardia Community College. In the fall of 1985, Boston University and the Massachusetts chapter of American Women Composers sponsored the Women's Music Festival, the largest ever in New England. Concerts like these make it possible for many people to hear women's music. Said Elizabeth Vercoe, a composer and co-director of the festival, "There is a great deal of music that is well worth hearing."

Conducting: the last bastion

Women have been virtually shut out of permanent positions as orchestra conductors, which Lehmann calls "the last bastion of male supremacy." A number of talented women today are beginning to batter down the bastions.

Eve Queler left the New York City Opera after five years as assistant conductor because director Julius Rudel would not allow her to conduct. In 1976, she was the first woman to conduct the Philadelphia Orchestra.

Victoria Bond, still in her 30s, already has a string of firsts: first and only woman to receive a doctorate in conducting from the Juilliard School, first woman appointed to the conducting staff of a major orchestra, the Pittsburgh Symphony, via an Exxon/Arts Endowment grant. In 1985 she conducted the Empire State Youth Orchestra.

Judith Somogi is the first woman to conduct at the New York City Opera (in 1974) and the first to conduct in a major Italian opera house. She made her symphonic debut in 1975, conducting the Los Angeles Philharmonic.

In 1985 the highest ranking woman conductor in the country was Catherine Comet, an associate conductor for the Baltimore Symphony.

Other prominent women conductors are Margaret Hillis, director of the Chicago Symphony Orchestra Chorus, which she founded, and Rachel Worby, former Exxon/Arts Endowment Conductor with the Spokane Symphony Orchestra. In 1985 JoAnn Falletta won the Stokowski Conducting Prize, a debut with the American Symphony Orchestra at Carnegie Hall, and the Toscanini Conductor's Award. For the past six seasons she's been music director of the Queens Philharmonic and in 1985 was conducting the Denver Chamber Orchestra.

Blanche Moyse, the 75-year-old director of the New England Bach Festival, recently made her New York conducting debut at the Symphony Space in New York City.

Margaret Harris has broken a variety of records by

being the first black woman to conduct the Chicago Symphony (in 1971) and to premiere her own piano concerto with the Los Angeles Philharmonic (in 1972). Carolyn Hills, founder of the New York Music Society and music director of the Livingston (N.J.) Symphony Orchestra, believes women won't get extensive opportunities to conduct in the major symphony orchestras until these groups appoint women as associate conductors and music directors.

Before 1970, the only two women well-known as conductors were Sarah Caldwell and Antonia Brico. In the early '70s, Caldwell, founder and director of the Opera Company of Boston, appeared on the cover of Time magazine. In 1976 she was the first woman to conduct the Metropolitan Opera. Brico organized and has conducted the Brico Symphony orchestra in Denver for over 30 years. Only recently did the Denver Symphony ask her to guest-conduct.

In 1975, none of the 33 major, 95 metropolitan or 42 urban orchestras then belonging to the American Symphony Orchestra League had a woman in the position of music director or conductor.

"In 1970," said Barbara Jepson in the Feminist Art Journal, "the very idea of a female auditioning for admission to a prestigious conservatory as an orchestra conducting major was apparently considered ridiculous." Queler recalled suggestions that she wear a tuxedo or conduct topless, or conduct a women's symphony if she wanted employment in her profession.

Women caucus for change

Many traditional musicians' organizations in the last 15 years have formed women's caucuses or committees to agitate and advocate on behalf of women musicians. Both the College Music Society and the American Musicological Society scheduled sessions on women at joint meetings. Another example is the 802 Women's Caucus of Allegro, founded in 1983. The women members set up mechanisms to "blow the whistle" when they ran into sexual discrimination or harassment. Their caucus encouraged them to start contracting their own work, an area few women had ventured into. They spoke out about working conditions that specifically affected women, educating the public and networking.

Problems the women voiced ranged from union letters addressing them as "Dear Brother," to men's refusal to hire women brass players because "women can't push." The Interguild Women's Caucus, an interdisciplinary performers' group, set up a "pass system" to pass on information about "persons in hiring capacities who sexually harass those seeking employment."

The new rock

Perhaps one of the most amazing transformations of the last 15 years is that of women in rock music—one of the "most influential strongholds of knee-jerk misogyny."

The new breed, recently profiled in Newsweek, are strong women with power, their own ideas and their own sense of style. Cyndi Lauper told Newsweek reporters, "I try to beget strength and courage and purpose. I want to show a new woman."

In January, Ms. named Lauper Woman of the Year, and Gloria Steinem, a Ms. editor, "applauded the fresh new atmosphere at some rock concerts." Women now are even seen giving the downbeat.

The Newsweek article concluded, "Today, although the corporate elite that presides over pop music is still dominated by men, the developments of the last three decades have made it possible for women performers to choose from an increasing range of styles, sounds and images—and to exercise more control over their careers."

In pop music, women singers have always had a degree of access and by 1978 were commanding 40 percent of the pop charts. It was a different tune for women songwriters, who failed to garner the placement of a single representative in the Songwriters Hall of Fame when it opened in New York in 1977. Now there are a growing number of highly successful female professionals turning out songs.

According to Paulette Weiss, writing in the Music

Educators Journal, "As the doors have opened in all areas of the music business, women have not hesitated to walk in, becoming disc jockeys, recording engineers and producers." But not without a struggle. Liz Saron, an engineer at a traditional sound studio, remembered a recording session with Mick Jagger: "He said he felt women had no place in the studio and should be home making quilts."

Theatre: A Foot on the Stage

Two Pulitzer Prizes for playwrighting, more opportunities for women as directors, producers and set designers, better roles—things are definitely improving for women pursuing traditional routes to success in theatre.

Beth Henley for "Crimes of the Heart" and Marsha Norman for "'night, Mother," won playwrighting's top prize in 1982 and 1983. Hopefully this indicates not only that more women are winning prizes, but also that more women are getting their plays produced. Of several hundred plays produced in New York City between 1969 and 1975, only 7 percent were written by women. In all the years from 1921 until 1958, women playwrights won only five Pulitzers.

Minority women playwrights, too, have had some recent successes, among them: Maya Angelou, Sonia Sanchez and Ntozake Shange. The latter's 1976 Broadway production, "For Colored Girls Who Have Considered Suicide When the Rainbow Is Enuf," aroused controversy and, according to Claudia Tate, editor of Black Women Writers at Work, "fell victim to a media blitz and was, thus, transformed and exploited." But Shange followed up with successful dramatic productions in 1977, 1978, 1979 and 1980.

These black women are creating drama that is continuing to, in the words of actress Michele Shay, "dissolve the resistance to finding the common ground," as did Lorraine Hansberry's 1959 "A Raisin in the Sun." That first, successful black, straight play on Broadway "opened up the world of black theatre." It "helped create the civil rights movement of the '60s," wrote Gregory Mosher, artistic director of the Goodman Theatre in Chicago, where a revival of "A Raisin in the Sun" opened in 1984.

Actresses, too, who have always been part of the theatre, had a tough time finding good roles a decade ago. 1970 census figures showed that about half of all actresses worked less than 28 and one-half weeks and earned less than $5,021. An analysis of some 350 Broadway and Off Broadway plays produced between 1953 and 1972 showed that only one-third of the available roles called for women. And many of those roles were demeaning. As Megan Terry, widely-known feminist playwright, observed, "In the masculine-oriented theatre, there are only three kinds of women—the bitch, the goddess and the whore with the heart of gold."

According to Elsa Rael, an actress who founded the POW (Professional Older Women's) Theatre to feature middle-aged actresses, the harshest discrimination is directed toward actresses over 40. POW Theatre's 1984 playwriting contest had only one requirement: the play's central character must be a woman over 50. The winning plays were read by Kim Hunter, Beatrice Straight, Ruby Dee, Frances Sternhagen, Zohra Lampert and Viveca Lindfors, and directed by Josephine Abady, Tisa Chang, Susan Einhorn, Sue Lawless and Dorothy Lyman.

Women as directors, designers

Women also found doors closed when they tried to move into positions as directors, producers, designers and technicians. In 1975, an informal woman's group, Action for Women in Theatre, surveyed 50 nonprofit theatres across the country. According to a report in "The Creative Woman," published in 1975 by the National Commission on the Observance of International Women's Year, they found that of the hundreds of plays produced by these theatres in the previous six years, only 6 percent were directed by women. Over half—26—of the theatres hired no women directors. Even more significant, then, are the Obie Awards that went to JoAnne Akalaitis in 1976, and to Elizabeth Swados in 1978, for distinguished directing.

Women directors are still few and far between. Of 261 plays produced on Broadway during the past five seasons, only nine of them—about 3 percent—were directed by women.

The League of Professional Theatre Women, which recently collected the statistics, questioned 47 established women directors, an overwhelming majority of whom reported that "a lack of trust in women's leadership and traditional male domination in the field" were the main stumbling blocks for women trying to climb the career ladder.

Other obstacles were:

- Discrimination during early training in both liberal arts and professional theatre programs. (Most respondents, for example, had been encouraged to pursue acting instead of directing.);
- Male networks or cliques from which women feel excluded;
- Tokenism in hiring;
- Job discrimination often carried out by women against other women. (Although women are generally more helpful to women directors than men are, women in hiring positions may still be reluctant to hire women directors.)

The same may be true for women scenic designers. No one seems to know exactly why so few women get hired for this position when they comprise 50 percent of costume designers and are also well represented in lighting design. Is it because fabrics and light are considered soft, pliable feminine materials?

Nancy Reinhardt, one of a 1985 panel of designers discussing the problem, felt "guardedly optimistic" about the future for women scenic designers. Marjorie Bradley Kellogg, another panelist and designer, noted that, away from Broadway, "discrimination against women is not as severe, but where real money is involved, the problem is more pronounced."

Other designers who took part in the discussion were Adrianne Lobel, Carrie Robbins and Heidi Landesman, who won a breakthrough 1985 Tony for set design.

In 1984 a survey by the Director/Designer Caucus showed that for women in scenic design, there are only 2.7 percent on Broadway; 25 percent Off and Off-Off Broadway; 27 percent in regional theatres, and 45 percent in "other" theatres.

Fifty-three percent of those queried noted discrimination against women in their training, 32 percent said they had experienced no discrimination, and 15 percent said maybe they had experienced discrimination.

In hiring, 33 percent had experienced discrimination, 40 percent said they had not experienced discrimination, and 27 percent said maybe they had experienced discrimination.

Ninety-three percent of the women polled said there existed old boy networks from which they were excluded. Asked if they thought women were under represented in their field, costume and lighting designers said no, but 90 percent of the scenic designers said yes and 10 percent were not sure.

Committee for Women

The Dramatists Guild, a mainstream group, established the Committee for Women in 1979 to "encourage and nurture female playwrights and to investigate those problems particular to women writing for the stage."

Gretchen Cryer, who founded the committee, said during a speech in 1981 at a symposium on women playwrights that "women's accomplishments in the theatre are the result of both powerful self-reliance, often in the face of hostility, and of mutual support for each other."

According to a 1984 article by Phyllis Paullette in Art and Artists, Peggy Gold, poet, playwright and current chairperson of the Committee, stated, "There is no debate that women have had a more difficult time getting their work produced than men have. Prospects seem to be better for women now than ever before."

The Committee's 1982 annual event was "Marketplace," an opportunity for playwrights to meet directors. Hundreds of both attended. In 1983 a "political cabaret" offered 12 selections from members' plays and was "a huge success." The group's Play Bank makes scripts by women playwrights available on request to any professional, university or college theatre.

Another long-established theatre group, the American Theatre Association, founded in 1936, has sponsored programs on black theatre; drama by, with and for the handicapped; senior adult theatre; and women's theatre, which "reflects the Association's commitment to the issues and concerns of the profession."

The focus of ATA's Women's Program is "increasing the voice and the visibility of all women in theatre. It encourages opportunities and involvement for women from performers to directors, designers to administrators. Women playwrights and their work receive special emphasis..."

Women's Program

According to the ATA, the Women's Program has developed national and regional communications networks between women in academic and professional theatre, and sponsors projects such as the pre-convention workshops for Women in Theatre that provide national forums for discussion and exchange. The program sponsors a newsletter, a play bank of scripts by women writers, and a resource directory of women in theatre that details their professional interest and qualifications.

Karen Boettcher-Tate of Portland, Oregon, won the first Jane Chambers Playwriting Award presented by the Women's Program of the ATA in honor of the late feminist playwright. Her play, called "Grandma Shot the Cat," recounts the tales told by her grandmother-in-law. In all, Boettcher-Tate has published 14 scripts. An earlier one, "Enemies: A Vietnam Journey," won second place in both the David Library Award on American Freedom and the Lorraine Hansberry Award.

Film: Small Successes

Traditional criticism of establishment films—those out of Hollywood or Europe—is consumer-oriented. It serves mainly to help moviegoers select the films they want to see. Most of the critics, whether men or women, show no feminist orientation. But there are a few—Molly Haskell and Marjorie Rosen come to mind—who do comment on mainstream films from a feminist perspective, though they may prefer not to call themselves feminist critics.

Whether called feminist critics or traditional critics, film reviewers have had a powerful impact in recent years. Turning the spotlight on mainstream films that exploit women as victims of violence, horror or pornography, they have clearly succeeded in raising public awareness of the whole porn issue.

Traditional distributors, many of whom turned down feminist films in the early '70s, are now much more likely to include at least feminist documentary films in their general collections. These films now have a recognized commercial audience. Some establishment distributors recognized the commercial potential of the feminist movement as early as 1973.

Traditional institutions also succumbed to feminist pressure to exhibit women's films. In 1972 and '73, feminists and women artists in New York demonstrated for equal representation at leading cultural institutions. This led to the inclusion of women's art films in various exhibits and programs.

In the winter of 1973, for example, the Whitney Museum in New York screened over 50 new documentary and avant-garde films by women at a special women's film program. In the same year the New York Cultural Center sponsored a week-long program of women's avant-garde films. In general, feminist filmmakers were not forced to create their own exhibitions from scratch.

The Whitney Biennial began including film in 1979. According to the Village Voice, April 23, 1985, it has "been less a leader than a follower of fashion....Over half the filmmakers included in the '79 and '81 Biennials had their work certified by the Anthology Film Archives, super-8 wasn't included until 1983, narratives and documentaries were all but nonexistent."

Meredith Monk's 20-year retrospective show of her films and videotapes ran through March 1985 at New York's Whitney Museum of American Art. Monk's show was part of the series, "New American Filmmakers."

Television also produced films by and about women. An example was television station WNET in New York which broadcast the first series of films on art produced by American Public Television and concentrating solely on women artists. In portrait style, "Originals: Women in Art" explored not only the lives and achievements of a number of outstanding women artists, but also some of the issues women have faced in being recognized as artists.

Perry Miller Adato produced three of the seven films: on Helen Frankenthaler, Georgia O'Keeffe and Mary Cassatt. Nancy Baer produced a film portrait of Alice Neel, Susan Fanshel and Jill Godmilow collaborated on filming Louise Nevelson and Mirra Bank made "Anonymous Was a Woman."

On the other hand, while traditional outlets were sometimes accessible, there were still problems. Standard booking and screening arrangements are quite different for independent films compared to movies. Movies can command continuous showings. Non-theatrical films are usually one-shot screenings. In addition there are huge variations in the suitability of screening locations. Feminist films benefit from discussion after the showing, and this is difficult if the room or the time schedule do not lend themselves to discussion.

Television as symbol

There is always a conflict between the desire to reach large numbers of people and the desire to combine screening and discussion. Television reaches the widest audience of all, but discussion afterward is virtually impossible for more than a few on camera.

Despite these limitations, television is important to feminist filmmakers both financially and symbolically.

Films shown on TV have a greater chance of being reviewed, for one thing. Most of the one-shot television programs have been in response to feminist pressures. In 1973, for example, women in Boston publicly protested neglect of their work by station WGBH.

But even when television stations do bow to pressure and broadcast women's films, feminist goals may not be fulfilled. "Specials are important in providing visibility for feminist films...but are also an effective way of limiting them to occasional and irregular showings," said Jan Rosenberg, author of <u>Women's Reflections: The Feminist Film Movement.</u>

An exception to the occasional and irregular format was the feminist television series, "Women Alive!" regularly scheduled and cosponsored by Ms. and a local public television station.

Pressuring television stations to broadcast women's films is one tactic and trying to get hired by the networks is another. But the hidden agenda linking both situations is the same: discrimination. The Women's Committee of the Writers Guild of America West published a study in 1984 documenting the extent of discrimination against women writers in television from April 1, 1982 through March 31, 1983. Here are their key findings:

- Out of all prime-time network television programming, males wrote 83 percent and females wrote 17 percent of the scripts.

- Even in studios which employed more women writers than men, men received more of the on-screen writing credits.

- Out of 75 network prime-time series shows, 37 shows had no women receiving on-air writing staff credits (story editor, story consultant, executive story consultant). Five of these shows were credited solely by women, or a woman writer in partnership with a male writer.

"While television exhibition is important on its own terms, it may also be a bridge from documentaries to movies, which remain a primary goal for many filmmakers," said Rosenberg.

Over the last decade and a half, women have been moving into positions of authority and power in the Hollywood film industry. Editing and costuming were two obvious areas in which women made early progress because both were considered women's skills.

Verna Fields and Dede Allen stand out as editors. Fields edited "American Graffiti" and won an Oscar for editing "Jaws" in 1975, while Allen has achieved a kind of cult status for her editing of such films in the '70s as "Little Big Man," "Slaughterhouse Five," "Serpico," "Night Moves," "Dog Day Afternoon," "The Missouri Breaks," and "Slap Shot."

Hollywood scenarios

As Irene Wolt points out in the December 1984 issue of American Film, getting a chance to work as a woman director in Hollywood has been a much rockier road. Martha Coolidge ("Valley Girls," "Joy of Sex") was told flatly when she started out that "You can't be a director." Production designer Polly Platt ("Terms of Endearment") used to say she couldn't be a director because she wasn't tall enough "to put my arm around Clint Eastwood's shoulder and walk him off the set during a crisis."

Even women who have made it to the top through traditional film channels often have to form their own production companies to produce films they want to make. Recent examples are Barbra Streisand, who won a 1984 Crystal Award for "Yentl," and Jane Fonda, Goldie Hawn and Jane Alexander.

Statistics in a 1984 article in American Film indicated that in the '80s, directing, writing and photographing feature movies is still considered men's work. In 1983:

- Female directors accounted for only 2 percent of the days worked on feature films;

- Fewer than 15 percent of all the feature films made from April 1982 to April 1983 were written by women;
- There is only one female director of photography in the American Society of Cinematographers;
- Of 683 members of the Producers Guild, fewer than 100 are women;
- Fewer than 10 percent of network and studio executives are women.

It's the old double bind: You don't get hired because you don't have experience and you don't have experience because you can't get hired.

Amy Jones ("Love Letters," "Slumber Party," "Massacre") described the Hollywood studio system as "staggeringly patriarchal and anyone who pretends it isn't is kidding themselves."

Challenging discrimination in the courts

The facts have been documented. Six female members of DGA, going through 30 years of Directors Guild deal memos, found that of 7,332 feature films released from 1949 to 1979, women directed only 14. Of 6000 prime-time television hours produced since 1949, women directed only 115. (Ida Lupino, who owns her own company, directed 35 of those.)

The women in the Directors Guild, the Writers Guild and the Screen Actor's Guild have been actively seeking measures to equalize hiring conditions in their respective fields. In 1984 the DGA filed class action discrimination suits against two of Hollywood's major studies, Warner Bros. and Columbia, and was considering suits against 19 other companies.

In 1985 the DGA was still awaiting a judge's opinion, not on the suit itself, but on the counter-claim by Columbia and Warner Bros. "that the Guild itself is discriminatory and therefore cannot properly represent the class," said Susan Smitman, a DGA representative closely involved with the case. It's quite possible that a ruling unfavorable to the DGA will stall the suit, without ever dealing with the basic claim of discrimination.

The Women's Committee of the Writers Guild of America West is also considering filing charges of sex discrimination in the hiring of screenwriters.

Preparing for top jobs

Other mainstream organizations are beginning to participate in helping women prepare themselves for the top jobs in Hollywood. The American Film Institute's Directing Workshop for Women has given women of proven accomplishment in the film industry—producers, actresses, writers, editors, studio executives—the opportunity to gain the necessary skills to direct in film and television.

Jan Haag, workshop head, has received support from the Rockefeller and the John and Mary R. Markle Foundations for the project. During the pilot phase, 15 workshop members completed 18 videotapes.

Another traditional institution, the Center for Advanced Film Studies, numbers 623 graduates, of whom six recent women graduates have had directing successes: Amy Heckerling ("Fast Times at Ridgemont High" and "Johnny Dangerously"); and Shelly Levinson, who received an Academy Award in 1981 for "Violet." Nancy Nickerson, co-producer of "The Silence," was nominated for an Academy Award in 1983 and won a Gold Award and Special Jury Award at the 1983 Houston International Film Festival, as did Ellen Sandler as director and Marcia Shia and Kim Thomas as co-producers of "When the Bough Breaks."

People in the industry are optimistic about women's progress. Producers Guild president Renee Valente thinks it's just a matter of time. She sees "many many more" women directors over the next decade as those now entering the field gain experience. Barbara Peeters, who has recently been hired to direct for television, says, "They are hiring more women." Kaye Cooper, director of the American Film Institute's Directing Workshop for Women, notes "a slight improvement."

Marcia Nasiter, first woman vice president at United Artists (in 1974), believes there are going to be more women directors just as there are going to be more women in all areas of business. So does Lynn Littman

("Testament"). In 1973, she said, there were no women executives at all. Emmy award-winning producer and director Joelle Dobrow says, "There's been some improvement."

Director Susan Seidelman ("Smithereens" and "Desperately Seeking Susan"), however, sounded a cautionary note in the December 1984 issue of American Film. "Right now there's a lot of talk about women who are directing films, as there was eight years ago. Then it was short-lived. I'm hoping now that this is a real change, that it isn't just Hollywood trying to go with the trend."

A final comment by Smitman: "Although things have improved slightly throughout the Industry since we started making noise back in 1978, there has really been no substantial change. Over the past year, things have actually shown a downturn—especially in the Director category."

Literature: Legacy, Celebration and Backlash

What happens when a television anchorwoman and a glamorous physician fall in love? Or a Virginia belle rejects her Southern beaux for her Indian captor? The answer is that millions of women will buy these books to find out. Romances, spelling relief from reality, are selling like over-the-counter happiness pills and some writers like Danielle Steel, the author of (most recently) Changes, and Janelle Taylor, author of Savage Conquest, are bobbing for weeks at the top of The New York Times best seller list.

In Reading the Romance, Janice A. Radway said such books "confirm the validity of the traditional female role in the patriarchal society." Does the coincidence of the demand for romance fiction during the same 15 years that saw the feminist revolution signify anything more than "improved marketing techniques"? Radway thinks it does. Feminism, she said, "has created ambivalence and anxiety for lots of women about the rightness and legitimacy of the female role."

The demand for romances is so insatiable that both would-be and professional writers are attending workshops or reading how-to books to learn the formula. The money may persuade many to reassure American housewives about traditional values, but no romances have as yet won traditional prizes. Women writers in other genres, however, have done just that.

Women win

Women won both the fiction and first work of fiction categories of the 1984 American Book Awards (formerly the National Book Awards). Harriet Doerr, a 74-year-old Californian, won for her first book of fiction, Stones for Ibarra, and Ellen Gilchrist won for her fictional Victory Over Japan. One other woman was nominated.

Other prizewinners in 1984 were Katherine Soniat, who won the First Camden Poetry Award; Anne Carson and Nancy Esposito, who won Colladay Awards from Quarterly Review of Literature; and Louise Erdich, who won the National Book Critics Circle Award for the most outstanding work for fiction for 1984. Lindsay Knowlton won the 1984 Word Works Washington Prize.

Women did not, however, win a representative share of the 1985 NEA creative writing and poetry fellowships. Fourteen creative writing fellowships went to women, 37 to men; 13 poetry fellowships went to women, 36 to men, a percentage in both categories of about one-third.

1983 saw seven women winning American Book Awards for hardcover and paperback fiction, first fiction, biography and hardcover and paperback children's literature.

Women have almost always won for children's literature, but in other categories, previously, women have walked away with fewer prizes.

Other prizes have also gone to women in the last few years, although summary figures are difficult to come by. In 1984, Eudora Welty won the Elmer Holmes Bobst award for fiction. Women also won Guggenheim fellowships and prizes or awards from the MacArthur Foundation, Discovery, PEN, Poetry Center, Yale Younger Poets, American Academy and Institute of Arts and Letters, Associated Writing Programs, Iowa School of Letters,

McGinnis Memorial Award, Lavan Younger Poets Awards,
Lenore Marshall/Nation Prize, Redbook, Saxifrage Prize,
Denny Poetry Award, Dos Passos Prize, Kafka Prize, and
General Electric Foundations Awards for Younger
Writers. Women also won 38 of 110 NEA poetry
fellowships for 1984.

In a funding venture benefiting fiction writers of both
sexes, the Literature Program of the NEA inaugurated a
cooperative effort with the PEN American Center to bring
fiction back to the pages of newspapers. Twenty-eight
women were among the 62 authors from 26 states that
won the second year's competition.

Prestigious Pulitzer Prizes went to women for fiction
in 1973 and 1983 (bringing to six the number of women
winners since the award began); for drama in 1981 and
1983 (eight women in all); for poetry in 1982 and 1984 (12
women in all); for general nonfiction in 1975 and 1983 (five
women in all). Since the early 1970s, women,
unquestionably, have made an impact by following
traditional routes to publishing fame and fortune.

Women in men's worlds

Black women have made significant inroads into the
traditional publishing houses. Alice Walker, who won the
Pulitzer Prize in 1983 for The Color Purple, published that
book with Harcourt Brace. Stephen Spielberg hit traditional
movie theatres in December of 1985 with his outstanding
production of Walker's novel. It played to packed houses.

Toni Morrison, author of The Bluest Eye, Sula, Song
of Solomon, and Tar Baby, is an editor at Random
House. Women have also achieved positions of authority
and power in various mainstream literary organizations:
magazine groups, book clubs, publishing houses. Examples
are Robin Smith who has been president and general
manager of the Book Clubs Division of Doubleday &
Company, "the largest marketing operation of general
books in the U.S. industry." As director of the Literary
Guild, Rollene Saal "decides the fate of manuscripts for the
largest book club (1.5 million members) in the world." Kay
Sexton, vice president in charge of marketing for B. Dalton

Books, is perhaps the "most powerful tastemaker in book retailing today," according to an article in the 1984 Northwest Orient Airlines Magazine.

The influence of these women, however, has not apparently changed the ratio of women authors to men authors who achieve publication. A Book-of-the-Month Club ad in The New York Times in 1985 featured 84 titles, of which only 12 were written by women. Waldenbooks' best seller listing for the week ending April 13 showed one woman author out of 15 top selling trade paperbacks, two women authors out of 15 top selling hardcovers, and nine women authors out of 15 top selling mass paperbooks (a category including romances.)

The Columbia Economic Survey of American Authors, a summary of findings prepared for the Authors Guild Foundation in 1981, stated, "In terms of public esteem and prestige, authors rank among the top 10 percent of all occupations." Are women getting the money along with the esteem?

What writers earned

"Although income from writing is unrelated to authors' social origins, educational achievements and geographical location," the survey maintained, "it is not altogether free of social patterning."

Translated, that means women came up short: "The now familiar findings on differences in income between men and women in most occupations appear here too, although such differences are comparatively muted. For example, women authors earned a median of $4,000 from writing in 1979 as against the $5,200 median earned by men," the survey concluded. While significant, this is a smaller differential than the 40 percent difference which separates the median incomes of men and women in the general labor force.

Moreover, the survey claims, "The chances of an author being in the bottommost or the topmost income strata is only minimally related to gender."

Further, the researchers found no gender-related differences in income among those who work exclusively at writing, that is, the committed full-timers who spend 25 hours a week or more at writing and have no other paid positions: 12 percent of both men and women in this group earned $20,000 or more. It is notable, however, that 10 percent of the men and 7 percent of the women earned more than $50,000.

Do women get reviewed?

Are women reviewed as often in periodicals such as The New York Times Book Review, Publisher's Weekly and the library review journals? No statistics seem to be available. However, there are so many factors involved besides the sex of the author that it's doubtful if statistics would get at the root of the problem, which is that "politics"—publisher-editor or reviewer-editor connections—so often determine which books get reviewed. Again, old boy networks seem to have more clout than new girl networks.

Most book review periodicals seem to pursue at least an appearance of fairness. For example, The New York Times recently printed Andrew Hacker's review of Robin Morgan's Sisterhood Is Global. He called the book "a sometimes grim but always fascinating compendium on the worldwide condition of women." He also disparaged the book's statistics and concluded that Morgan didn't ask the assistance of women statisticians Janet Norwood at the Bureau of Labor Statistics or Arlene Saluter of the Census Bureau because the compilers of Sisterhood Is Global view women "who succeed in a man's world as themselves suspect."

Hacker also complained that women heads of state listed in the book are not cited as role models: "Too professional a tone may signify one has succumbed to the patriarchical mentality, wherein, as Robin Morgan puts it, the standard for being human is being male." Hacker added, "Insofar as this is so, the women's movement wants more than fairer access to opportunities and power. It is asking that we reconsider our most basic presumptions about how we analyze the world."

Ellen Goodman, in her nationally syndicated column of Jan. 21, 1986, wrote about the continuing need for women writers "to keep counting." She referred to the mid-January meeting of the PEN International Writer's Congress in New York: "...women writers including Betty Friedan, Gail Sheehy, Grace Paley and Margaret Atwood added up the panelists for the meeting and then divided the total by two: two sexes. There were 120 men speaking to the group and only 20 women." When Friedan went to deliver the imbalance sheet to PEN President Norman Mailer, he reportedly laughed and said, "Oh, who's counting?" Goodman concluded: "It was, of course, the minority who was counting. It always is."

Forging Alternative Links

Visual Arts: Another Vision

While progress has been made by women in traditional art institutions, it has been slow and erratic. Many women, some from a theoretical standpoint, some because of their pragmatic assessment of the odds against them, elected to establish their own institutions.

Ellouise Schoettler, executive director of the Coalition of Women's Art Organizations, in her 1981 testimony before the House Interior Appropriations Subcommittee, put the matter plainly. "Early in the 1970s, women in the arts, disadvantaged by a traditionally male-favoring arts establishment, recognized that to achieve substantial careers...they would have to develop alternative opportunities....Through determined entrepreneurship, women in the arts established organizations, alternative exhibition centers, arts centers and publications which have fostered their career development and emergence as full participants in the arts community..."

Art history and art criticism

Feminist art history and criticism, an unprecedented outpouring of alternative scholarship, probably began in 1971 at the same time Linda Nochlin, now distinguished professor of art history at the City University of New York, not only asked but answered the question, "Why Have There Been No Great Women Artists?" Since then enterprising scholars have investigated the lives of women artists, past and present, reevaluated their work and their contributions, and invented new ways of looking at and thinking about art that have changed forever perceptions of what art is.

In a subsequent 1979 essay, "Toward a Juster Vision: How Feminism Can Change Our Way of Looking at Art History," Nochlin asked if genius is sex-linked. "What if Pablo Picasso had been a girl?" Her answer: "Pablita's opportunity to achieve greatness would have been in jeopardy since she might have been home washing dishes."

Nochlin's writings, along with other trailblazing books, articles, dissertations and papers, have formed a new body of revisionist art history, effectively countering the all-male version promulgated in such still ubiquitous tomes as Janson's History of Art or Hauser's The Social History of Art.

After Nochlin's 1971 bombshell, Elton C. Fax published Seventeen Black Artists, recognizing minority men and women. Then in 1974, Eleanor Tufts published Our Hidden Heritage, suggesting that the appropriate question is not "Why have there been no great women artists?" but rather: "Why is so little known about the great women artists of the past and present?"

In 1975 came Cindy Nemser's interviews with contemporary women artists. Titled Art Talk: Conversations with Twelve Women Artists, it also reacted to Nochlin's premise that there have been no female equivalents for Michelangelo, Leonardo, et al. Nemser maintained that female esthetic accomplishments had been intentionally overlooked by historians and critics. She also charged that her book was attacked and panned by art magazines, ignored by The New York Times and refused display space in New York City museums because of its all-woman theme.

Other significant contributions were Two Centuries of Black American Art, by Davis Driskell, and the book, Women Artists written by Karen Petersen and J.J. Wilson. In 1978, Elsa Honig Fine's book, Women and Art, well-suited to classroom use, encompassed women artists from the Renaissance to those currently active.

In 1979, Eleanor Munro's Originals: American Women Artists, presented revealing in-depth interviews with women artists. All of these books are valuable not only for their text, but also for their illustrations, said art historian H. Diane Russell. "Indeed, one of the most important developments of the past decade," she explained, "is the greatly increased availability of illustrations" of the works of women artists.

Other books traced various threads. Madlyn Millner Kahr explored the Danae myth through works of various women artists. Editors Elsa Honig Fine, Lola B. Gellman and Judy Loeb put together a useful compendium on the visual arts, and Claire R. Sherman and Adele M. Holcomb authored Women Scholars and the Visual Arts.

Lucy Lippard's From the Center, published in 1976, presented criteria for evaluating art from the standpoint of "female imagery." Her latest book is Getting the Message? A Decade of Art for Social Change. She writes on art and politics monthly for In These Times.

Judy Chicago's 1975 book, Through the Flower provided an autobiographical perspective. Her 1979 "The Dinner Party" detailed the history of the creation of the work of art by that name and her 1985 "Birth Project" did the same thing for her most recent collective art work.

Other important books were Germaine Greer's The Obstacle Race; Feminism and Art History, a series of essays edited by Mary Garrard and Norma Broude; the dictionary of women artists born before 1900, edited by Chris Petteys; the epic tome, almost ten years in the making, American Women Artists, by Charlotte S. Rubinstein, published in 1982; and Gayle Kimball's important Women's Culture: The Women's Renaissance of the Seventies, published in 1981.

Dissertations and papers

Dissertations and papers presented at various conferences have also played their part in disseminating information about rediscovered women artists. Such forgotten or excluded artists as Judith Leyster, Marguerite Gerard, Mary Cassatt, Rosa Bonheur, Alice Neel, and more, have been restored to their rightful places. Other writers focused on artist wives of famous male artists like Elaine DeKooning and Lee Krasner, who died last year shortly after the Museum of Fine Arts in Houston and New York's Museum of Modern Art both displayed her first retrospective exhibit.

Women themselves have resuscitated neglected women artists in significant numbers over the last 15 years. Muriel Magenta, an art historian now on the faculty of Arizona State University, remarking on this phenomenon, commented that "these same scholars 20 years ago would probably have researched the accomplishments of male artists. Prior to 1970, selecting the work of a female artist as the subject of a thesis, book or important article would have been avoided and possibly considered imprudent. Any significance female artists might have contributed to the history of Western European art was generally disregarded in scholarly circles. Thus the feminist movement has been a decisive factor in terms of influencing the new scholarly interest in the historical contributions of women artists."

H. Diane Russell said the same thing, with a difference, in her 1980 review article in Signs. "During the past ten years, the currents of scholarship on women and the visual arts have flowed continuously but erratically. Whether this scholarship has sufficient force to sustain itself, and whether it can avoid the insular character of traditional art history are pressing questions. We know more about women artists than ever before: their practical difficulties in securing artistic training, their remarkable fortitude in overcoming obstacles from pregnancy to brutal misogyny, and their achievements."

Uncountable numbers of popular articles also appeared during the '70s, honing in at shorter length on the problems women artists faced. Nemser's "Art Criticism and Women Artists" took male reviewers to task for implying that women artists are incapable of serious art. When they discuss women at all, she maintained, they focus on the woman's teacher (usually male), on her male lovers, her male-attended salons, or the story of her life, but not on the works themselves.

Periodicals

To disseminate the flood of alternative scholarship, an astonishing number of alternative art journals made a beginning in the '70s. The Feminist Art Journal, Womanspace Journal and Womanart, all now defunct, were three of the early ones. Women Artists News, Helicon Nine, Calliope, Woman's Art Journal, Calyx, Heresies and Chrysalis were just a few new journals.

In the Feminist Art Journal, started in 1972 by Cindy

Nemser, Pat Mainardi and Irene Moss, for example, Mainardi helped establish the premise that women's quilts were art; Gloria Orenstein examined women's themes, Schwartz uncovered the sexual prejudices of male art critics, and numerous other authors scrutinized museum personnel practices, reported on sex differences in reviews, documented a "feminine sensibility" or researched the lives of forgotten women artists, most of whom juggled their creative drive with external demands for domestic services.

Though it concentrated on the visual arts, it also covered theatre, dance, literature and music. It ceased publication in 1977 amid a confusion over goals.

Among the newest periodicals is Sage, a biannual scholarly journal concerning black women. Edited by Patricia Bell-Scott and Beverly Guy Sheftall, it began publishing in April of 1984.

Newsletters of the various alternative organizations also carried the message of expanding explorations into women's art history, as well as women's setbacks and triumphs.

The 1978 edition of the Index to the Directory of Women's Media listed 31 women's art, music, literary and film periodicals. The 1985 Index listed 462 women's art periodicals, more than any past year. The Index also listed 116 women's presses and publishers (compared with 47 in 1978), 67 art/graphic/theatre groups (compared with 44), 31 film groups (compared with 17), 35 music groups (compared with 36), 26 video and cable groups (compared with 13), and 80 women's bookstores.

Networking tools

The Directory and its Index are invaluable networking tools, as was the earlier 1971 women's slide registry initiated by feminist author and art critic Lucy Lippard. The purpose of both was the essential one of making women's art accessible. Eleven slide registries and slide resources were listed in Cynthia Navaretta's 1979 Guide to Women's Art Organizations. And in 1984, The National Center on Arts and Aging formed a Slide Registry for Older Adults. Containing one to three slides and a

resume of art background for each artist, the slide registry
is used for selecting works for NCAA gallery exhibits and is
available to all public and private institutions interested in
exhibiting works of older artists.

Galleries

In the '70s, women artists realized that it was
statistically unlikely that their pictures would ever be hung
in traditional museums or galleries. If they wanted
exposure, they would have to become their own best
friends. This meant curating, dealing, critiquing, promoting
and running their own art businesses. It was the only way
to gain some control over their opportunities for exhibiting
and selling their work.

In New York City, in 1972, Barbara Zucker and
Susan Williams founded A.I.R., one of the earliest
alternative galleries, with a contingent of 20 women
artists, each of whom would be guaranteed one one-woman
show a year. Soho 20 sprang up the same year. Soon
women's galleries opened in other parts of the country:
Artemesia, Inc. and Artists Residing in Chicago (A.R.C.) in
Chicago in 1973, and others in Boston, Providence, Atlanta,
Minneapolis, Washington D.C. and elsewhere.

In the Midwest, the Women's Art Registry of
Minnesota, founded in 1974, is one of the largest feminist
art collectives. Late in 1984 they published "a major
document in the history of feminism and American art," a
96-page catalog providing the first comprehensive
documentation of their history. Feminist writer Robin
Morgan wrote the foreword for the catalog, which treats in
depth 37 works of women, spanning 200 years, that opened
at the Minnesota Museum of Art in 1984. At the opening,
art historian Linda Nochlin talked on "Women, Art and
Power."

Exhibits

Tired of waiting for museums to do it, women also
began to put together their own art exhibits. From 1971 to
1979, Cynthia Naravetta's Guide listed 37 exhibits. Muriel

Magenta commented on "the myriad of contemporary women's art exhibitions presented locally, nationally and internationally," in her article, "Feminist Art Criticism." She pointed out, "The number and quality of women's art exhibitions has increased dramatically over the years and has reached astounding proportions which extend ... to even remote communities."

Of course the most significant exhibit, and THE historic art event of the '70s, was the 1976-77 exhibition curated by Linda Nochlin and Ann Sutherland Harris. Titled "Women Artists: 1550 to 1950" it included 158 drawings and prints by 84 European and American artists. Large crowds flocked to the various cities on the traveling exhibit's itinerary: Los Angeles, Austin, Pittsburgh and Brooklyn. Newspapers covered the event and the catalog, as H. Diane Russell pointed out, "is a prodigious work, one that will continue to be consulted for many years." She added that although the catalog deserves a thorough review in an art history journal, it has yet to receive one.

The Woman's Building

In 1973, the Woman's Building, an outgrowth of Womanspace, the creation of a coalition of Los Angeles women artists, was started by Judy Chicago, Sheila de Bretteville and Arlene Raven. Built around the Feminist Studio Workshop School for Artists, it became a pioneering center of women's culture.

As one example of its usefulness to women artists over a decade later, its slide collection of historical and contemporary women artists is the country's largest. It is used by teachers, curators, researchers, artists and students.

The Women's Studio Workshop, founded in 1974 "to support and encourage the creation of contemporary art works," was dedicated to arts education. According to the literature, it has been for the past 10 years "a center of critical dialog in the arts. Ongoing programs include W.I.N.G.S. (Women Invent New Gallery Spaces), Women's

Work in Film and Video, Visiting Artists and Artist-in Residence Program, workshops and lectures."

Ariel Dougherty, development director of the workshop, said that in 1984 WSW and the Woman's Building (Los Angeles), Women and Their Work (Austin, Texas), and Women Make Movies (New York City) received Apple II computers, printers, modems and software from the company "as the beginning of a national network of women's art organizations." In another joint project, they are working to create a national database on women artists.

"Women Choose Women," featuring the works of 109 contemporary women artists, opened at the New York Cultural Center in 1973. Women in the Arts spearheaded this important exhibit of paintings, the first major show of work by women artists in an establishment big-city center. In 1974, the Museum of Philadelphia's Civic Center mounted "Women's Work: American Art in 1974." It featured 81 works of contemporary women artists, selected entirely by five women curators, Adelyn Breeskin, Anne D'Harnoncourt, Lila Katzen, Cindy Nemser and Marcia Tucker. Grace Glueck of The New York Times described it as a "heartening idea of the number of very good women artists around, and the strong highly individual work they are producing."

At the same time in Philadelphia, Cindy Nemser's show, "In Her Own Image," occupied the Fleisher Art Memorial. Its purpose was to counter the stereotyped images of women as femme fatale or child-woman that male artists have perpetuated over the years.

Later, Diane Burko, a Philadelphia painter, organized a city-wide exhibit, "Philadelphia Focuses on Women in the Visual Arts," in which every major cultural institution in the city eventually participated.

The "Year of the Woman" exhibit, held at the Bronx Museum of Arts in the spring of 1975, coincided with the celebration of the United Nations International Women's Year.

In the fall of 1975, an all-woman exhibition called "Works on Paper" was mounted at the Brooklyn Museum, an institution whose special exhibitions, prior to 1970, featured men only. Josephine Withers, noted art historian,

curated a show called "Women From the Vaults" in
1979. She discovered the art in storage areas of museums.

Views by Women Artists

In 1982, "Views by Women Artists," a series of 16
independently curated theme shows, was held in New York
City in conjunction with the annual meetings of the
Women's Caucus for Art, the Coalition of Women's Art
Organizations and the College Art Association. Scattered all
over the city, the individually curated shows featured over
400 women artists. In addition to organizing "Views," the
coordinating NY/WCA asked traditional New York City
galleries to show women artists during that same
period. Over 150 complied.

Sabra Moore wrote in the 1981-82 Woman's Art
Journal: "The ideas for the show grew out of a reaction to
the political climate—the image projected by the Moral
Majority that a woman should return to the home." The
event emphasized equality among artistic points of view,
and proved the economic and physical feasibility of
organizing a large project through small parts. "Views by
Women Artists" was "able to build...an entire women's art
system outside the regular one."

Unfortunately, "there was virtually no coverage of
these events in the daily newspapers," said Paula
L. Chiarmonte, art historian and art librarian. Lawrence
Alloway also criticized the critics for their lack of response:
"I think the silence is part of the critics' persistent
obtuseness to the links between art and society, especially
concerning women," he wrote in "Where Were You on the
Week of the 23rd," in the Village Voice.

Schools

Before 1973, the first alternative art school was
founded by Judy Chicago, who designed the first women's
studies program at California State College at Fresno, in
1970. She invented new techniques for releasing the energy
of her students; consciousness raising, psychodrama and
research into the history of great women artists of the past

were among her pioneering methods.

The next year she invited Miriam Schapiro to visit. Later Schapiro and Chicago set up the Feminist Art Program at the California Institute of Arts in Valencia. That experiment resulted in the now-famous Womanhouse (1972). Charlotte Rubinstein, in her book American Women Artists, called it "a female fantasy environment of women's lives, hopes, despair and frustration."

In Womanhouse, the female students decorated each room with feminine images. In the kitchen, for example, associations with mothers and mothering inspired the breast-like eggs attached to walls and ceiling. As Chicago noted in her book, Through the Flower, when both men and women attended her art classes, the women felt inhibited. Thus Womanhouse was a chance "to do art without a man judging it."

Although it existed only a month, Womanhouse rallied the feminist art movement. For the thousands who visited, it became a model and symbol for the Los Angeles women's art community. It gave women artists all over the country the experience of the power that can be generated when women develop their own institutions. Schapiro commented later, "You go from simple collaboration to the network. And it's from the network that you're going to get the big historical changes."

Feminist Art Institute

On the opposite coast is the New York Feminist Art Institute, founded in 1978 by women who went through the traditional art schools of the '50s and '60s. About 300 women from 18 to 70 attend the evening and weekend classes, workshops and special events each semester.

Executive director and one of the founders, Nancy Azara, explained the curriculum. "We wanted to have courses that would be instrumental in developing the artist as a person." The faculty's guiding imperative, she said, "is that they help each student find and explore her own personal imagery and learn the skills necessary to express those images."

Women's rebellion against discrimination, fueled by the new art history and criticism, led naturally to a revolution in art teaching. New courses of study began to appear. Athena Tacha Spear, in her publication, Women's Studies in Art and Art History, observed that feminist art instructors were actively seeking to rewrite the history of women in the arts through new courses for and about women artists.

Some of these new courses included: "Seminar on Women and Art," taught by Linda Nochlin at Vassar; "The Art of Women and a Feminist Perspective on Art," taught by Mary Garrard at the American University in Washington, D.C.; "Women, Art and Feminism," taught by Lise Vogel at Boston University and Massachusetts College of Art; "Women and the Arts," taught by Joyce Kozloff at the School of Visual Arts; and such studio workshops for women artists as those of Rita Yokoi at the California State University in Fresno and the Feminist Studio Workshop program led by Judy Chicago, Sheila de Bretteville and Arlene Raven.

In Cynthia Navaretta's 1979 Guide to Women's Art Organizations were listed five national women's visual arts organizations and 98 state ones. Certainly the numbers have soared since the early '70s.

One of the most prominent groups, the Women's Caucus for Art, a national organization of women art professionals, has over 2500 members in 17 state chapters. Among them are women artists, art historians, museum curators, critics and educators. At its 1979 convention in Washington, D.C., President Carter presented WCA awards to five distinguished elder women artists: Isabel Bishop, Selma Burke, Alice Neel, Louise Nevelson and Georgia O'Keeffe.

In her final editorial late in 1984, outgoing WCA president Muriel Magenta listed future goals of the organization she characterized as "still the leading organization within the feminist art movement." The goals are broader than the 11 recommendations of the Committee on the Arts and Humanities adopted by the National Commission on the Observance of the

International Women's Year. The WCA goals are:
- providing equal exhibition opportunities;
- promoting fair distribution of grants and funding;
- educating the general public to women's artistic contributions;
- lobbying for equitable employment of women on university and college art faculties;
- expanding the dominant esthetic to encompass all forms of creative expression;
- formulating and supporting legislation relevant to their goals;
- achieving representation and visibility for women's art work;
- promoting opportunities for realistic economic survival in the arts;
- encouraging a nonsexist approach to art curriculum at all educational levels.

In 1983, Magenta reported, the WCA, affiliated with the College Art Association of America, gained 655 new members. The group moved into new offices at Moore College of Art in Philadelphia, with space to house their archives and the comprehensive slide and publications library of members' work.

To increase their networking potential, in 1982, the group distributed their first National Network Directory. Since 1982, their newsletter has been replaced by a publication called Hue Points, with a magazine format.

Art groups join forces

In 1977 Judith Brodsky of the WCA urged the formation of a Coalition of Women's Art Organizations to unite the efforts of the many groups working toward similar goals. Co-founder Cynthia Navaretta, editor of Women Artists News, served as first pro tem chair. Over 200 such groups—women's art collectives, cooperative galleries, publications devoted only to women's art and women's art schools—were scattered throughout the country. The combined membership of these groups then was nearly 100,000. These figures did not include women in the performing arts or in music.

The coalition, headed in 1985 by Dorothy Provis of
Port Washington, Wisconsin, has emerged as the major
national women's organization in the arts representing
women to the federal government. Because of the large
number of organizations, boasting a combined membership
of 75,000, it can command the attention of Congress and
government agencies.

Their accomplishments have been impressive. The
CWAO scheduled five speakers before regional hearings on
the White House Conference on the Arts and in 1978
organized the first national lobbying day in Washington,
D.C. Some 200 delegates descended on the Capitol to rally
their legislators on behalf of good arts legislation. This was
the first direct input to Congress on the concerns and issues
of women in the arts. The CWAO also met with NEA on
matters directly concerning women and art, and with other
government agencies, established the women's ARTSPACE
at the IWY conference in Houston and organized women to
march for ERA in July 1978. They held their first national
conference in 1979.

Black women artists, led by Faith Ringgold, formed
Women Artists and Students for Black Art Liberation and
later an exhibition group called Where We At.

Conferences of women artists over the past decade
and a half have served many needs: networking, confidence
building, developing cohesiveness and unity, mutual
support, a sense of sisterhood, and providing
inspiration. Navaretta's Guide lists ten between 1972 and
1978, not counting annual repeats of the same conference.

A women's museum

One institution that has made significant strides in the
1980s is the National Museum of Women in the
Arts. Combining traditional, mainstream methods of raising
funds with its core goal to exhibit art by women that never
gets displayed elsewhere, the institution is part alternative
and part traditional.

First Lady Nancy Reagan served as patron of the Third Annual Benefit in April of 1985 and the evening produced over $75,000 for the museum. Yet museum founder, Wilhelmina Cole Holladay, was motivated to focus exclusively on the collection of women's art when she found not a single woman artist listed in the establishment source, Janson's <u>History of Art</u>.

Museum membership in the summer of 1985 stood at 213 individuals and corporations as founding members and 12,000 members, a dramatic increase of 2000 percent over the previous year.

Supported by the mainstream American Association of Museums as a long overdue project, the National Museum of Women in the Arts will house the Holladay Collection, an incomparable body of some 400 works from 16 countries by over 200 women artists who lived from the 16th century to the present. Its library resources will serve as an advanced study center for students of art by women. It is hoped that the museum's permanent home after 1986 will attract 500,000 visitors annually. Its first exhibit, "American Women Artists 1830-1930," will open in April of 1987.

Music: Alternatives for Women

In David Ewen's long-used volume of biographies of 17 of the world's outstanding <u>Twentieth Century Composers</u> there is not one woman.

Sound familiar?

As in the visual arts, the primary goal of scholarship, according to writer Elizabeth Wood, in her 1980 review article in Signs, "has been the revival of the life and work of exceptional [women] composers."

A common thread running through these recovered women's lives is the supportive, secondary roles that women musicians have played, as wives or younger sisters of composers or as "bearers rather than creators of musical traditions."

From 1975 to 1980, checklists, editions, handbooks, dictionaries, discographies and bibliographies of both published and manuscript sources contributed to a cross-fertilizing harvest of women's music history and criticism.

A "model of the new feminist scholarship" is Women in American Music: A Bibliography of Music and Literature, edited by Adrienne Fried Block and Carol Neuls-Bates. Wood calls this monumental source "indispensible to future American research and to the growing number of courses in music history and women's studies." Unpublished dissertations and research papers further expand the knowledge of women's contributions to composition, performance and applied music. Aaron Cohen has put out an enormous bibliography of living women composers and their work.

Jeannie G. Pool, in a 1979 article in Music Educators Journal, also comments on the amount of material that each year "becomes available on the subject of American music, including bibliographies, histories, biographies, biographical dictionaries and continuous oral history."

She indicates that courses on women in music history are "springing up" at high schools, colleges and conservatories, and concludes that the "discovery of a history of American women composers offers a potential source of personal strength for women musicians of all ages."

Other important books have been Unsung: A History of Women in American Music by Christine Ammer and Women Making Music: Studies in the Social History of Women Musicians and Composers, edited by Jane Bowers and Judith Tick.

Common themes and patterns

These books have uncovered "common themes and patterns of discrimination in attitudes toward the nature of women's work in music; the circumstances in which women have made music; and the thorny issue of whether women have a distinctive style," said Wood.

Two more recent books are Contemporary Concert Music by Women, compiled and edited by Judith Lang Zaimont and Karen Famera, and The Musical Woman: an International Perspective, a proposed three-volume work by

Judith Lang Zaimont with Catherine Overhauser and Jane
Gottlieb.

In one way or another, many of the published books
have examined the basic assumptions, familiar to visual
artists, that there have been no "great" women composers;
that both instruments and instrumental styles and
techniques have been sexually stereotyped; and that women
write sentimental songs rather than symphonies.

With centuries of historical precedent behind it, the
situation was largely unchanged in the early '70s. Women
had to find other ways to pursue their music and the
feminist movement inspired and emboldened them.

As Elizabeth Wood put it, "Through alternative
strategies, women have devised conditions in which they
can both continue to work and exercise influence."

Women have always had easier access to alternative
closed systems such as all women music clubs, orchestras
and private teaching. Historically, however, according to
Wood, these alternative organizations have not had much
impact on either traditional institutions or the public's
perceptions of women musicians.

In many ways, "Today's feminist scholars echo late
19th century women activists by forming their own
academic forums and colloquia and sponsoring their own
concerts, festivals and lecture-recitals to read papers and
perform music," said Wood.

The National Women's Music Festival, first held in
Champaign, Illinois, in 1974, became an annual event. The
first festival, publicized only by word of mouth, drew about
100 women. More than 1,000 women attended the third
event and attendance has been increasing ever since. At
least 15 other festivals between 1974 and 1979 carried on
the work.

A national conference on women in music took place
in the spring of 1985 at the University of
Kansas. Undertaken to "promote accomplishments of
women in education, performance, research and
composition," the event featured composer Judith Lang
Zaimont and historian Jeannie G. Pool.

For classical music, the most important woman's
record company is Leonarda, featuring premiere recordings
by historical and contemporary women composers. They

also publish music by men. Marnie Hall is the director and founder. Northeastern Records is producing a series on women's music that comprises perhaps one-third of the catalog. Da Capo Press is republishing music from the past by composers like Fanny Mendelssohn and Clara Schumann. In addition to art music, folk music, musical theatre and various forms of popular music have flourished in the '70s and early '80s completely outside of established musical institutions. "They were nourished and sustained by grass roots publications, women-directed recording companies and women-promoted organizations," wrote Wood in her Signs article.

Jeannie G. Pool, in her 1977 Women in Music History, listed 19 record companies devoted to "recordings by women for women." Among these is Olivia Records, an alternative recording company that in 1983 moved toward a mainstream market when it introduced its sister label, Second Wave Records. Though Olivia's focus remains on adult contemporary music, Second Wave "offers a distinctly different approach by recording a wide array of musical styles." According to President Judy Dlugacz, "With Second Wave, we are working to further women artists without restricting the recording process to women only."

Fallen Woman

In Madison, Wisconsin, the decade-old Fallen Woman Productions is one of the community's oldest feminist institutions and has prospered since its early days. Unlike cooperative feminist production companies, Fallen Woman is a private business, designed to provide women's music and produce local feminist cultural events on a profit basis.

Periodicals

Disseminating and commenting on news of all the activity in alternative music called for periodicals devoted to it. Some of these were Pan Pipes, Paid My Dues, Calliope, Written Word Collective, Ear Magazine Women's Music and the Feminist Art Journal. Occasionally mainstream music periodicals published articles or special issues on women's music.

During the past 15 years, alternative organizations have offered support and services. Some of these are American Women Composers, Inc, the International League of Women Composers, National Federation of Music Clubs, Society of Black Composers and Women of Music of Chicago.

American Women Composers was founded in 1976 by Tommie Ewert Carl to help women get their works published, broadcast, performed and recorded; to collect scores, tapes and discs for an archive for the works of women; and to make the general public aware of women as composers, performers and conductors.

The International League of Women Composers, founded by Nancy Van de Vate in 1975, has as its principal aims to improve and advance commission, recording and performance potentialities for women composers. The organization schedules chamber music concerts and has an ongoing series of one-hour radio programs of music by members. It also functions as an information clearinghouse and resource center.

In the current Index/Directory of Women's Media, 35 music groups are listed. In Cynthia Navaretta's 1979 Guide to Women's Art Organizations were listed 3 composers organizations; 29 performing groups (including such now famous ones as Sweet Honey in the Rock); 3 performance booking agencies; 14 recording and distributing companies; 16 festivals, concerts, conferences or symposia held between 1974 and '79; and 8 women's resource organizations.

In addition there was a special project to study country and western music's perspective on women and influences on the socialization of Southern women.

The New England Women's Symphony, established in 1978, played works only by women composers and invited only women to conduct the orchestra. It did allow men to play; auditions were screened and several men joined. Kay Gardner, composer, conductor and flutist, was music director and principal conductor of the symphony. Unfortunately, the group has since disbanded. However, the

Bay Area Women's Philharmonic is now going into its sixth season.

Theatre: Feminist Drama

The proliferation of alternative feminist theatre has typified the last decade and a half in the theatre arts. According to Linda Walsh Jenkins, co-editor of Women in American Theatre, the first feminist theatres emerged in the early 1970s. It was artists determined to change the status quo who began to take over the mechanisms of counter-culture, anti-establishment theatre groups, already familiar and in place from the '60s. While the longevity of specific alternative groups may have been problematical at first, clearly feminist theatre is flourishing today. (Sixty-seven art/graphics/theatre groups are listed in the 1985 Index/Directory of Women's Media.)

"There is now a history, a vocabulary, a body of writing, a political and artistic impact emanating from the movement," wrote Jenkins in 1981.

These feminist theatres, springing up spontaneously all over the country, shared the common goal of creating display space, and hence an audience, for feminist drama. By definition, feminist drama values women's experience and places women's mental and physical struggles and growth at the center of the drama rather than as tangential to the struggles of the male lead.

Such theatre, said feminist playwright Megan Terry, "spread the psychic news" about women's lives, women's stories, women's artistry.

Having an alternative feminist theatre movement meant that women no longer had to write plays men would approve of. By 1979, 90 such feminist theatre groups—from Tucson to Minneapolis, and New York to Los Angeles—dotted the country. In 1981 there were 112, according to Navaretta's guide.

Some are women-only companies that perform for women-only audiences; some are women-only companies that perform for mixed audiences; and some are mixed companies that perform for mixed audiences.

Two types of theatres

Philosophically, theatres break down into two types. The first seeks to provide a showcase for women in the theatre, an alternative employer for women playwrights, directors, producers, set designers, actors and so on. They prefer women artists and plays that present women in nonstereotypical ways.

These more moderate groups, though less numerous, are among the oldest and best known. Some, such as Women's Interart in New York City, the Los Angeles Feminist Theatre, the Women's Project of the American Place Theatre, and the Washington Area Feminist Theatre, tend to organize themselves like traditional theatre groups. Because display of the work is the main objective, they use traditional criteria to select the plays they produce. They hope to gain notice from establishment media. Often, they have relatively stable organizations, permanent homes and a measure of financial stability.

The second type of women's theatre group is committed to raising the consciousness and improving the lives of women in general, not just women in the theatre. These groups may appear to be short-lived and have no organizational form or permanence. They reject the hierarchical organization typical of mainstream theatre groups for a collective model featuring cooperation among equals and interchangeable roles, both on and off stage—a deliberate counter to the traditional ideas of male-dominated structures.

Collective improvisation

As Susan Suntree wrote in "Women's Culture," "Women's theatre groups are notably collective in their approaches to shaping a piece. Experiment and improvisation are often mentioned as working methods, as opposed to the usual assumption that a director will define the performance—though a director, perhaps with newly defined status, is commonly included. Some groups choose a director for a particular piece or members take turns directing. A few groups have writers as part of the ensembles and perform from scripts; others collaborate on a piece and write it as it develops." These techniques are now used by some mainstream theatres as well.

Some theatre groups specifically explore alternative sexuality, minority experience or nontraditional lifestyles. These more radical groups create solidarity among members, but encourage rebellion against traditional standards. Their purpose is not to persuade but to shock audiences into new ways of perceiving. Predictably, they are more often ignored by traditional media and theatrical organizations.

Actually, both types of feminist theatres have been largely ignored by established reviewers, critics and scholars. Certainly national newspapers and magazines have not reported the country-wide phenomenon of their unscripted, unrehearsed emergence. Of more than 15 feminist theatres active in New York City between 1969 and 1977, The New York Times and the Village Voice regularly reviewed only the productions of the Women's Interart Theatre. During the same period, only five articles in traditional periodicals attempted to deal with women's theatre nationwide. Even underground newspapers and radical feminist publications provided only sparse coverage.

Performance: The Public Art

There are many definitions of performance art. Moira Roth, author of The Amazing Decade, called it "a hybrid form which combines visual arts, theatre, dance, music, poetry and ritual."

Kay Larson, in her 1980 Artnews article, described it as "a mixture of narrative, visual and conceptual esthetics—body art with words." Performance art's ability to exaggerate the incongruities between social roles and the individual, she said, makes it especially useful to women.

For the purposes of this paper, video art will also be considered as a type of performance art, "the most promising and potentially the most revolutionary art medium of this—or any former—era," according to David A. Ross, curator of video, film and performance at the Long Beach Museum of Art.

Contemporary performance art had its roots in the

"happenings" of the '60s, and the much earlier performances of the Futurist, Dada and Surrealist movements. "Today's performance art is direct experience, not easily written about or recorded," wrote Claudia King in the 1980 bulletin, "Art Documentation." Unstructured, sometimes without a script, and certainly not replicable like a staged performance, each event is unique, "an unfolding of personal or group consciousness."

It is revolutionary and at the same time a throwback to the art forms of primitive societies. "Each contemporary performance is a reenactment, a recreation of life," wrote King. "Each member of the audience responds to the artist's communication, transforming it in accord with personal experience and political orientation."

It has certainly been reinterpreted by the feminist artist movement. Southern California, with its strong, informal collective artists organizations, such as Mother Art and The Feminist Art Workers, established in 1974, is the location of much activity. In 1978 The Los Angeles Woman's Building scheduled a major conference, with exhibition and performances. And in 1978, Linda Burnham founded High Performance Magazine in Los Angeles.

More and more women artists over the past decade have used this new medium to explore their creativity, changing both its content and its form.

For the people

Because they had no access to mainstream institutions to display their art, they intentionally bypassed traditional settings to bring their message to all kinds of people, some of whom would never set foot in a museum. The windows of Bergdorf Goodman on Fifth Avenue in New York City, the steps of the Los Angeles City Hall, metropolitan sidewalks, the beaches of California, an artist's garage, all were stages for performance art.

Thus performance art emerged, like a goddess from the sands of the California beaches, as an alternative institution in itself. In 1979, the New Orleans exhibition, "A Decade of Performance Art," curated by Mary Jane

Jacob, brought together many of the themes and forms the art had assumed.

A listing of performance history from The Amazing Decade shows 10 performances in 1973, 11 in 1975; 16 in 1976; 21 in 1977; 10 in 1978; 15 in 1979. Site works and other innovative forms became environmental projects, sometimes using plants, fish or living elements to make a statement about ecology or appearing suddenly as a "farm" alongside a freeway.

According to David Ross, Eleanor Antin, whose performance works employed alter-ego characters, uses video art to frame her work and direct her audience. In "The Adventures of a Nurse" (1976), Antin presents a series of the nurse's fantasies. The taped video version is more than just a document of her live performance, but actually gains credibility thanks to the audience's familiarity with the conventions—camera shots and cuts—of television.

Alexis Smith, Nancy Angelo and Candace Compton, Lynda Benglis, Antoinette DeJong, Cynthia Maughan, Susan Mogul, Barbara Smith, Joan Logue, Linda Montano, Lisa Steele and Suzanne Lacy are included in Ross's Southland Video Anthology.

Film: Women Make Movies

In her 1981 book Women's Reflections: The Feminist Film Movement, Jan Rosenberg covered the independent women's film movement in compelling detail. It takes criticism and history, she said, to legitimate an art movement. And film critics help explain it to the public. She divided feminist film critics—Molly Haskell, Marjorie Rosen, Sharon Smith, Claire Johnston and E. Ann Kaplan are among the best known—into those primarily oriented toward establishment movies from Hollywood and Europe and those oriented toward feminist documentary and avant-garde films.

Rosenberg pointed out that the two main types of independent films—documentary and avant-garde—have a closer analogy to the publishing world than to the commercial Hollywood film industry. Documentary films, so far the dominant form, are analogous to nonfiction writing and avant-garde films to poetry. In most cases, their economic support comes from different sources.

Funding for the less accessible (some say elitist) avant-garde film typically came from a filmmaker's family and friends, while documentaries often received funding from government sources. These sources increased their funding throughout the '70s. The National Endowment for the Arts, for example, spent $1.26 million to fund films in 1971 compared to $7.6 million in 1976.

According to Ariel Dougherty, now development director of Women's Studio Workshop in Rosendale, New York, "Women have probably had their largest impact" in documentaries in which they were able to make "particular political statements" targeted at a "broad spectrum of women."

Distribution

While criticism set the tone for the feminist film movement, filmmakers themselves were coming to grips with the practical realities. The impetus to create alternative institutions was the same for filmmakers as for visual artists: the total lack of opportunity via traditional outlets. In the early '70s, established film distributors simply dismissed women's films with a patronizing, "It's a very nice film, dear, but it's not commercial." Most were blind to the growing force of the women's movement.

As Rosenberg noted in 1971, women produced 36 films. By mid-1976, the number of filmmakers had grown to over 200 and by 1977 at least 250 films were being marketed as feminist films.

As in other arts, women had to invent and then make routine alternative ways of reaching audiences, and because feminist film distribution took shape outside of existing structures, it was the most autonomous of the film support systems. Today, 22 profit-making and nonprofit companies or cooperatives handle the multifaceted task, compared to 17 listed in the 1978 Index/Directory of Women's Media. Some filmmakers also distributed their own films.

Between 1971 and 1975 women surged to the forefront of independent film production. By 1975, five major feminist film cooperatives had been formed: New Day Films, Women's Film Coop (now defunct), Iris Films, Women/Artist/Filmmakers and Women Make Movies. Each played a crucial political and educational role in defining the significance of the women's movement and also in providing the practical and mechanical services critical to economic survival.

Women Make Movies was founded in 1972 "by two women film teachers (Ariel Dougherty and Sheila Paige) who offered workshop training in film and video production to neighborhood women," according to Dougherty's unpublished account. "Between 1972 and 1976 over 40 films and video pieces were created and over 500 women, including mothers, grandmothers, housewives and students, received training..."

New Day Films was also formed in 1972 by four filmmakers as a distribution cooperative. Convinced of their audiences, they chose to take "complete control of the distribution of their films."

Iris Films, wrote Dougherty, was an alliance of three women from Los Angeles and two from Washington, D.C., who planned to produce a film together. "They soon realized that producing films was only half the battle and committed themselves to exhibiting, distributing and promoting women's films as well."

Feminist film coops organized film festivals, special showings, how-to-do-it sessions and conferences and put out publications on alternative distribution. They made it possible for the films to reach their small intended audiences and for the filmmakers to earn enough money to continue making films.

Film festivals

Around the country, local, national and international film festivals "became the major forum for introducing a great number of women's films to an audience." While it is impossible to estimate the numbers of these festivals, Kristina Nordstrom, director of the two largest festivals, estimated that at least 40 to 50 festivals occurred between mid-1972 and late 1976. During those years major festivals were held in New York, Boston, Philadelphia, Washington, D.C., Chicago, San Francisco, Los Angeles, Jacksonville, Fla., and Northampton, Mass.

The Flaherty Film Seminar in 1971 provided a meeting ground for women who later became involved in the First International Festival of Women's Films, conceived by Nordstrom and held in New York in June 1972. The latter "focused national attention on the burgeoning women's film movement and provided a model of that type of exhibition." The Second International Film Festival was held in New York in 1976. Together the two festivals showed more than 100 films.

In February and March of 1975, the Conference of Feminist Film and Video Organizations, sponsored by Women Make Movies in New York City, and The Feminist Eye Conference in Los Angeles, together attracted over 325 feminists involved in all aspects of media production from the United States, the United Kingdom and Australia. They represented the "enormous swell of grass roots activity in the early 1970s," wrote Dougherty.

One of the things that came out of the two conferences, she said, was the identification of Media Report to Women, a monthly fact tabloid written by Donna Allen out of Washington, D.C., "as a major informational communications tool."

Other gatherings had significance for feminist filmmakers, even though the numbers of women's film collectives began to fall off in the late '70s. All such festivals fulfilled several major networking functions. They informed wider audiences of the large number of feminist films available, disseminated practical information about rental prices and processes, introduced filmmakers, critics and distributors to new works and to each other and promoted sisterhood within the collective movement.

In addition, festivals rallied, identified and solidified audiences, usually college students, mostly women in their 20s and 30s. "More than anything else," said Jan Rosenberg, "the institutionalization of the feminist

movement within colleges and universities has created a
new market for feminist resources."

Other alternative film periodicals besides Media
Report to Women helped disseminate the news. Women and
Film began publication in Los Angeles in 1972 as "the only
major written forum for the discussion and development of
feminist filmmaking," said Dougherty. Newsletters,
catalogs and other publications also came from newly
founded media groups such as Filmwomen of Boston, New
York City Newsreel (later Third World Newsreel), Women's
Film Co-op (of Connecticut and Massachusetts), The Twin
Cities Women's Film Collective, and the Amazon Media
Project.

In 1974, wrote Dougherty, Jump Cut began
publication. It contained "feminist film criticism, coupled
with a Marxist perspective" and reviews of Hollywood
films, television and independent films...." Videoletters, a
bi-monthly exchange of videotapes among women
filmmakers in 13 U.S. cities and their counterparts in
London and Toronto, was a short-lived attempt to
"exchange news and information among feminists
throughout the world."

At the end of 1975, Women in Film ceased
publication. The following year, several former Women and
Film members founded Camera Obscura, a journal of film
theory. Now the leading journal of feminist film theory, it
has helped stabilize the movement.

According to Dougherty, "by 1976 a number of
women's media groups which had blossomed in the early
1970s began to fold or disband. They had served their
primary function of providing women with skills and
self-confidence. Women were beginning to specialize....We
demanded greater professionalism of ourselves....We needed
larger and larger budgets....And the economy was
beginning to sag. In spite of this, some organizations, such
as Iris Films and Women Make Movies, continued to
prosper and grow, distributing feminist work, and new
groups, such as Iris Video in Minneapolis, were formed."

Dougherty thinks that despite the difficulty of getting
funding, women's films and videos have continued to
improve and find wider audiences. To achieve this, women

have had to make some connections with both alternative and traditional institutions.

Literature: New Outlets for Women's Books

Underpinning the alternative strategies in literature is feminist criticism, a phenomenon that paralleled the "extraordinary flowering of women's writing in the '70s and '80s." In a December 1984 New York Times article, Elaine Showalter, a professor of English at Princeton University and the editor of The New Feminist Criticism, said: "Feminist critics and scholars such as Sandra Gilbert, Susan Gubar, Annette Kolodny, Josephine Donovan, Barbara Christian, Nancy Miller, Nina Auerbach, Carolyn Heilbrun, Cheryl Walker and Patricia M. Spacks, who study the modes of women's writing in history and the themes, images and structures that have emerged from the tensions between the female literary tradition and the cultural mainstream, have enlarged our sense of what women's writing has been and what it can be."

While Showalter questioned whether we can know if the term "women's writing" has any "intellectual, moral or historical validity without serious study of hundreds of writers and works," she affirmed that "The feminist study of women's literature has outlined a great tradition, as capacious and diverse as men's writing." This study has recovered and reevaluated women's writing in the past, but has yet to resolve the conflict between women who write—but refuse to call themselves women writers—and women who write purposefully about "women's lot" and call themselves feminists. Showalter charged that many women who refuse to call themselves women writers only illustrate how thoroughly they have been taught to denigrate women's art and how "important art and literary power in our society are still firmly linked to masculinity." She said suitable topics and important traditions are still "defined as masculine" and "the female witness...is still not accepted as first-person universal. Women telling stories about themselves or others are not trusted; they are judged as limited, evasive, neurotic, hysterical, deceitful, immature or prejudiced—the essence of what critics call unreliable narrators."

The masculine perspective, she went on, is considered the human perspective, the male predicament, the human condition. "No quantity of detail about Rabbit Angstrom's basketball games, midlife crisis or Toyota dealership can diminish John Updike's title to universality," she wrote.

Redefining women's art

In concluding her article, Showalter said women writers and feminist critics have different tasks but must both redefine women's art if prejudices that put "female" at one end of the spectrum and "universal" at the other are ever to be erased. She called on women writers to "affirm both their womanhood and their esthetic freedom." She said they must follow the example of Gloria Steinem who, on her 40th birthday, responded to the compliment that she didn't look her age with, "This is how 40 looks."

In the same way, Showalter said, when women are "complimented" by being told "they don't write like women because their work is so powerful or original or profound, they must respond, 'This is how women write'."

Joanna Russ, in her ironically titled 1984 book, How To Suppress Women's Writing, said men have always maintained that women can't write at all. And they have an answer for every fact to the contrary.

What if a woman has written? The male establishment denies she was the agent. She had listened to the talk of her husband's brilliant friends (Mary Shelley), or some "man inside her" wrote it, or "it wrote itself."

But if she has written it all by herself, she shouldn't have. What kind of a person is she? She can't be virtuous if she knows enough to write about those things.

But what if she has known enough to write about those things? Then they are the wrong things to write about: the drawing room, the family, the kitchen, courtship, dailiness. "Poor Jane Austen could paint only miniatures."

But what if readers like her book? Then she doesn't deserve the credit. She's someone else's wife (Zelda

Fitzgerald) or was a spinster (Emily Dickinson) or crazy
(Sylvia Plath).

But what if she isn't any of these? Point out she wrote
only one book (Gone With the Wind). One book doesn't
mean she's a real writer.

The seven percent solution

If all these rationalizations fail, there is only one thing
left to do, said Russ ironically. "Give women's work a
limited exposure." Russ proceeded to cite surveys of
anthologies that vary the authors and texts included but
keep the "total representation of women writers at about 7
percent—a different 7 percent as generations or editors
change, but still 7 percent."

Russ concluded that women writers have always
found it hard to write, because of the above myths, the lack
of role models, "because they deny that they are really
women or that they write like other women or about
women's subjects" or "because they get out of the major
genres and turn to diaries or letters or science fiction or
mysteries."

Or because they had failed to establish alternative
routes to getting their work published. That "because," as
the last 15 years have shown, has now been remedied.

Articulating and publicizing

The establishment of feminist presses, like the
founding of the women's reports, newsletters and
magazines, is a phenomenon of the last 15 years. The 1985
Index/Directory of Women's Media lists 116 women's
presses and publishers, the pivotal institutions, said Robin
Morgan in her 1981 interview with Gayle Kimball.

In a survey of feminist book publishers released in
1978, Polly Joan and Andrea Chessman reported that 82
presses in the United States and Canada were publishing
books covering women's movement ideologies from "strict
feminist separatism to cooperative non-sexism." Some
presses specialize in poetry or novels, some in nonsexist
children's stories. Some have men as partners. The names
of just a few of the presses include: Out and Out Books,

Shameless Hussy Press, Vanilla Press, Times Change
Press, Daughters, Inc. and Vanity Press.

According to the <u>Women's Book of World Records and
Achievements</u>, women began to revive and establish
women-oriented, women-owned and women-operated
publishing ventures as "a natural and essential requirement
of the women's movement for articulating and publicizing
grievances." As in most revolutions, the printed word was
crucial in mustering the troops. Lindsy Van Gelder, writing
in the November 1970 issue of Ms., said the feminist press
was "a cutting edge, a conscience...particularly around
1969 and 1970 when the printed word was feminism....it's
no accident that our first leaders were writers; there was a
hunger for information...."

That hunger was exacerbated by the traditional media
which virtually ignored women's news, or trivialized and
demeaned its importance by putting it on the "women's
pages." In addition, women realized that the power of the
press belonged to those that owned it.

Getting the word out meant establishing an
alternative press. The rise of art periodicals devoted to
women is one aspect of that awareness and urgency and is
dealt with in another section. Woman-owned book
publishing enterprises brought out works on the lives of
forgotten women, explored mother-daughter themes, and
circulated poetry, essays, fiction and nonfiction self-help
books, psychology, theory, humor, biography and
autobiography, art and poetry.

The Feminist Press

The Feminist Press, a publishing house specializing in
nonsexist textbooks and juvenile literature, was established
in 1970 by Florence Howe, who continues as its president.
It is dedicated to producing books for women's studies
courses, a phenomenon that burgeoned along with women's
presses.

The Feminist Press is the major nonprofit publisher of
nonsexist curriculum material and books on women. "It has
played a central role in shaping the women's studies
movement nationally," said Howe, pointing out that the

number of women's studies courses grew from 13 or 14 programs in 1969 to 432 in 1982.

In its 16 years of operation Howe has "guided a hundred or so new or previously out-of-print books by women to publication. The list is impressive, including authors Paule Marshall (Brown Girl, Brown Stones and Reena), and Meridel Le Sueur (Ripening). "We don't do books that will be best sellers," Howe observed in an interview in the Madison Feminist Connection in June of 1983. "We do what the classroom needs forever—feminist classics."

Howe did not start out to become a publisher. Inspired by a vision of a series of books about the lives of women, she was searching for a publisher. It soon became clear, however, that if she wanted to publish, she would have to start a press of her own. In 1970 the first book—Life in the Iron Mills by Rebecca Harding Davis—rolled off the presses. In 1971 she published a children's book, The Dragon and the Doctor, priced at $1. In 1983, the Feminist Press, which now brings out about a dozen titles per year, sold $377,000 worth of books, most in the $8.95 range.

In 1985 the Feminist Press moved to The City University of New York "to continue its program of service, research and educational publishing" according to the fall/winter catalog. Working with various CUNY colleges, the press will become "before the decade is out, the nucleus of a new City University Press."

Seal Press

Seal Press, on the opposite side of the country from The Feminist Press, was founded as a collective in 1976 by two women, Barbara Wilson and Rachel de Silva, joined later by Faith Conlon. Each of the founders contributed $40, as did their first author, and "not a single penny has been invested since." Ellen Herman described the modus operandi in her article in the February 1985 Women's Review of Books.

The women do their own layout, warehousing, bookkeeping, promotion and editorial work as well as some of the printing. Wilson "described their internal organization as organic and expressed a familiar ambivalence about the formalization of collective work arrangements that often coincides with a growth in staff or number of books. Apprentice members and student interns provide essential help in getting through the daily grind." Seal also employs some freelance bookkeepers and designers.

Seal pays a royalty to its authors and has just begun to cover small advances of $500 to $1,000. The unique advantage they can give their authors "is the chance to stay in print and develop an audience," a commitment, said Herman, "typical of feminist publishers, and a reflection of their political responsibility to the women's movement, not to themselves as solvent businesses."

Seal has sought a regional community as its audience, one structured by location. Other presses have targeted audiences of lesbians (Naiad), fiction readers, women of color (Kitchen Table), women's studies teachers (The Feminist Press), marxists (Monthly Review), or the new left (South End Press). A new press is Firebrand Books in Ithaca, New York.

Women's bookstores

According to Carol Seajay, a founder of Old Wives' Tales bookstore in San Francisco and editor of The Feminist Bookstore News, "Many of the 80 or so feminist bookstores that exist today in the United States are small, but most are mature businesses." (The 1985 Index/Directory of Women's Media listed 44 women's bookstores.) Whatever the current numbers, they arose to fill the need not met by mainstream booksellers. Their emphasis on books by and for women, their community orientation and their political perspective made them unique.

To broaden their appeal and pay the rent many sell records, periodicals, posters, pins, notecards, T shirts, and nonsexist children's books as well as books by and for women on virtually every conceivable topic. Many of their books come from feminist publishers, university presses and small publishers, according to a 1983 article in Ms. by Jeanne O'Connor.

The Crazy Ladies Bookstore in Cincinnati, for instance, carries books by and about "wimmin," lesbian/gays and men's consciousness raising. Turtle Grandmother Books mail orders works by women of color, specifically North American Indian women. The Bethune Museum-Archives stock educational materials, traveling exhibits and video tapes on black women and organizations from 1800 to 1980. Some bookstores serve food or sell women's crafts and records as well as books.

"Just about every feminist bookstore extends beyond selling to act as a community clearinghouse, a referral service and a social center," O'Connor wrote. While political motivations led to the founding of most women's bookstores, and collective models of organization kept them going, many today are remarkably successful. Some are now reorganized as nonprofit partnerships rather than collectives. Others have moved from hard-to-find locations that served more as clubs for an "in" group of women to Main Street locations that attract all kinds of people looking for books they can't find anywhere else.

Based on a study she conducted recently, Seajay estimated that "women's bookstores sold $4 million worth of books in 1981." And she added that they have begun to have considerable impact on mainstream publishers (men) who are beginning to bring out feminist titles of their own.

In 1976, the first "Women in Print" conference served as an important communications link for women publishers and booksellers. One result was The Feminist Bookstore News, a bimonthly networking publication that contains capsule descriptions of new books on the market and solutions to bookstore and business problems.

In Madison, Wisconsin, the Room of One's Own Bookstore celebrated its 11th anniversary in January of '86. The store, which is cooperatively owned and operated, sells a variety of books, including textbooks and nonsexist children's literature. Occasionally they sponsor poetry readings or author autograph parties.

Organizations for women writers

Cynthia Navaretta's 1979 Guide to Women's Art Organizations listed four alternative women writers organizations: the Feminist Writers' Guild of Berkeley, California, the D.C. Feminist Writers' Guild in Silver Spring, Maryland, the New York Feminist Writers' Guild in New York City, and The Woman's Salon, in Sea Cliff, New York.

The Berkeley group, organized in 1978 with more than 1000 members, pressures "national publications to review books by feminist presses and writers, to protest discrimination against women in the distribution of grant money, and to provide members with publishing information."

The Washington D.C. group "publishes a newsletter and maintains files on feminist agents, editors and presses." The New York City organization proposes "to correct the inequities of the reviewing and publishing system," and the Woman's Salon serves as an "alternative literary network to provide audience support and serious critical attention to the works of women writers."

Women's newsletters and periodicals—a good example is New Directions for Women—review a number of books on all topics by women writers in each bimonthly issue. Specific book reviewing periodicals also fill the gap left in coverage of women's books by traditional media.

Bibliography
Women and the Arts:
A Survey of Recent Progress

GENERAL

Allen, Martha Leslie, ed. 1985 Index/Directory of Women's Media, Washington, D.C.: Women's Institute for Freedom of the Press.

AP. "Reagan Proposes Big Slash in Arts Budget." The Capital Times, January 16, 1985.

Asinof, Lynn. "Big Changes in Companies Affect the Arts." The Wall Street Journal, April 24, 1984, p. 1.

Berman, Avis. "A Decade of Progress." Artnews, October 1980, pp. 73-79.

Chiarmonte, Paula L., ed. "Women Artists: A Resource and Research Guide." Art Documentation, October 1982.

Dettbarn, Susan, researcher. "The Arts Administrator--Job Characteristics." Madison: Association of College, University and Community Arts Administrators, 1983.

Farbman, Steven and Kimel, Earle. "The Arts Stand at Back of the Line for Dollars." The Washington Post, July 19, 1982, p. 5.

Glueck, Grace. "Women Artists '80." Artnews, October 1980, pp. 58-63.

Kimball, Gayle, ed. Women's Culture: The Women's Renaissance of the Seventies. Metuchen, N.J. and London: The Scarecrow Press, Inc., 1981.

Larson, Kay. "For the First Time Women Are Leading Not Following." Artnews, October 1980, pp. 64+.

Magenta, Muriel. "Feminist Art Criticism: A Political Definition." The Journal of the Theory and Criticism of the Visual Arts, Arizona State University, 1981.

Malone, Julia. "After ERA: A Search for a New Direction Begins." The Christian Science Monitor, June 25, 1982, p. l.

National Commission on the Observance of International Women's Year, 1975. The Creative Woman: A Report of the Committee on the Arts and Humanities.

National Commission on the Observance of International Women's Year, 1975. The Spirit of Houston: An Official Report to the President, the Congress and the People of the United States. March 1987.

National Endowment for the Arts. "Employment Trends Among Artists." Cultural Post, June 1983, p. 5.

National Endowment for the Arts. "Council Discusses Blind Judging." Cultural Post, June 1983, p. 7.

National Endowment for the Arts. Research Division Report 7. "Minorities and Women in the Arts: 1970."

National Endowment for the Arts. "New Dimensions for the Arts 1971-1972."

National Endowment for the Arts. "Museums USA, 1974."

National Endowment for the Arts. Research Division Report 12. "Artists Compared by Age, Sex and Earnings in 1970 and 1976, January 1980."

National Endowment for the Arts. Research Division Note 4. "Women and Minorities in Artist Occupations." July 4, 1983.

Navaretta, Cynthia, ed. Guide to Women's Art
Organizations and Directory for the Arts. New York City:
Midmarch Associates, 1982.

O'Neill, Lois Decker, ed. The Women's Book of World
Records and Achievements. Garden City, New York:
Anchor Press/Doubleday, 1979.

Reiss, Alvin H., ed. Arts Management, Summer 1983,
pp. 1-4; September/October 1983, pp. 1-4;
November/December 1983, pp. 1-4; January/February
1984, pp. 1-4.

Rom, Cristine C. "One View: The Feminist Art Journal."
Woman's Art Journal, Fall 1981, Winter 1982, pp. 19-24.

Russell, H. Diane. "Art History." Signs, Spring 1980, pp.
468-481.

Salmans, Sandra. "Big Business Tightens Its Arts Budget."
The New York Times, February 20, 1983.

Shaver, Carl. Money Talk.

Van Wagner, Judy K. Collischan, ed. Women Shaping Art:
Profiles of Power. New York: Praeger, 1984, pp. 3-6.

Weil, Rose R., ed. CAA Newsletter, Fall 1984, pp. 8-9.

Wisconsin Humanities Committee exhibit. "Black Women:
Achievements Against the Odds," Summer 1984.

Also correspondence with and/or literature and/or statistics
from:
    American Association of Museums.
    Association of College, University and Community
        Arts Administrators.
    Marge Campane, Community Arts Management
    Program.
    Center for Arts Information.
    Center for the Study of Women and Society.
    College Art Association of America.

Ruth Mayleas, program officer, The Ford
  Foundation.
National Endowment for the Arts.
Cynthia Navaretta, editor, Women Artists News.
Office of U.S. Congressman from Wisconsin Robert
  W. Kastenmeier.
Dorothy Provis, Coalition of Women's Art
  Organizations.
Ellouise Schoettler, Coalition of Women's Art
  Organizations.
The Sophia Smith Collection-Women's History
  Archive.
Kendall Taylor, Director, Arts Management
  Associates.

CRAFTS AND QUILTS

Bodine, Sarah. "At Long Last Art: A New Home for the
Crafts." Vantage Point, September/October 1984, p.16.

Kassell, Paula. "Quilting--Communal Creativity." (A review
of The Artist and the Quilt, edited by Charlotte Robinson.)
New Directions for Women, March/April 1984, p. 5.

MacDowell, Marsha; MacDowell, Betty; and Dewhurst,
C. Kurt. Artists in Aprons: Folk Art by American
Women. New York: E.P. Dutton with Museum of American
Folk Art, 1979, pp. x-xviii.

Mainardi, Pat. "Quilts: The Great American Art." The
Feminist Art Journal, Winter 1973, pp. 1, 18-23.

Robinson, Charlotte, ed. The Artist and the Quilt. New
York: Alfred A. Knopf, 1983.

VISUAL ARTS

Alloway, Lawrence. "Where Were You on the Week of the
23rd?" The Village Voice, March 2, 1982.

Bennetts, Leslie. "Judy Chicago: Women's Lives and Art." The New York Times, April 8, 1985.

Blum, June. "Women and Success at the Brooklyn Museum." The Feminist Art Journal, Fall 1975, pp. 14-15.

California Commission on the Status of Women. "A New Journal on Black Women." California Women, October 1984. p.6.

Cameron, Julia. "Women's Art Museum? A Gentle Dream Finally Begins to Take Shape." Chicago Tribune, February 16, 1986, p. 6, section 13.

Chicago, Judy. "A Female Form Language." Women's Culture: The Women's Renaissance of the Seventies, edited by Gayle Kimball, pp. 60-72. Metuchen, N.J. and London: The Scarecrow Press, Inc., 1981.

Cox, Meg. "Art Expo: Popcorn and Picassos at the Navy Pier." The Wall Street Journal, May 22, 1984, p. 28.

Dickinson, Eleanor. 1979 notes on interview with H.J. Janson. Washington, D.C.: College Art Association Convention, February 1, 1979.

Dickinson, Eleanor. "Statistics: Sex Differentials in Art Employment and Exhibition Opportunities." February 24, 1978.

Fine, Elsa Honig. "One Point Perspective." Woman's Art Journal, Fall/Winter 1981-82.

Fine, Elsa Honig. "One Point Perspective." Woman's Art Journal, Spring/Summer 1985.

Finger, Anne. "Jersey Embroiders Chicago." New Directions for Women, January/February 1984, pp. 13-14.

"Women Finally Get Some Respect in World of Art." The Capital Times, March 9, 1985. (Reprinted from Harper's Bazaar.)

Hoelterhoff, Manuela. "MOMA's Coming Out Party: Art in a Glass House." The Wall Street Journal, May 15, 1984, p. 28.

Moore, Sabra. "Views by Women Artists." Woman's Art Journal, Fall/Winter 1981-82.

National Museum of Women in the Arts News, Spring 1984, Winter 1984/85, Spring/Summer 1985.

Nemser, Cindy. "Book Review" (A review of Through the Flower: My Struggle as a Woman Artist by Judy Chicago.) The Feminist Art Journal, Spring 1975, pp. 44-45.

Newfield, Marcia. "Overdue Applause Greets Black Artist." New Directions for Women, March/April 1985, p. 4.

Nochlin, Linda. "Why Have There Been No Great Women Artists?" Artnews, January 1971, pp. 23-29 +.

Nochlin, Linda. "Toward a Juster Vision: How Feminism Can Change Our Way of Looking at Art History." Feminist Collage. New York and London: Teacher's College Press, 1975, p. 5.

Olin, Ferris. "Galleries: Some Vital Statistics." Art Documentation, October 1982, pp. A-18, A-19.

Orenstein, Gloria. "Art History." Signs, Winter 1975, pp. 505-525.

Roos, Sandra. "Women's Imagery/Women's Art." Women's Culture: The Women's Renaissance of the Seventies, edited by Gayle Kimball, pp. 42-60. Metuchen, N.J. and London: The Scarecrow Press, Inc., 1981.

Ross, David A. Southland Video Anthology 1976-77. Long
Beach Museum of Art, 1977.

Rubinstein, Charlotte Streifer. American Women
Artists. Avon, 1982, pp. 374-381.

Schoettler, Ellouise. "Testimony Before the House
Appropriations Committee, Sub-Committee on the Interior."
April 18, 1978.

Schoettler, Ellouise. "Washington Letter." Women Artists
News, June 1978, p. 11.

Stockinger, Jacob. "Museum Will Put Women Artists in
Spotlight." The Capital Times, September 9, 1985, p. 40.

Taylor, Kendall. "Risking It: Women as Museum Leaders."
Museum News, February 1985, pp. 20-33.

Weinstein, Joyce. "Women Artists Picket MOMA." Women
in the Arts Bulletin, September/October 1984, pp. 1-2.

Also correspondence with and/or literature and/or statistics
from:

> Artemesia Gallery, Chicago.
> Coalition of Women's Art Organizations.
> Muriel Magenta, Women's Caucus for Art.
> The National Museum of Women in the Arts.
> Georgia O'Keeffe exhibit catalog.
> The Studio Museum in Harlem.
> The Woman's Building.
> Women in the Arts Foundation.
> Women's Art Registry of Minnesota.
> Women's Caucus for Art.
> University of California at Los Angeles.

DANCE

Kendall, Elizabeth. "Dancing: A Ford Foundation Report."
December 1983, p. 41.

Kisselgoff, Anna. "Has the Dance Boom Run Its Course?" The New York Times, March 3, 1985.

Kisselgoff, Anna. "Diversity Is the Word for American Dance Today." The New York Times, March 10, 1985, p. 19.

Kisselgoff, Anna. "At the Heart of Martha Graham's Drama." The New York Times, April 14, 1985, p. 10.

Kronen, H.B. "Editorial." Dance Scope, September 1980.

"Martha Graham Reflects on her Art and a Life in Dance." The New York Times, March 31, 1985.

Reynolds, Nancy, ed. The Dance Catalog: A Complete Guide to Today's World of Dance. New York: Harmony Book, 1979.

Satin, Leslie. "Dance." Guide to Women's Art Organizations. P.O. Box 3304, Grand Central Station, New York, NY 10163, 1979, pp. 41-42.

Shewey, Don. "Enriching the Stage Through Music and Dance." The New York Times, March 10, 1985, p. 4.

Siegel, Marcia B. Watching the Dance Go By. Boston: Houghton Mifflin Company, 1979.

Vaughan, David. "Twyla Tharp: Launching a New American Classicism." Dance Magazine, May 1984, pp. 54+.

Also correspondence with and/or literature and/or statistics from:

> Committee on Research in Dance.
> Gill Miller, chairwoman, Department of Dance, Denison University.
> Performing Arts Research Center, New York Public Library.

Joan Woodbury, professor of dance, University of Utah.

MUSIC

Abeles, Harold F. and Porter, Susan Yank. "So Your Daughter Wants to Be a Drummer." Music Educators Journal, March 1977, pp. 48-49.

Adam, Margie. June 1977 interview. Women's Culture: The Women's Renaissance of the Seventies, pp. 158-160. Metuchen, N.J. and London: The Scarecrow Press, Inc., 1981.

American Theatre. "Operatic Workout." March 1985, p. 24.

Block, Adrienne Fried and Neuls-Bates, Carol, eds. Women in American Music. Westport, Conn.: Greenwood Press, 1979, pp. xxvi-xxvii.

Borroff, Edith. "A Conference on Women in Music: A Progress Report." College Music Symposium, vol. 22, no. 2, (1982), pp. 161-5.

Evans, Janet. "To Be or Not to Be Bias...That Was the Question." The School Musician, August/September 1982, pp. 42-43.

Gardner, Kay. Letter. Women's Culture: The Women's Renaissance of the Seventies, edited by Gayle Kimball, pp. 157-158. Metuchen, N.J. and London: The Scarecrow Press, Inc., 1981.

Gotzler, Karen, ed. "Fallen Woman Productions." Forte, November 1984, pp. 7+.

Greenberg, Gilda M. "Women in Major Symphonies: Why a Minority?" International Musician, April 1982, p. 5+.

Grimsted, Karen. "Mooncircles." Women's Culture: The Women's Renaissance of the Seventies, edited by Gayle Kimball, p. 157. Metuchen, N.J. and London: The Scarecrow Press, Inc., 1981.

Henahan, Donal. "Women Are Breaking the Symphonic Barriers." The New York Times, January 23, 1983.

Hoelterhoff, Manuela. "The Sills Regimen Shapes Up City Opera." The Wall Street Journal, September 19, 1984, p. 28.

Hume, Paul. "Sisters of the Symphony." The Washington Post, November 15, 1981.

Jepson, Barbara. "American Women in Conducting." The Feminist Art Journal, Winter 1975-76, pp. 13-18, 45.

Jepson, Barbara. "Music By Women: a Fall '76 Roundup." The Feminist Art Journal, Winter 1976-77, pp. 40-41.

Jepson, Barbara. "After the Pulitzer, Then What?" The New York Times, October 28, 1984.

Julius, Ruth. "Showcasing Women Composers." The Feminist Art Journal, Summer 1977, pp. 38-40.

Kozinn, Allan. "An American Woman Conductor on the Way Up." The New York Times, March 24, 1985.

Lehmann, Phyllis. "Women in Orchestras: The Promise and the Problems." Symphony Magazine, December 1982, p. 12.

Miller, Jim, et al. "Rock's New Women." Newsweek, March 4, 1985, pp. 48-57.

Miller, Dr. Karl F. "Pulitzers in Music" a letter to the editor. The New York Times, December 23, 1984, p. 10.

National Association of Schools of Music. "Music in Higher Education. 1981-82."

Neuls-Bates, Carol. "The Status of Women in College Music: Preliminary Studies." College Music Society Report Number 1 (1976).

Neuls-Bates, Carol. Women in Music. New York: Harper and Row, 1982, pp. xii-xvi, 325-331.

"Where Is 20th Century Music Now?" The New York Times, June 24, 1984.

Pool, Jeannie G. "America's Women Composers." Music Educators Journal, January 1979, pp. 28-41.

Pool, Jeannie G. Women in Music History: A Research Guide. Ansonia Station, P.O. Box 436, New York: Author, 1977.

Presslaff, Hilary Tann, ed. "Opinion and Commentary." International League of Women Composers Newsletter, Summer 1984.

Pucciani, Donna. "Sexism in Music Education: Survey of the Literature 1972-1982." Music Educators Journal, September 1983, pp. 49-51+.

Renton, Barbara Hampton. "The Status of Women in College Music 1976-77: A Statistical Study." College Music Society Report Number 2 (1980).

Rich, Alan. "High Notes at the City Opera." Newsweek, October 8, 1984, pp. 80-81.

Sandow, Gregory. "The Passionate Conductor." The Wall Street Journal, November 5, 1984, p. 22.

Scovill, Ruth. "Women's Music." Women's Culture: The Women's Renaissance of the Seventies, edited by Gayle

Kimball, pp. 148-162. Metuchen, N.J. and London: The
Scarecrow Press, Inc., 1981.

Seashore, Carl E. "Women in Music: A 1940 Perspective."
Music Educators Journal, January 1979, pp. 42 +.

Seligmann, Jean and Witherspoon, Deborah. "High Notes
at the City Opera." Newsweek, October 8, 1984, pp. 80-81.

Sterritt, David. "Exploring All the Human Voice Can
Do--With Whimsy and Wonder." The Christian Science
Monitor, March 1, 1985, p. 21.

Stockwell, Norman. "Ronnie Gilbert: Carrying a Banner
Once More." Feminist Connection, September 1984, p. 25.

Tick, Judith. "Passed Away Is the Piano Girl: Changes in
American Musical Life, 1870-1900." The New Grove
Dictionary of American Music. London: Macmillan Co.,
1986.

Tick, Judith. "Women and Music." Manuscript.

Van Tuyl, Laura. "More Applause, More Royalties for
Women Composers." The Christian Science Monitor,
October 3, 1985. p. 1+

Weiss, Paulette. "Women in Music: A 1978 Perspective."
Music Educators Journal, January 1979, pp. 43-45.

Wood, Elizabeth. "Women in Music." Signs, Winter 1980,
pp. 283-297.

Yourke, Laurel. "Thank Heaven for Ronnie Gilbert."
Feminist Connection, October/November 1984, p. 26.

Also correspondence with and/or literature and/or statistics
from:
    American Symphony Orchestra League.
    American Women Composers.

Adrienne Fried Block, Committee on the Status of
  Women, CMS.
The College Music Society.
International League of Women Composers.
Local 802 Women's Caucus-Allegro.
National Association of Schools of Music.
Nancy B. Reich, Committee on the Status of Women,
  CMS.
Elizabeth Vercoe, International League of Women
  Composers.

PERFORMANCE ART

Baracks, Barbara. "Deja WOW." The Village Voice,
October 14-20, 1981, p. 103.

Baracks, Barbara. "WOW Funky & Feminist." The Village
Voice, October 7-13, 1981, p. 93.

Larson, Kay. "For the First Time Women Are Leading Not
Following." Artnews, October 1980, pp. 64+.

Lippard, Lucy R. "Feminist Space: Reclaiming Territory."
The Village Voice, November 29, 1983, p. 120.

Lippard, Lucy R. "Time Will Tell." The Village Voice, June
19, 1984, p. 100.

Lippard, Lucy R. "The Politically Passionate." The Village
Voice, February 21, 1984, p. 90.

Roth, Moira, ed. The Amazing Decade: Women and
Performance Art in America 1970-1980. Los Angeles:
Astro Artz, 1983.

Also correspondence with and/or literature and/or statistics
from:

    Vicki Patraka, Women's Caucus, American Theatre
    Association, Bowling Green University.

COMEDIANS

Berger, Phil. "The New Comediennes." The New York Times Magazine, July 29, 1984, pp. 26-32+.

Gresham, Cyane. "Humorist Kate Clinton: Making the Grownups Uncomfortable." Feminist Connection, December 1984, p. 19+.

Gussow, Mel. "Whoopi As Actress, Clown and Social Critic." The New York Times, October 28, 1984.

Haun, Harry. "Whoopi's One of a Kind." New York Daily News, reprinted in The Wisconsin State Journal, November 25, 1984.

Israel, Lee. "Joan Rivers and How She Got That Way." Ms., October 1984, pp. 108-114.

Katz, Debra Morgenstern. "Women Who Get the Last Laugh." McCalls, March 1983, p. 62.

Klein, Julia. "The New Stand Up Comics." Ms., October 1984, pp. 116-126.

Klein, Stewart. "The Queens of Comedy." Harper's Bazaar, August 1983, pp. 166+.

Nemy, Enid. "Whoopi's Ready, But Is Broadway?" The New York Times, October 21, 1984.

Trott, Walt. "Last Laugh Duo Brings Off-Beat Comedy Antics to Bunky's Stage." The Capital Times, September 4, 1984.

THEATRE

American Theatre. "Older and Better." March 1985, p. 24-25.

American Theatre. "Make New Sounds." November 1984, p. 5+.

Chinoy, Helen Krich and Jenkins, Linda Walsh, eds. Women in American Theatre. New York: Crown Publishers, Inc., 1981.

Flierl-Steadman, Susan M. "Award-Winning Playwright Finds Support, Encouragement in ATA Women's Program." Theatre News, January/February 1985, p. 5.

Gussow, Mel. "New Group to Offer Plays by Women." Women: Their Changing Roles. Elizabeth Janeway, ed. New York: Arno Press, 1973, p. 355.

Kellogg, Marjorie Bradley. "Women's Caucus Puzzles Over Lack of Set Designers." Variety, January 12, 1983, p. 220.

Kellogg, Marjorie Bradley. "Betting On a Dark Horse." American Theatre, May 1984, pp. 28-29.

Malpede, Karen. Women in Theatre. New York: Drama Book Publishers, 1983.

O'Quinn, Jim, ed. "Combining Forces." Theatre Communications, January 1983, pp. 12-16.

O'Quinn, Jim, ed. "Women Directors: Why So Few?" Theatre Communications, February 1984, pp. 12-13.

O'Quinn, Jim, ed. "Festival Showcases Women." Theatre Communications, March 1984, p. 8.

Paullette, Phyllis. "How to Make It in the Theatre." Art and Artist, February/March 1984, p. 7.

Rich, Frank. "Theatre's Gender Gap Is a Chasm." The New York Times, September 30, 1984.

Ross, Laura. "Designing Women." American Theatre, January 1985, p. 35.

Shay, Michele. "Make New Sounds." American Theatre, November 1984, pp. 5+.

Suntree, Susan. "Women's Theatre: Creating the Dream Now." Women's Culture: The Women's Renaissance of the Seventies, edited by Gayle Kimball, pp. 106-117. Metuchen, N.J. and London: The Scarecrow Press, Inc., 1981.

Also correspondence with and/or literature and/or statistics from:
    American Place Theatre.
    American Theatre Association.
    At the Foot of the Mountain.
    Gladys Crane, Department of Theatre, University
      of Wyoming.
    The Dramatists Guild.
    League of Professional Theatre Women.

FILM

American Film Institute. "New Opportunities for Women."

Dougherty, Ariel, with contributions from Frances Reid, Michelle Citron, Julia Lesage and Candace Compton. "Thirteen Years of Feminist Media Making in the United States." 1981, manuscript.

Fein, Esther B. "How 'The River' Came to the Screen." The New York Times, December 16, 1984.

Gabler, Neal. "Women in the Director's Chair." (Interview with Lynn Littman.) Sneak Previews. Madison, Wisconsin: WHA-TV, June 28, 1984.

Gent, George. "Women Filmmakers: Doors Opening." The New York Times, June 15, 1972.

Hoberman. J. "Hearing Voices." The Village Voice, April 23, 1985.

Indiana University. Women's Films: A Critical Guide, 1975.

Kay, Karyn and Peary, Gerald, eds. Women and the Cinema: A Critical Anthology. New York: E.P. Dutton, 1977.

Lyons, Jeffrey. "Women in the Director's Chair." (Interview with Marcia Nasiter.) Sneak Previews. Madison, Wisconsin: WHA-TV, June 28, 1984.

Rosenberg, Jan. Women's Reflections: The Feminist Film Movement. Ann Arbor, Michigan: UMI Research Press, 1983.

Wetmore, Patricia C., ed. Women's Films: A Critical Guide. Indiana University Audio-Visual Center, 1975, pp. vii.

Wolt, Irene. "All Dressed Up With No Place to Go." American Film, December 1984, pp. 58-61.

Zimmerman, Debra S. "Women Make Movies, Inc." Manuscript.

Also correspondence with and/or literature and/or statistics from:
American Film Institute.
American Women in Radio and Television, Inc.
Center for Advanced Film Studies.
Conference of Feminist Film & Video Organizations.
Directors Guild of America.
Ariel Dougherty, development director, Women's Studio Workshop.
Ishtar Films.
National Association of Broadcasters.

Women Make Movies.
WTTW - Chicago.
University of Wisconsin-Milwaukee Women's
International Film Festival.

TELEVISION

Buck, Jerry. "Women Still Have a Long Way to Go." The
Capital Times, 1985.

DeVries, Hilary. "Women Wrestle with New Image." Green
Bay Press Gazette, July 4, 1984. (Reprinted from the
Christian Science Monitor).

Feinsilber, Mike. "TV Finally Portraying Women More
Honestly." The Capital Times, December 7, 1984.

Hyman, Jackie. "Lavin Says Alice Ends Next Season." The
Capital Times, August 10, 1984.

Kerr, Peter. "Women in Take Charge Roles Stride into TV's
Limelight." The New York Times, September 16, 1984.

Trafford, Abigail, et al. "She's Come a Long Way--or Has
She?" U.S. News and World Report, August 6, 1984.

Also correspondence with and/or literature and/or statistics
from:
American Women in Radio and Television.
National Association of Broadcasters.
Jean Gaddy Wilson, School of Journalism,
University of Missouri-Columbia.

LITERARY ARTS

Arthur and Elizabeth Schlesinger Library. "The Feminist
Press and Other Organizations." Newsletter, Fall 1984.

Ashworth, Debora. "Madonna or Witch: Women's Muse in

Contemporary Poetry." In Women's Culture: The Women's
Renaissance of the Seventies, edited by Gayle Kimball, pp.
178-186. Metuchen, N.J. and London: The Scarecrow
Press, Inc., 1981.

Brewer, Darylin, ed. "Grants and Awards." Coda,
April/May 1985, pp. 22-24; February/March 1985,
pp. 20-23; September/October 1984, pp. 18-20; June/July
1984, pp. 19-22; April/May 1984, pp. 19-22;
February/March 1984, pp. 19-21.

Bunkers, Suzanne. "In Search of Our Mother's Garden."
Feminist Connection, December 1984, p. 9.

Cornish, Sam. "Middle-Class Souls on Ice." The Christian
Science Monitor, March 1, 1985, p. B1.

Gaylor, Annie Laurie. "Book Review: Marshall's New
Collection Is Memorable." (A review of Reena by Paule
Marshall.) Feminist Connection, March 1984, p. 17.

Gaylor, Annie Laurie. "Florence Howe: Feminist Movement
Builder." Feminist Connection, June 1983, pp. 26+.

Gilbert, Sandra M. "Feisty Femme, 40, Seeks Nurturant
Paragon." (A review of Reading the Romance: Women,
Patriarchy and Popular Literature by Janice A. Radway.)
The New York Times Book Review, December 30, 1984,
p. 11.

Glasgow, Joanne. "If It's Great, A Man Inside Her Wrote
It." (A review of How to Suppress Women's Writing by
Joanna Russ.) New Directions for Women,
January/February 1984, p. 19.

Hacker, Andrew. "The Whole Feminist Catalogue." (A
review of Sisterhood Is Global, edited by Robin Morgan.)
The New York Times Book Review, January 27, 1985,
p. 12.

Heilbrun, Carolyn. "Discovering the Lost Lives of Women."

The New York Times Book Review, June 24, 1984, p. 1+.

Herman, Ellen. "Seal Press: An Object Lesson." The Women's Review of Books, February 1985, pp. 13-14.

Hohenberg, John. Pulitzer Prizes. New York and London: Columbia University Press, 1974.

Howes, Carey. "Vanessa Bell: A Robust Life of her Own." (A review of Vanessa Bell by Frances Spalding.) New Directions for Women, January/February 1984, p. 16.

Kingston, Paul W. et al. "The Columbia Economic Survey of American Authors: A Summary of Findings." Center for the Social Sciences, Columbia University, The Authors Guild Foundation, February 1981.

Lipsyte, Marjorie. "Perfectly Ripened Prose." (A review of Zami by Audre Lorde.) New Directions for Women, January/February 1983, p. 12.

Morgan, Robin. "Defining Women's Culture." In Women's Culture: The Women's Renaissance of the Seventies, edited by Gayle Kimball, pp. 30-42. Metuchen, N.J. and London: The Scarecrow Press, Inc., 1981.

Murray, Maureen. "Three Sisters Share Their Art with Students." New Directions for Women, January/February 1983, p. 8.

National Endowment for the Arts. "Employment Trends Among Artists." Cultural Post, June 1983, p. 5.

National Endowment for the Arts. "Short Fiction Again to Appear in Newspapers." Cultural Post, June 1983, p. 1+.

National Endowment for the Arts. "Council Discusses Blind Judging." Cultural Post, June 1983, p. 7.

Newspaper Enterprise Association, Inc. World Almanac and Book of Facts 1985. New York: 1985.

O'Connor, Jeanne. "What Makes a Feminist Bookstore Special? 88 Different Answers." Ms., September 1983, pp. 79-82.

Showalter, Elaine. "Women Who Write Are Women." The New York Times Book Review, December 16, 1985. p. 1+.

Sutin, Lawrence. "Turning the Pages: A Nonfiction Account of the Publishing Industry." Northwest Orient, August 1984, p. 32.

Tate, Claudia, ed. Black Women Writers at Work. New York: Continuum, 1983.

Trimmer, Joseph F. National Book Awards for Fiction. Boston: G.K. Hall & Co., 1978.

"Walker Goes Home to Royal Welcome." USA Today, January 20, 1986, p. 2D.

Also correspondence with and/or literature and/or statistics from:

    The Feminist Press.
    The Authors Guild.

CONFERENCE PARTICIPANTS

<u>Authors of Conference Papers</u>

TISA CHANG, Artistic/Producing Director, Pan Asian
    Repertory Theatre, New York, NY; presentation as
    Conference panelist, "The Messages and Concerns of
    Women of Color."

RUTH C. DEAN, former arts policy reporter for <u>The</u>
    <u>Washington Star</u>, freelance writer on the arts;
    presented Conference paper, "Women in the
    Performing Arts: Whither the Year 2001—A
    Catalytic Force in the Artistic Firmament, or Still
    Riding in the Back of the Bus?"

ELIZABETH DURBIN, author, researcher, editor of
    cultural publications; presented Conference paper, "A
    Report on Survey of Decade-Long Progress."

MARYO EWELL, Director of Community Programs,
    Colorado Council on the Arts and Humanities; writer,
    lecturer, consultant on arts in the community;
    presented Conference paper, "The Beloved
    Community: Toward a Feminist Definition of
    Community Arts."

FLORENCE HOWE, author, editor, founder and co-director
    Feminist Press, early leader women's studies
    movement; presented Conference summary paper.

ELIZABETH JANEWAY, novelist, social critic, writer on
    women's issues; presented Conference paper, "A
    Language for Women and What That Doesn't Mean."

JEAN LaMARR, Native-American printmaker/community
    artist; member Minority Women Artists, Paiute, Pit
    River, Susanville Indian Rancherio; presentation as

Conference panelist, "The Messages and Concerns of Women of Color."

PAULE MARSHALL, novelist; Visiting Professor of English, Virginia Commonwealth University; presented Conference paper, "A Black Woman Writer Thinks Back Through Her Mothers."

NELLIE McKAY, Associate Professor, Afro-American Studies and Women Studies, University of Wisconsin; presentation as Conference panelist, "The Messages and Concerns of Women of Color."

ROBIN MORGAN, poet, playwright; journalist, contributing editor to Ms. Magazine; presented Conference paper, "Women's Culture and Building the New Society."

GLORIA ORENSTEIN, Associate Professor in The Program for the Study of Women and Men in Society, University of Southern California; Co-creator of the Woman's Salon for Literature in New York; presented Conference paper, "Re-emergence of the Goddess in Contemporary Feminist Art and Literature."

ANNE-IMELDA RADICE, Administrative Director, The National Museum of Women in the Arts, Washington, D.C.; presented Conference paper on The National Museum.

SOPHIE RIVERA, Hispanic-American photographer, New York; presentation as Conference panelist, "The Messages and Concerns of Women of Color."

BARBARA ROWE, actress, playwright; creator and presenter of one-person portrayals of outstanding American feminists, via Cameo Productions, Elmhurst, IL; presented Conference dramatization, "Le Jour et La Nuit of Miss Mary Cassatt."

Group Discussion Leaders and Rapporteurs

MARY BARRETT, Professor of Art, University of
Wisconsin-River Falls; group discussion rapporteur,
"Goals and Strategies for the Future."

KIRSTEN BECK, New York communications consultant;
writer and lecturer on cable television, other new
technologies and their relationships to the arts; group
discussion leader, "Arts in Mass Media."

CARA CHELL, Associate Dean, Letters and Science,
University of Wisconsin-LaCrosse; group discussion
rapporteur, "Economic Perspective."

BARBARA COLTON, Professional actress, National First
Vice President of Actors Equity; former theatre
panelist, National Endowment for the Arts; group
discussion leader, "Goals and Strategies for the
Future."

LESLEE NELSON CORPIER, Associate Professor Visual
Arts, Division of University Outreach, University of
Wisconsin-Madison; member Conference Advisory
Committee; group discussion rapporteur, "Visual
Arts."

NANCY DEUTSCH, Continuing Education Services,
University of Wisconsin-Madison; group discussion
rapporteur, "Goals and Strategies for the Future."

KAREN DOBBS, Vice President for Programs, American
Symphony Orchestra League, Washington, D.C.;
group discussion leader, "Economic Perspective."

ARIEL DOUGHERTY, Development Director, Women's
Studio Workshop, Rosendale, New York; group
discussion rapporteur, "Arts of the New
Technologies."

SUSAN FRIEDMAN, Professor, English and Women
Studies, University of Wisconsin-Madison; group

discussion leader, "Political Perspective."

FANNIE HICKLIN, Associate Dean of Faculties, Chair Department of Theatre and Dance, University of Wisconsin-Whitewater; group discussion rapporteur, "Goals and Strategies for the Future."

MARGOT KERNAN, photographer/video-artist; writer on film; organized national conference on women's video film; group discussion leader, "Goals and Strategies for the Future."

GAYLE KIMBALL, Women's Studies Program, California State University-Chico; editor, Women's Culture: The Women's Renaissance of the Seventies; group discussion leader, "Aesthetic Perspective."

ESTELLA LAUTER, Professor, Communication and the Arts, University of Wisconsin-Green Bay; author Women as Myth Makers: Poetry and Visual Arts by Twentieth Century Women; group discussion leader, "Goals and Strategies for the Future," and group discussion rapporteur, "Aesthetic Perspective."

RHODA LERMAN, biographer, novelist and playwright; group discussion leader, "Literary Arts."

GLORIA LINK, Professor and Coordinator of Theatre, University of Wisconsin-Oshkosh; group discussion rapporteur, "Arts in Mass Media."

MARGARET LYNN, Executive-Director, American Theatre Association; group discussion leader, "Educational Perspective."

NELLIE McKAY, Associate Professor, Afro-American Studies and Women Studies, University of Wisconsin-Madison; group discussion rapporteur, "Literary Arts."

KAREN MERRITT, Senior Academic Planner, University

of Wisconsin System; group discussion rapporteur, "Educational Perspective."

CYNTHIA NAVARETTA, Editor, Women Artist News, New York City; co-founder and first chair Coalition of Women's Art Organizations; group discussion leader, "Visual Arts and Crafts."

MARGOT PETERS, Professor of English, University of Wisconsin-Whitewater; biographer of women artists and winner of national awards for her books; group discussion rapporteur, "Goals and Strategies for the Future."

RHODA-GALE POLLACK, Chair, Fine Arts Division and Associate Professor Dramatic Arts, University of Wisconsin-Parkside; group discussion rapporteur, "Performing Arts."

PATRICIA QUINN, Adult Opportunity Office, University of Wisconsin-Eau Claire; group discussion rapporteur, "Goals and Strategies for the Future."

ANNE-IMELDA RADICE, Administrative Director, The National Museum of Women in the Arts, Washington, D.C.; group discussion leader, "Goals and Strategies for the Future."

ALICE RANDLETT, Associate Professor Learning Resources, University of Wisconsin-Stevens Point; group discussion rapporteur, "Institutional Perspective."

ELLOUISE SCHOETTLER, Associate Director, Focus International/American Women in Art; formerly Executive Director, Coalition of Women's Arts Organizations; group discussion leader, "Institutional Perspective."

SUSAN SEARING, Librarian, University of Wisconsin System Women's Studies Library; group discussion rapporteur, "Political Perspective."

JUDITH TICK, pioneer in women's studies in music; author of several books, including Women Making Music; group discussion leader, "Goals and Strategies for the Future."

JOAN WOODBURY, Professor of Dance and Director University of Utah Ririe-Woodbury Dance Company, Salt Lake City, Utah; group discussion leader, "Performing Arts."

Other Conference Participants.

MARGIE ADAM, feminist singer, composer, pianist, Berkeley, CA.

MARGARET WALKER ALEXANDER, novelist and poet; Professor of English and Director of Institute for the Study of the History, Life and Culture of Black Peoples, Jackson State College, Mississippi.

MARILYN ANDERSON, visual artist, Women's Art Registry of Minnesota.

BARBARA AUBIN, mixed media artist, member National Women's Caucus for Art, Chicago, IL.

KAREN AXNESS, co-owner Room of One's Own, feminist bookstore, Madison, WI.

LORNA BOURG, Assistant Executive Director, Southern Mutual Help Association, Jeanerette, LA; author Planation Portraits: Women of the Louisiana Cane Fields.

JACQUELINE BRADLEY, television and movie actress, member Executive Committee and co-chair Women's Committee, Screen Actors Guild, New York, NY.

SISTER VERONICA BRUTOSKY, C.S.J.,
Founder/Director International Registry for Religious
Women Artists, Fresno, CA.

BUTO, special assistant, Women's Art Registry of
Minnesota, Minneapolis, MN.

BETTY CRALL BUTTERBOUGH, writer on dance,
Indianapolis, Indiana.

KATHRYN CLARENBACH, Professor Political Science and
director Women's Education Resources, Division of
University Outreach, University of
Wisconsin-Madison; Conference Co-Director.

LINDA CLAUDER, Manager of Projects and Production,
WHA and Wisconsin Public Radio; Associate
Professor, University of Wisconsin-Extension.

KRISTINE COTTOM, President WAVE, women's art
gallery, St. Louis Park, MN.

KAREN COWAN, Professor Dance, Division of University
Outreach, University of Wisconsin-Madison; Executive
Director Wisconsin Dance Council; dancer and
choreographer; member Conference Advisory
Committee.

GLADYS CRANE, Chair, Women's Caucus, American
Theatre Association, Laramie, NY.

ARLEY CURTZ, Executive Director, Wisconsin Arts Board.

BETSY DAMON, performance artist, one of the original
theorists of feminist art, attended '73 Conference; did
ritual piece called "5,000 year old Woman" on
Madison Avenue.

CHERIE DOYLE, curator, Women's Art Registry of
Minnesota and Macalester College.

HERMEINE EHLERS, Project Coordinator, Wisconsin
Women in the Arts.

SUSAN FARMER, Assistant Professor Art, Division of
University Outreach, University of
Wisconsin-Madison; painter; member Conference
Advisory Committee.

ELSA HONIG FINE, Editor and Publisher, Woman's Art
Journal; author book on women artists, Knoxville, TN.

CAROLE FISHER, artist/educator, Women's Art Registry
of Minnesota, Minneapolis, MN.

REGINA FLANAGAN, photographer, program coordinator,
Wisconsin Arts Board.

RONNIE GEIST, Media Director, Women's Interart
Center, New York, NY.

KRIS HIGGINBOTHAM, publications designer, University
of Wisconsin-Madison.

FRIEDA HIGH-WASIKHONGO, graphic artist, woodcuts
and pastels; Associate Professor of African and
Afro-American Art, Department of Afro-American
Studies, University of Wisconsin-Madison.

WENDY HO, Ada James Women's Center, Madison, WI.

SUE HOUSER, Treasurer, Women's Caucus for Art,
St. Louis, MO.

PAT HUTCHINGS, Coordinator Department of English,
Alverno College, Milwaukee, WI.

TONI INTRAVAIA, dance notator, Carbondale, IL.

EDWARD KAMARCK, Professor Theatre Arts, Division of
University Outreach, University of
Wisconsin-Madison; playwright; administrator,

researcher, writer and editor in the arts; Conference
Co-Director.

JOAN LAZARUS, Assistant Professor Theatre Arts,
Division of University Outreach, University of
Wisconsin-Madison; specialist on youth theatre;
member Conference Advisory Committee.

GENEVIEVE LEWIS, administrator of creative writing
programs, Division of University Outreach, University
of Wisconsin-Madison; editor and writer; Conference
Coordinator.

MARGOT LEWITIN, Artistic Director, Women's Inter-Arts
Center, New York City, NY.

SUE MABERRY, Administrative Director, The Women's
Building, Los Angeles, CA.

BARBARA MANGER, Artist, member planning committee
'73 conference; founding member and former state
coordinator Wisconsin Women in the Arts, Milwaukee,
WI.

RUTH MAYLEAS, Program Officer, Education and Culture
Program, The Ford Foundation, New York, NY.

MARIA MAZZARA, visual artist, Women's Art Registry of
Minnesota, Burnsville, MN.

GILL MILLER, chairwoman, Department of Dance,
Denison University, Granville, OH.

ANNA B. NASSIF, Professor Dance Choreography,
University of Wisconsin-Madison.

MARY PALM, Secretary-Treasurer, Wisconsin High School
Forensic Association, Division of University Outreach,
University of Wisconsin-Madison.

VICKIE PATRAKA, Women's Caucus, American Theatre Assoc., Bowling Green University, Bowling Green, OH.

ELAINE PERRET, high school art teacher, St. Clair, MI.

JACQUELINE PERRET, teacher of creative writing, University of Miami, Coral Gables, FL.

JAYNE POOR, Professor of Dance, Rockford College, Rockford, IL.

DOROTHY PROVIS, National President, Coalition of Women's Arts Organization.

JULIET (McNamara) RAGO, Professor of Art, Loyola University of Chicago, member National Women's Caucus for Art, Evanston, IL.

JANE ROBERTS, composer, music teacher, lyricist, poet, playwright; Homewood, IL.

JOAN ROOT, painter, New York City, NY.

PHYLLIS JANE ROSE, actress, director Foot of the Mountain Theatre, feminist theatre, Minneapolis, MN.

BETTY SALAMUN, Artistic Director Dancecircus, Milwaukee, WI.

TED SHANNON, former Dean and Emeritus Professor Education, University of Wisconsin-Extension; administrator of arts and humanities programs; member Conference Advisory Committee.

LIBBY SHAPIRO, professional French Horn player; member Woman's Caucus of Local 802 of Musician's Union, New York City, NY.

ANNIE SHAVER-CRANDALL, Vice President Eastern Region, Caucus for the Arts, New York, NY.

DIANA SNYDER, Professor of Dance, University of
Illinois, Champaign, IL.

JUDITH STANLEY, Professor of English, Alverno College,
Milwaukee, WI.

RITA STARPATTERN, Director, Women and Their Work,
Austin, TX.

SANDRA TAYLOR, visual artist, Women's Art Registry of
Minnesota.

EVELYN TERRY, printmaker, Milwaukee; participant '73
conference; co-organizer of August 1984 exhibit at
UW-Milwaukee: EROTICA - Woman Creating Beyond
the Sexual.

MARIAN THOMPSON, Professor Family Living
Education, University of Wisconsin-Madison; editor
Wisconsin Women and Public Policy.

CONNIE THREINEN, program coordinator Women's
Education Resources, Division of University Outreach,
University of Wisconsin-Madison; co-author Ten Years
of Title IX.

MARLYS TRUNKHILL, singer, Green Bay, WI; has
performed with the New York Philharmonic, Boston
Symphony, NYC Opera, Boston Opera Company, and
the American Opera Society.

ELIZABETH VERCOE, composer, member Executive
Board, International League of Women Composers;
Chair, MA Chapter of American Women Composers,
Concord MA.

GENEVIEVE WHITFORD, poet, Madison, WI.

KARON WINZENZ, curator of Art, Assistant Professor
Communication and the Arts, University of
Wisconsin-Green Bay.

LOUISE WITHERELL, Professor Humanistic Studies,
University of Wisconsin-Green Bay.

SHIRLEY WITHERSPOON-LINDSTROM, blues-jazz
singer, Minneapolis, MN.

JUDITH LANG ZAIMONT, composer, member Executive
Board, International League of Women Composers;
Baltimore, MD.

INDEX